The Brook

by

Barbara Lyons

TOPGALLANT PUBLISHING CO., LTD.

HONOLULU, HAWAII

1976

First Printing 1976

TOPGALLANT PUBLISHING CO. LTD.
845 Mission Lane
Honolulu, Hawaii 96813

Printed in the United States of America

Library of Congress Cataloging in Publication Data

Lyons, Barbara.
  The brook.

  1. Lyons, Barbara—Biography—Youth. I. Title.
PS3562.Y448Z52   398'.092'4 [B]   75-42444
ISBN 0-914916-10-6

Contents

FOR A.B.S.
Brave as man is, soft as woman
HENRY WADSWORTH LONGFELLOW

AND W.O.S.
Look forward and upward

Where does the line fall between
what happened and what might have happened?
Or between the way people were,
and the way they are remembered?
As one looks back fifty years,
more and less, it seems to me
that if the spirit of those days
so long ago can be recalled or imagined,
even for a few moments,
that is the important thing.

Brookside ¹ Now

A few years ago, I made a pilgrimage that I had taken in spirit a hundred times. With my husband, I visited the place that is now the Sacred Hearts Convent in Honolulu.

It was on a day when students were entering or returning to the school, so there was a good deal of bustle, but the face of the nun who greeted us was serene under her starched coif and veil. She led us through the wide hallway to the outdoor gallery that ran the length of the central part of the large building, and from which a wing extended at either end.

"Go wherever you like," she said, but added with a glance at my husband, "except to the wing where the Sisters have their rooms."

"Of course, we won't go near there," he said gravely. "My wife wants particularly to walk around the yard."

"And to go down to the brook."

"The yard is changed," went on the nun, as if I hadn't spoken. Perhaps the words had only sounded in my mind. "We had to level off much of the grounds when the Convent was built. And to sacrifice seventeen trees."

Seventeen trees . . . trees climbed so many years ago. Seventeen! We went down a broad flight of steps to the courtyard at the rear of the Convent building, and walked slowly through it to the slope that descended beyond. There were royal palms off to the left—not all of them, though. The entrance to Brookside had been between pillars of the gray stone wall that bordered Nuuanu Avenue, and the driveway had been lined with the straight, proud trunks of these stately palms.

Looking toward the barred gateway, I saw clearly for an instant on the old driveway a small girl in overalls, riding an ancient mare. Was it Holly? Or me . . . Robert could have been in the kamani tree, waiting for his turn on Jenny. Or spinning tops with Randy near the back steps, or fishing in the brook.

The old entrance looked as if it remembered a time when it hadn't been barred, when the Hupmobile or the Pierce-Arrow was driven through it, Nagata spruce in his uniform and cap at the wheel. Now, the Convent was reached by way of Bates Street, around the corner from the old entry—opposite the steps and path from the street, that had led past the poinciana regia tree to Grandpa and Grandma's house.

The kamani in the Brookside yard, with its glossy foliage—one could hide in that tree; its leaves were large and many. Some of the great ingas still marched down the slope; the golden shower at the top seemed to miss the little arbor that had stood beside it. There were mangoes still, and tall curving coconut palms that we used to walk up as far as we could with bare feet, and where we found lizard eggs in crevices of the brown bark.

We reached the monkey-pods too soon, I thought—there had been a long, slow sweep to the giant trees and the brook, and it was with a shock that I came to the stone steps. The nun had mentioned "leveling off."

But the firm, new bridge might have been the old plank I remembered—once on it, I didn't see it. The water circled slowly about its stones as it had done so many years ago, coming toward me as before at its own leisurely pace. The constant murmur and gentle splash was in my ears. It had been here, in the air above the brook, all those years that I had been away . . . Looking toward the high arch of the tunnel under Nuuanu Avenue, I felt again the excitement of being in it, with the rumbling of streetcars overhead; a sound that somehow never disturbed the essential quiet of that place, even accented it.

Monkey-pods along the banks, a dozen of them, spread their branches to make the brook a dark, secret place. A place to catch 'opae with Robert, Randy, and later little Ka-chan. A place to swim, when rainfall from the mountains swept down the Valley, raising the brook along its banks until one could find a pool, or make one with stones, while water now surged by. At these times the brook spoke of the wildness of its origins, and I exulted in the dashing water and miniature cascades of spray over the stones. Again, on a day when sunlight streaked through the branches to make sparkling patches on its surface, it was gay, and I would find myself humming some tuneless song.

More than anything, in all its moods, this was an untroubled place. A place to be alone. To walk from bridge to tunnel by way of the stones, testing to see which were firm; to sit among the vari-colored impatiens blossoms and the clover and reeds of the bank and breathe in their damp fragrance, and to search for a four-leaf clover; to read, to think, to not think; to listen to the waters of the earth and marvel that they coursed by forever, like a life without end.

Before we left the Convent we went to the chapel at its far side, situated where Kirey's cottage had been. She would have liked that.

Ten or twelve nuns knelt at prayer in the lofty room. The afternoon sun streamed across the pews, over the bowed, veiled heads, and glinted through stained glass. Was this, and the kneeling nuns, what made the chapel a radiant place, and a tranquil place?

But that was the way Brookside always had been. A quality of radiance and tranquility, combined, and with this a sense of life being lived. All the living that had gone on here! Now the girls, whose chatter was remote from the chapel, supplied the living force, balanced by the calm, orderly presence of the nuns. The spirit of Brookside had come down through the years, I thought, from the time when a ship's captain and his wife, my great-grandparents, had built a house here and made it their home.

I had been afraid to go back to Brookside, and longed to with an intensity that made me dream of it, dozens of times. I had dreamed of going up to the door, being admitted, and finding all strange. Well, it *was* changed. The high, square old house was gone, replaced by the Convent. And the yard, all but the brook, was greatly changed. It was mostly level now, and seventeen of its trees were no more, trees known to me as one knows a tree in childhood.

But we were lucky. Brookside had not been cut up into small lots, as had happened to so many of the old homes of Honolulu. And there still belonged to it that special quality of aliveness that had been there those many years ago, and surely before, held now by the nuns in their gentle hands.

Brookside ²Then

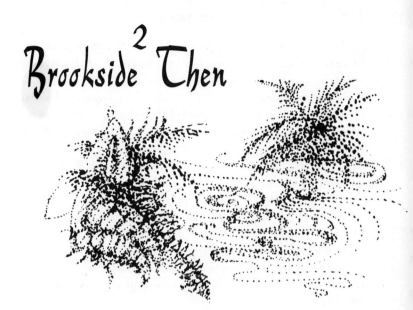

" . . . *Hato pop po*
Mame ya hoshii ka
Sora yaru zo."

Otoru was singing softly as she gave me my bath. I loved the off-key tones of her light voice.

When she had wiped the soap off my face with a wet wash cloth, I asked, "What does it mean? What's it about?"

"That's the pigeons, cooing."

"Like the ones we have in the yard?"

"Yes, and on the roof sometimes."

"Teach me the song?"

"All right. Now turn over."

She went on singing as she soaped my back.

"Minna de nakayoku
Tabe ni koi."

Otoru always let me have a swim when she had pulled out the plug and hung it by its chain around the faucets. As the water gurgled out, I slid back and forth in the big white tub,

5

sloshing waves up its sides, then climbed out to be enveloped in a large fluffy white towel. The mat on which I dripped had a raised design and the word "BATH" on it.

Otoru was so pretty in her bright kimono, its sleeves pinned together back of her shoulders so they wouldn't get wet, and the obi tight at her waist in a wide band. Her black hair was piled high on her head. She was nineteen, grown up, but she liked to play games with me, and teach me to write my name in Japanese characters. It was fun to have her bathe me, which Kirey couldn't do because of her bad back.

Dressed in pajamas and my kimono, I jumped down the step from the bathroom to the Japanese matting of the stair-hall and ran around the curve of the bannister.

"Tell Robert I'll be getting his bath ready," Otoru called. Wobert could take his own bath now, but she let the water in for him.

I went through the screen door to the inner hall, yelling, "Wobert!" and along it to the nursery. I let the nursery door bang loudly, and then couldn't resist pinching Wobert as he leaned over to get clean pajamas from his bureau.

Kirey, coming through the door from her bedroom in her long, starched dress, said, "Nincompoop!" and I glanced at the high stool that stood against the wall.

"Run along now, Robert. Soap well. And no splashing onto the floor."

Wobert couldn't pinch me back because she was right there. He scowled at me and went out of the room, trailing pajamas and kimono.

Kirey said, "Clean child!" to me. She seemed not even to have thought of the stool. Usually when I did something that made her call me "Nincompoop," she tied me onto a white stool with black stockings, and I would contemplate the pictured nursery rhymes of the wallpaper until she untied me. These were in a border of the blue paper, near the ceiling, and I'd sit there singing to myself, "Little Bo-peep has lost her sheep . . . " and feeling woeful until I came to " . . . wagging their tails behind them." I'd follow the pictures all the way around the four walls, regarding Miss Muffet, and Jack pulling out the plum, and Little Boy Blue fast asleep.

Kirey's white hair was drawn up and coiled into a neat bun at the top of her head, secured by large bone hairpins. She smelled of Yardley's English Lavender. There was something so comforting in the sight and smell of Kirey that it never would have occurred to me that she could be anywhere but at the center of my world, Brookside. She stood very straight always, partly because of the corsets that supported her bad back, and also because she was a straight-standing person. A pair of pince-nez was fastened to her bosom; they pulled out on a chain from a gold pin with her initials on it: A B K. Kirey's face was kind, blue eyes smiling, but when she told you to do something and said, "No nonsense, now," there was no nonsense.

Kirey was an Englishwoman, a maiden lady who had come to Hawaii by way of New Zealand. She was an R.N.— "That means a nurse," she explained—and before she came to live with us, she had been Lady Superintendent of Nurses at Auckland Hospital. We had a picture of her in a dark nurse's uniform with white cuffs, and a white cap right on top of her head and tied under her chin. She was standing beside a round table, with her hand on the back of a chair. She looked very nice—I loved that picture—but different. "I was much younger when it was taken," she said.

When Kirey reached Hawaii, she had nursed at various sugar plantations near Hilo and along the "Scottish Coast." She would tell us about places called 'Ola'a, Pepe'ekeo, Hamakua. "I feel at home with the Scots," she told me. "I took my training in 'Auld Reekie,' you know."

"Are you going downstairs yet?" I asked her now.

"In a minute. Run catch Otoru, if you like."

Kirey knew that I didn't like going down by myself. I

waited at the top of the flight for Otoru. She didn't have to start Holly with her bath; Holly could let her own water in now.

I loved the wide, carpeted stairway with its two turns, but it seemed a very long way down and I was glad to have Otoru beside me. The hall at the bottom was well enough lighted through the front door and windows to the lanai, but in the long living room, the lamps had not yet been lit. I held Otoru's hand as we crossed the end of it, past Munna's piano, and went through the dining room to the pantry. The round "children's dining table" there was set for four, us three children and Kirey.

"What are we having for supper, 'Toru?"

"Soup, bread and milk, and baked apples."

"I don't like baked apples."

"And cookies."

"Oh." That was better. "Can I go and look at Ah Loi?"

"Yes, come along."

I scampered out across the wide back porch to the kitchen door, and peered in at him while 'Toru went in. He was at the wood stove, tall and scary looking as ever, his long black queue hanging down behind the funny little skull cap he wore. I wished I dared go and yank at his queue. He didn't even glance at me. Ah Loi never let us into the kitchen when he was there.

"He doesn't like it here because Daddy won't let him smoke opium," Holly had said.

"Why doesn't he go away, then?"

She shrugged. "I wish he would, so we could go in there with Misao and 'Toru."

Misao came into the kitchen now from the little inner pantry, and smiled at me. Misao was just as pretty as Otoru. They were sisters, and Misao was married to Nagata, the chauffeur. She wore more subdued kimonos than Otoru did, because she was married. She was going to have a baby, and pretty soon she wouldn't be working in the house. We'd miss her—but, a baby! And we could run over to see it, and her. She and Nagata lived in a cute little house near the garage.

There was a good smell coming from the stove. "I

wouldn't keep the old crotchet if he weren't such a good cook,'' Munna would say.

At supper, Kirey had some of whatever it was that smelled good, and tea from her teapot, while we had our bread and milk. Bread and milk was delicious, though, probably better than what she had.

"Kirey, can I have some Cambric tea?"

"Not at supper, child. And we say, 'may.'"

"Tomorrow afternoon?"

"We'll see."

Wobert said, "Daddy and I went down to the brook when he got home from work, and we threw stones in. He was teaching me how to skip stones."

"I can remember when you used to say 'tones,'" Holly said.

Wobert received this remark in dignified silence.

"Did you skip any?" she asked.

He shook his pale, almost-white head. "No. But Daddy said I'm learning."

"Elbows, Robert," Kirey said quietly, and he quickly put his hands in his lap. He had finished his bread and milk—he was always the first of us to be pau eating.

After supper, we went into the living room to see Munna and Daddy. Sometimes they sat in the little den before their dinner, but tonight they were at the far end of the long room, past the white pillars at either side. Here, there were two velvety sofas and some big chairs, and beyond them was the windowed alcove with the Cold Lady in it. She was made of white marble and stood on a high pedestal, holding a pitcher on her head. "Rebecca at the Well," Munna said her real name was. Holly had named her the Cold Lady.

Munna was saying, "We've got to tell them," but when she saw us, she smiled her bright smile and held out her arms. Holly ran and jumped into them, then Wobert did, and then it was my turn. She was wearing something long and rose-colored, not a dress, and as always, she smelled very sweet. Not the lavender smell that was Kirey's, something different.

Holly hugged Daddy, too, but when he held out a hand to me, I edged away.

Daddy raised and lowered his eyebrows at me and then at Munna, and said to her, "Baba has a way of wriggling off behind the nearest piece of furniture to escape undue familiarity on the part of her male parent."

Sometimes I wanted so much to sit on his lap that I could hardly stand not to. But he wasn't around all day like Munna, and I was a little afraid of him. He was much taller than Munna, and very slim, with blond hair above a high forehead, and blue eyes that made me almost brave enough to go up to him.

"I think tomorrow," he said over our heads to Munna. "Not at night."

Holly said, "Not what at night?"

Holly had long, spiraly brown curls that Otoru brushed morning and night till they shone, and twisted them round her slender fingers. Then she put a wide flat bow on Holly's head, so that it stuck up from the back, pink or blue or yellow. No one would have dreamed of putting a bow on my short, straight hair—least of all me. It looked just right on Holly, though.

Munna beckoned to her and said, "Come tell me about school today."

Holly was in first grade at Miss Maxfield's school. Wobert and I were going to kindergarten sometime.

Munna moved over and Holly sat with her in her chair. While they were talking, I thought about kindergarten, but not very hard. It seemed a long time away. My mind wandered to Jenny. We rode her every day, and nothing had ever been so much fun. I could hardly wait until tomorrow, so I could ride her!

When Kirey came and said "Bed-time," Munna looked at her with an unhappy kind of face.

Kirey was reading *The Adventures of Buster Bear* to us. When we were in bed, she sat in her chair on the sleeping porch and pulled her glasses out on their chain. Kirey had a rocking chair in her bedroom, but otherwise always sat in a straight-backed one. My bed was in a corner, and Holly's and Wobert's on the other side of the room. Each of us had a very small Oriental rug at the side of the bed.

"Little Joe Otter was fairly bursting with excitement," Kirey read. "He felt that he had the greatest news to tell since Peter Rabbit had first found the tracks of Buster Bear in the Green Forest . . . So he hurried to the Smiling Pool . . ."

When Munna came up to kiss us good night, she smiled very sweetly at Kirey and put an arm around her shoulder to hug her. They said nothing to each other, but it seemed to me that something was strange. It made me feel rather anxious as I said my prayers. "God bless Munna and Daddy and Kirey, and Holly and Wobert, and Grandma and Grandpa and Mutie, and 'Toru and Misao and Nagata. And Ah Loi." Kirey had said that Ah Loi should be blessed, too.

Kirey tucked me in when Munna had gone, and her eyes were sad, even though she was smiling. She took Teddybear off his little chair and put him under the covers with me.

"What's the matter, Kirey?" I asked, suddenly fearful.

I saw that her eyes shone bright as she leaned over to kiss me. "Good night, child," she whispered.

"Kirey . . . " But she was turning to Wobert's bed.

When she switched off the light, I asked, "Will there be clunder tonight?" The only thing I could think of to explain my fearfulness was that there was going to be a thunderstorm.

She came to my bed and said softly, "No, there won't be. See all the stars in the sky?"

The sleeping porch where the three of us slept was above the front lanai, jutting out from the rest of the house. The walls were high, with screening around the top half, so that you saw only treetops and sky from it. Kirey and I looked up through the screens at the stars together.

"That's the Little Dipper, do you remember? When there is thunder," she went on, "you mustn't be frightened. It's when we need rain badly that thunderstorms come, to give us lots all at once.'' She stroked my hair back off my forehead, and patted Teddybear. ''Don't forget that your guardian angel is near, taking care of you.''

There was a light on in the nursery just back of the sleeping porch, and I lay looking through a window above my bed at the border of pictures. ''Hi, diddle diddle,'' I sang to Teddybear, my eyes on the cow jumping over a crescent moon. ''The cat and the fiddle . . . ''

Then I listened to the creakings of the house. Often these were friendly sounds, as if Brookside were talking to itself—about us, what else? But tonight the crack of a floorboard on the porch, the groan of a beam, the subdued rattling of a window somewhere made me uneasy.

Kirey had left the door to her room open as usual, next to the nursery. She read late at night, and was awake when we went to sleep, and again before we woke in the morning. I got out of bed suddenly and went to her door. She was at her desk, writing a letter, but she turned and got up right away.

''Can't sleep?'' she asked.

''No . . .''

She took me onto her lap, and sang as she rocked me:

> *''Now the day is over,*
> *Night is drawing nigh . . .''*

I looked round at all of her things that I knew so well. The white-painted bed had a board under the mattress, and on the table beside it was her watch in its gold case; she kept it five minutes ahead—''Like the King of England.'' Her Holy Bible was on the table too, and a volume called *British Poets*. There were Chinese vases and a nest of mother-of-pearl inlaid teak tables that she had bought at Ah Inn's store, and small Oriental rugs that lay on the Japanese matting. She used to say, ''I can't seem to help being extravagant when I'm at Ah Inn's. But 'What for no?' One needs to be extravagant sometimes.'' She had given some of the things she had bought to Munna, and a tiny ivory figure to each of us children. Mine was a coolie in a wide pointed hat, pulling a ricksha.

Pictures on the wall were of her family in England, a friend in Edinburgh whom she called "The Wee Sprite," and a man who lived in New Zealand. These were framed in panels of heavy wood. There were plants in pots with figured designs, again from Ah Inn's; she had a watering can for these, which she filled at the washstand in a sunny alcove off a corner of the room. In turns she put the pots at the windows that got the morning sun. "The growing sun," she said.

There was always a bunch of sweet-smelling flowers that she had cut. I leaned against her corseted bosom, and contentment crept over me. Kirey was there—she was always there—and everything was all right.

She finished the song with:

> ". . . *Thine Angels spread*
> *Their white wings above me,*
> *Watching round my bed.*
> *Amen.*"

I lay against her for a while, with the tune going through my head as she rocked. At last I said sleepily: "Tell me about Boots and Shoes."

"When I was a little girl in Yorkshire, we had two fox terriers, and their names were Boots and Shoes . . . "

When Kirey put me back to bed, Holly and Wobert were both asleep. "Is my guardian angel still here?" I whispered.

"Yes, darling. Always near, watching over you. Remember."

I turned and thrust my nose into the safe smell of Teddybear.

After breakfast, Munna called us into the den off the living room and told us that Kirey was going to leave Brookside. I looked at her fixedly, unable to understand what she was saying. Kirey *leaving Brookside*. No, it couldn't be. Kirey belonged at Brookside, just as the rest of us did.

"You all know that Kirey has a bad back. Well, the doctor has told her now that she must be very careful of it, and that she mustn't work any more."

Work? Kirey work? What was Munna talking about?

I tried to pinpoint the conclusive argument that was churning around in my head. "Kirey lives here!" I shouted.

Munna took me onto her lap and said gently, "She's not going far away, and she'll come to see us often. Very often," she added firmly.

Holly was saying, "Where is she going?"

"She'll have a nice little house at a place called Cottage Grove, right here in Honolulu. We'll go to see *her* often, too."

I flung myself off of Munna's lap and out of the room, shouting, "Kirey! Kirey!"

She called from the top of the stairs and I stumbled up the long, turning flight, sobbing.

The rest of the day had a dreamlike quality. We did the same things as usual, but nothing seemed right. There was an undercurrent of strangeness; all was unreal.

Each of us had a ride on Jenny. Nagata saddled and bridled her for us because we couldn't reach up that high, and he lifted me on, too. When Jenny had first come, we had ridden her only on the driveway—from the garage to the house, past it and along to the front gate on Nuuanu Avenue, then back and around to the curved drive that had two entrances on Bates Street. Now we rode her on the grass, too, down the hill to the brook, under the big trees, all over the yard. Usually it was the most fun of anything we did, but today I hardly noticed what I was doing. The clop, clop of hoofs on gravel, their muffled thud on grass scarcely penetrated my consciousness.

Later we went over to Grandma and Grandpa's house, across Bates Street from the back of Brookside. Through the little iron-railed gate on our side, carefully across the quiet street, up the stone steps that were shaded by a poinciana regia tree, like a giant red and green umbrella. Some of the delicate blossoms lay scarlet upon the sharpness of gravel, and automatically I picked them up and placed them on the grass.

Grandma and Grandpa were there on the lanai. There were two lanais at this house, an open one with railings that went round the corner toward Nuuanu, overlooking the big breadfruit tree, and which led to the formal front door. Then there was the enclosed lanai where Grandma and Grandpa always sat, with a long koa table between their two rocking chairs, a big lau hala mat on the floor with Oriental rugs on it, and floods of light coming in through the windows. The window wall behind the koa table was curved, Grandpa's rolltop desk was against the back wall, the front one had in it the door that we always used.

Grandma said cheerily, "Well, Kirey! Are you all packed?"

Grandma was always cheery, a short, plump little woman who wore long, crackly dresses; always smiling, often gently teasing—but today, she seemed to smile when perhaps she didn't want to.

Grandpa got up from his chair and I ran over to throw my arms around his knees, clad today in white. In summertime, he wore white suits, or dark trousers with a white linen or pongee coat and vest. And always high shoes, buttoned or with elastic at the sides, and when he went out, a Panama hat. Grandpa had silvery, silky hair, and a large white moustache that was tickly when he kissed you.

"Merry Sunshine!" It was his name for me, but that day I felt like anything but merry sunshine. He patted my head.

"I'm keeping our cribbage score, Miss Kire," he said. "Don't imagine that you can escape our tournament by moving a few miles away!"

A few miles . . . I went back to Kirey and held on tight to her hand.

"Run out and ask Ara for some cookies, Robby," Grandma said. "Go along, all of you."

As we went, we heard her telling Kirey that Mutie was out,

at a Humane Society meeting. "You should have seen her yesterday!" she added, laughing. "She ran out onto the Avenue and poked her umbrella at a wagon driver who was beating his horse."

There was always a round tin of oatmeal cookies on the bottom shelf of the safe in the pantry, where we could reach it if Ara wasn't there. But he had heard us coming, and was opening the screen door of the safe.

"You like cooky?" His round face beamed on us. We loved Ara, and wished we could have a houseboy. Not instead of Misao or 'Toru, of course. But a kind man, clean in starched white jacket and trousers like Ara, would have made us not mind Ah Loi so much. Perhaps when Misao had her baby . . .

I knew the cooky would be delicious, but only seemed to want to nibble around the edges. This house, too, had been infected by the unrealness of the day; nothing was as usual.

As we stood at the top of the steps and Kirey was saying goodby, Grandpa took her hand in both of his and said, "We'll miss you, all of us—the old, the young, the fat, the thin, the short, the tall."

Grandma kissed her and said, "You won't be far away. We're not losing you, Kirey."

"No, indeed!" said Grandpa. "When you're hungry for these children, come to see them—and don't forget us ancients across the street."

When we got back to Brookside, Kirey's trunk and valise were standing in the hall.

Munna called Kirey into the den and we could hear them talking in low voices. Then Kirey said, "Let her come! It will be better for her to know exactly where I am, from the start."

The little house at Cottage Grove was very nice. Already Kirey's things were in the tiny sitting room: her vases and little Chinese figurines, her tea set near the window, the two panels of wood-framed photographs on the walls. There was the nest of three teak tables and, of course, her potted plants and some flowers. Kirey loved plants and could make anything grow.

"Let's have tea in my new house," she suggested. "Now all of you sit down and I'll have the kettle on the boil in the twinkling of an eye."

She went into the little kitchen, and after peering into it—there wasn't room for anyone but Kirey—I sat with Munna, Holly, and Wobert, and looked round at the known things in their unfamiliar surroundings.

Kirey brought in the teapot and the hot water, put them on the tray and sat beside it, and lifted the lid of the teapot. "Nine stirs is as good as a spoonful of tea," she said, stirring with a silver spoon.

She poured Cambric tea for the three of us, choosing each delicate china teacup with care and adding hot water and lots of cream and sugar to the inch or so of tea; then "real tea" for Munna and herself. Holly passed round the Huntley Palmer biscuits on a china plate, and the two grown-ups chatted as if this were quite an ordinary occasion, somehow making it even more strange.

When it was time for us to go, Munna and Kirey kissed each other, then Kirey kissed each of us children. I clung to her, and she went down the steps with me to the waiting auto.

She shook hands with Nagata and thanked him for bringing her and her belongings, and said, "You must bring Misao out to see me one day soon."

As the car drove off, I kneeled on the seat and looked out of the narrow back window for as long as I could see her, standing and waving at the steps of her new home.

A³ Woman who Teaches and Trains...

I woke that morning to Grandpa's whistle, and sprang out of bed and ran along the hall to the head of the stairs. Whenever Grandpa came to our house and saw nobody around, he whistled his special notes that said, "Are you there?"

"Happy birthday, Merry Sunshine!" he called, and I ran down to jump the last few steps into his arms. His cane was leaning against the wall, so that he could catch me.

"Let me see, now, how many years is it? You must be four years old today!"

"Grandpa!" I giggled. Of course, he really knew how old I was.

"What! Can it be *five*?" He looked perfectly astonished, convulsing me with further giggles. Putting me down, he said anxiously, "You won't forget our engagement for this afternoon, will you?"

As if I could! The Parade . . .

"And do you remember who's coming to tea?"

"Kirey!" I yelled, and turned somersaults down the length of the hall.

Grandpa had his cane again, and was at the front door. "I

wanted to see the birthday girl, first thing. By and by I'll be going down to meet Miss Melbehn at the boat, as your Daddy will be at work. An old man like me can show up late at his office, now and then." He started down the lanai steps, then turned to ask, "Would you like to ask Miss Melbehn to go to the parade with us and to come to tea? She may be lonely, her first day here."

"No!" I shouted. "No, no, no!"

He waved his cane and was off along the walk at the side of the house, that led to Bates Street. "If you change your mind, let Grandma and me know," he called back. I stood watching him as far as the elephant ear tree, at the little gate.

Miss Melbehn! *Why* did she have to come on my birthday? Especially, I didn't want her for tea at Grandma and Grandpa's. I wanted us to have Kirey to ourselves.

Oh, why did Miss Melbehn have to come at all! I went slowly up the stairs and to the nursery, where Otoru had left my clothes out for me on a chair. Otoru had been sleeping in the nursery since Kirey had gone to live at Cottage Grove. Now she'd be moving down to her own room, and Miss Melbehn— *she* was going to be in Kirey's room.

One of my bloomer suits today—pink. I got into it—no buttons, except the ones to undo on my pajamas—and slid down the bannister to see if it was breakfast-time. I hovered in the hall, peeking past the piano at the end of the living room to the big, light dining room.

Otoru was laying the table, and Munna stood at my place with some flowers in her hands. I mustn't look! I strolled over to the front door and gazed out across the lanai to the driveway, the granite steps to the lawn beyond, and far away, the beginning of the hillside above the brook. It was a sparkly day, the right kind of day for a birthday.

Behind me, Misao said, "Happy birthday!" and began to strike the breakfast gong. The four notes rose and fell as her gong stick tapped the bars and blended together to make a lovely chiming sound.

Then Munna came, and everyone was there—Daddy, and

Holly, and Wobert—and we went into the square, high-ceilinged room where there were flowers around my place at the table, and a stack of packages on a little table beside it.

Most of them were wrapped in white tissue paper, of which Munna always had a good supply on hand. (At Christmas, there were red and green as well.) These birthday ones were tied with different colors of yarn, the kind she was always knitting.

I eyed the pile sidelong, but didn't begin opening things until Munna said: "Well, birthday girl! Don't you want to see what your presents are? I'm dying to know!"

At the top of the pile was a small package with a card written in Munna's large, upright hand. In the box was a plain gold circlet that slipped easily over my hand. A bracelet, like Holly's! This was the only one from Munna and Daddy that had a card on it, so I knew it was their "main present." One of the others was a doll, and I said, "Thank you," but I really didn't like dolls very much. It was just like one that Holly had whose name was Violet, so I thought, I'll call her Rose.

From Holly there were paper dolls, from Wobert a fishnet tied to a bamboo pole. I could see that he had made it himself, and also wrapped it, and could imagine him frowning as he tied the lopsided bow of blue ribbon. Misao and Nagata's present was in a narrow box; it was a fan, which spread out to show white birds on blue paper, and white clouds, and a stream below. It was beautiful. 'Toru had given me a tiny doll in a glass and red lacquer box, that looked exactly like a small Japanese girl dressed up in kimono and obi. From Grandma and Grandpa there was a book called *The Dutch Twins*, and Grandma had written: "They're five years old, just like you!" Mutie's present was a string of beads, of course—blue ones. The necklace was very pretty.

At the very bottom of the pile was a large, flat, heavy package, with a card on it in a small, neat kind of curly handwriting that I knew well: Kirey's. Daddy helped me to open this one. It was a picture of a nurse with a little boy who had curls and who was very dressed up in a long coat with fur around the bottom and collar, and a hat edged in fur, too. He and his nurse were crossing a street while a policeman made all the buggies and carts and hansom cabs, with horses harnessed to them, stop until they got across. Daddy read the words at the bottom of the picture: "His Majesty, the Baby." A picture of my own! To hang on the wall near my bed—I knew just the place for it.

Otoru and Wobert helped me to carry all the things upstairs. When they had gone, I opened the door from the nursery to Kirey's room. New furniture had been put in it for Miss Melbehn. Hatred for her surged through me. Why should she be in Kirey's room! And I supposed she'd be eating with us, and putting us to bed . . . If she read us a story, I wouldn't listen. I'd put my fingers in my ears.

Through the window across the room, I could see Grandpa's auto turning into the driveway from Nuuanu. She was here, then. Where was the fishnet? I'd take it and find Wobert, and we could try it out in the brook. I grabbed it up and ran down the hall.

But I was caught. From partway down the stairs, I saw them coming up the lanai steps: Grandpa with his cane, holding the arm of a tall, thin woman. Munna's quick footsteps sounded, going toward the front door.

I ran back up and along the bannister to the "telephone corner," just opposite the bathroom, and from there ducked into the doorway that led to the attic stairway, and sat on one of the lower steps. There were voices below, then Munna and the thin woman were coming up the stairs. Munna was saying, "You must be tired after your long trip," and a foreign-sounding voice replied, "It would take more than a journey to tire me. I live sensibly and keep very well." The screen door to the inner hall opened and closed.

After a little while, Munna seemed to be going down by

herself. I opened the door cautiously and heard her in the hall, thanking Grandpa for having met Miss Melbehn.

Grandpa said he had been very glad to do it, then his voice lowered to a hoarse whisper. I leaned over the bannister to hear what he was saying. It ended with, "My first impression is that you needn't worry about Dan's flirting with her."

When it was quiet, I scuttled down the stairs, past the piano, and to the back porch by way of the passage that went by the "closet under the stairs."

Seeing Wobert under the monkey-pod tree, I shouted to him and he waited while I ran down the steep back steps. "She's here! Let's go down to the brook and we can try my new fishnet. She'd never find us there!"

Lunch wasn't birthdayish, the way it should have been.

Miss Melbehn sat next to Daddy, and Wobert was on her other side. I was right across from her. She sat in her chair very primly. Her back looked rigid. It wasn't the same way that Kirey sat up straight. You noticed Miss Melbehn's cheekbones because she was so thin, and her mouth closed tightly in a line. She was Danish, we had been told.

Munna talked a lot, asking Miss Melbehn about her trip from Winnipeg, and now and then saying something to me, with her gay smile, and I knew she was remembering it was my birthday. Daddy didn't say much, just wiggled his eyebrows at Miss Melbehn and asked her if it had been rough during the boat trip, or something about a lake in Canada. Much later I realized that he had been trying to help Munna, but that he had been nearly as awestruck by our new governess as we were.

Governess! What did we want a *governess* for. Munna had told us that she was a teacher, and that was what a governess was—a teacher who lived at home with you.

"But we're going to school by and by, like Holly," I had protested. "Wobert and me."

"I looked it up in the dictionary," Holly said. Holly had been reading now for two years, ever since she read *The*

Wonderful Wizard of Oz to herself when she was five. She could read big words, and everything. "A governess is 'A woman who teaches and trains children, especially in a private family.' "

I didn't want to be taught and trained. "We *are* going to Miss Maxfield's school, aren't we?" I asked anxiously.

"Yes," Munna said. "Miss Melbehn will take care of you, and help you with lessons, and things. Perhaps later she'll sometimes teach you, too. We'll all be glad to have her here, since Kirey has gone."

I choked now at lunch, thinking about it, and Daddy hit me on the back till I stopped. She didn't even bring me a birthday present! I thought, glaring across the table.

She was saying, "I have never been seasick," answering Daddy's question about the boat. "Many of the passengers were ill and were obliged to remain in their cabins. I was in the dining room for every meal." Her way of speaking was strange to us. She cut her words off short, somehow, and certain words she pronounced differently from the ways of other people we knew.

"Do they have good food on a boat?" asked Holly.

"It was adequate. I myself am always careful of my diet."

I stared at her, wondering how we could ever talk to her, then glanced at Wobert and caught a completely startled look on his face. He was gazing open-mouthed at Miss Melbehn. What was the matter with him? He couldn't be *that* surprised that she never got seasick.

Dessert was ice cream and chocolate sauce, two scoops apiece, the way it always was on birthdays, and on every Wednesday and Sunday. There was a birthday cake too, of course. It was decorated with pink icing and had six pink candles on it.

"One to grow on," said Munna. "Now make a good wish."

I sat gazing at the six wavering flames. A *good* wish, yes! You only got this chance once a year. What should it be?

Everyone was quiet, and I realized they were all watching, waiting for me to wish.

"Hurry up!" said Wobert. "The candles will burn right down to the cake, if you don't look out."

My mind was an utter blank. I shut my eyes for a couple of seconds, as if I were wishing, then blew. With all my huffing and puffing, two of the candles were still flickering when my breath was gone.

"It won't come true for two years!" shouted Wobert.

"What was your wish?" asked Miss Melbehn.

I was tongue-tied, and didn't look at her.

"She mustn't tell," Munna said, "or it won't come true. Now cut the first slice for yourself, and Misao will do the rest."

After lunch, Wobert said to me, "You know what? When she was talking in that stuck-up way about not being seasick, I kicked her under the table and she *kicked me back*. Without even looking at me."

This somehow disturbed my picture of Miss Melbehn. Looking so stiff and yet doing such an unexpected thing . . . I stood watching her go up the stairs. She had a look of being alone.

I took Rose outside and showed her around the yard. For a doll, she wasn't bad. Maybe I'd play with her sometimes. She was made of something that wasn't really hard, but still she couldn't be hugged the way Teddybear could. She was wearing a thin white dress that had lace or something around the edges, and so did the petticoat and panties, and she had white socks and shoes. Brown hair was painted on her head.

"You see, Rose, this is the front gate." I got up on the stone wall and sat her on one of the pillars. A streetcar went by, tinkling its bell, and the conductor waved at us. It had to slow down to get up Judd Hill.

"And right here is the Chinese cherry tree. We can sit in it and watch autos come in through the gate." We waited among the slender leaves for a while, but nothing came in and there was no one around. Only a few mynah birds, chattering as they flew into the clump of bamboo at the other side of the drive. I picked and ate one of the shiny little orangey-red cherries, shaped like a Chinese lantern with round, fluted sides.

We went down along the grass slope below the wall to the brook, where the bridge went over Nuuanu. The bridge, and the wall here, were very high. "Miles high," I said to Rose. "Well, not *miles*." But we had to lean way back to see the top of the wall. We walked on the wide-bladed buffalo grass under the big trees, with the brook below us, and then down the steps to the wooden bridge. Just to the edge. Rose might be scared if we went out onto it. I looked down at the dark water, flowing faster than usual it seemed under the plank, and could feel my heart beating. Back up the steps, we followed the little 'auwai at the bottom of the yard; it streamed down to join the brook. Across this narrow rush of water were trees and bushes growing so close together that you couldn't see very far into them. "A wilderness," Munna called it. It was part of the yard but we weren't allowed to go in there.

At the top of the hill we found a mango on the ground, but it was squishy with black spots on it. The mangoes on the trees here were much too high to reach. They looked good, turning yellow.

Fat Yama was raking leaves. He smiled and said, "Haro," but we didn't stop to talk to him. I didn't like Yama very much. He looked as if he smiled to be polite, not because he wanted to. Once I had heard Grandma saying to Munna, "Yama is an 'eye-servant.'" I hadn't known what that meant, but guessed that Grandma didn't think much of him, either.

Wobert was yelling for me. "Time to get ready for the Parade!"

The Parade! I ran all the way up to the house, and Wobert and I raced up the stairs and along to the nursery. Miss Melbehn was there, and we stopped short.

She was standing beside her suitcase, which lay open on a stand, putting things from it into the drawers of the chiffonier that had been moved into Kirey's room for her. What was it doing in the nursery? Some of her things, a pile of white cotton nightgowns and a grayish-blue shawl, were on the bed that Otoru had been sleeping in.

Miss Melbehn said, with a kind of smile, "I told your mother that I should prefer to sleep here, to be closer to you children."

"Oh."

Closer to us—we wouldn't like that. But she wasn't going to be in Kirey's room!

"I shall be able to supervise you more easily from here."

Wobert edged toward the door, and I would have backed out of the room if she hadn't just then taken a framed photograph out of her suitcase and placed it on the chiffonier. It was a family group, old-fashioned looking—father, mother, three girls, and a boy. She must have a family, strange though it seemed. The rest of them must be very far away. Which one of the girls could have grown up to be Miss Melbehn?

She stood for a moment looking at the picture, and her face was sad. I remembered how she had looked, walking up the stairs. Alone. Lonely—Grandpa had said she might be lonely at first.

"Grandpa's taking us to the Parade this afternoon," I blurted out. "He wants you to come, too, and to go to their house for tea."

She turned, with more of a smile this time. "I must get unpacked and settled in. But perhaps by tea-time . . . "

Otoru came in softly on her straw slippers. "Come, bath early today!"

The Parade was a wonder. We sat in a grandstand in a wide place off the street. Grandpa carried me because the steps were so high, and everybody was greeting him as we went up the rows of benches. "Hello, W.O.! Aloha, W.O.!" He stopped to talk to some of the people, and waved at others. Lots of them were Hawaiian ladies and men, wearing lau hala hats with flower leis on them, or feather leis. He spoke to some of them in

Hawaiian. We saw 'Toru with Misao and Nagata, and called hello to them.

There were just the three of us, and Grandpa sat with Wobert on one side and me on the other. Only three, because *Holly* was going to march in the Parade!

"When will Holly go by?" I asked excitedly. "Will she be first?"

"Perhaps not first, but we'll be seeing her!"

"Watch for the banner that says 'Lanai School' on it," said Wobert. "Lawrence is going to carry the banner. I know Lawrence."

At the beginning of the Parade were carts drawn by horses, all covered with flowers, every kind of flower you could imagine. "They're floats," Wobert said. "That's what you call them, floats." On one of them, a man and lady were dressed like a Hawaiian king and queen. They wore feather capes and leis, red and yellow, and sat on a mat of feathers. The man wore a high feather hat that Grandpa said was a helmet. On the next one, a Hawaiian man played an ukulele and sang, and a girl in a grass skirt danced the hula. She wore lots of plumeria leis, pink and rose and yellow and white.

"Where's Holly?" I asked. "When's she coming?"

"Don't worry, she'll be along! We'll be seeing her."

Next came men in uniforms, marching behind a band that played *Hilo March*. It made you want to march, too, to hear it! Some of the men were very old.

"That's the National Guard," Grandpa said. "And veterans—men who used to be in the Guard."

When the two flags were carried past, the Stars and Stripes and the Hawaiian flag, Grandpa stood up and took off his Panama hat and held it against his chest. Everybody else stood up, too.

There were ladies wearing black holokus and hats, with orangey-yellow leis. " 'Ilima," Grandpa said. "The flower of Oahu, and of royalty. Those ladies belong to the Ka'ahumanu Society."

"What's that?"

"It's named for a great queen, Ka'ahumanu. She was King Kamehameha's favorite wife."

"Did he have two?"

"More than that! Lots of them. But she was the one he loved best."

"Lanai School!" shouted Wobert.

There was Lawrence, in front with the banner, standing straight and tall. His class, kindergarten, came after him. Next first grade—and then Holly! She was looking right ahead and keeping time, with a serious face. Her curls bobbed against her back and shoulders. She didn't see us, but we clapped hard.

Last of all came the Pa'u Riders, one for each island—the Princess of that island. Oh, how beautiful they were, the horses and the riders! "It's an art, dressing a pa'u rider," Grandpa said. "Not many can do it properly." The satiny cloth—gold, red, purple, all colors—was wrapped intricately about each princess and fell in graceful folds to the stirrups, and below them.

The horses' coats were shining, and each was different— brown from light to dark, sorrel, chestnut, white, black, gray. And a black and white one. "A pinto!" cried Wobert. "That one's a pinto." All of the horses wore big, thick leis, and arched their necks and pranced as if they knew Princesses were riding them.

Grandpa told us which belonged to each island. "Golden 'ilima for Oahu, feathery red lehua for Hawaii. And a maile leaf lei for that horse, from the mountains on Hawaii."

"Which is Maui?" I asked. It was the only other island I knew, the one Daddy had grown up on.

"That's the Rose of Heaven, lokelani." The Maui Princess was wearing the most lovely, gleaming rosy-red, and her long wavy black hair shone, with a band of roses and green leaves round it.

One of the Princesses' leis was of berries instead of flowers, another was strands and strands of tiny pink seashells. The

Princess of Molokai wore white kukui blossoms, and her horse the big pale leaves of that tree.

"Last of all, Molokini," Grandpa said. "Molokini is hardly big enough, just a great rock, but we call it the ninth island."

We hated to have the Parade end. I heard a girl saying, "Oh, it was gorgeous!" Gorgeous. A new word, but it sounded the way the Parade had been. A gorgeous Parade. And it had happened on my birthday!

Grandma said: "Will you pour, Kirey?"

We were in the living room because it was a special occasion. Kirey was sitting in "her chair at Grandma's house," a mahogany one with arms and a straight back. Everything else was different that day, as we were in the long, rather dark, irregular-shaped room with its old-fashioned looking sofas and chairs. The floor was covered by Oriental rugs large and small, and many paintings hung on the papered walls. Even the ceiling was papered here, in a symmetrical design, and a chandelier hung from it in the part of the room where the piano was. The door and window frames were of a dark, plainly carved wood. Near the archway to the enclosed lanai stood a bronze statue of Nimrod.

Mutie was there, for once not up in her room stringing beads. She used to say, "It's making me lose my eyesight, but I can't help it." I loved to go to her room and see the boxes and baskets of beads, all shades. Sometimes she let me run them through my fingers, like colored waterfalls.

Holly told Grandma about marching in the Parade while Kirey poured, and Wobert and I helped Ara pass teacups and china plates with embroidered napkins. I could see that we were going to have gems, dark oblong-shaped muffins that I loved, and we never had except at Grandma's.

Kirey's voice sounded extra polite as she asked, "Sugar and milk, Miss Melbehn?"

"A teaspoonful of melk, if you please, and some hot water added. I take no sugar."

Oh, it was good to have Kirey there! I sat beside her and turned away from Miss Melbehn, and tried not to hear her talking to Grandpa. She was telling him how she had happened to go to Canada from Denmark. I wanted to forget her, forget that she was lonely, and that she would be there in the nursery when we went to bed.

Kirey was wearing one of her church dresses, gray silk, and the brooch that had braided strands of her mother's and her own hair showing through the glass.

"How is Teddybear?" she asked.

"Fine. Thank you for the picture."

"Do you like it? It came from London for you."

I wanted to tell her how much I loved it, and where Nagata had hung it for me, and was trying to think of words to say.

"Are you going to hang it near your bed?"

"It's there already!"

Kirey nodded, smiling, and even though I could hear Miss Melbehn telling Grandpa about Winnipeg, it didn't matter any more.

4
The
Baby Whale

Holly's voice startled me awake. "A *whale!*"

Sleep was gone in an instant. Had it come at last? Often while swimming in the shallow water near shore, or gazing from the beach across the bay to the long arm of the West Maui Mountains, I thought about whales and wondered if some day I would see one. Grandpa had taken us to the Bishop Museum in Honolulu, where an enormous whale was suspended from the ceiling. When you stood on a balcony, you could see its insides. But I had never seen a live one.

Wobert said from the doorway, "It's a baby. Washed right over the reef in the night!" He was gone, calling back as he ran, "Come see! Some baby!"

Holly dashed to the closet for her bloomer suit, and I scrambled out of bed. We didn't bother about shoes, so it didn't take long to dress. A *whale*. We ran across the lanai and out to the beach.

We had moved to Maui, the island where our father had lived before he and Munna were married. Munna had told us that Daddy hadn't been so well as he should be in Honolulu—

31

it was too hot, and he wasn't used to office life. So we were going to live on the mountain on a cattle ranch, but for the time being we were at the beach.

The whale wasn't in the water. Its great, sloping gray back glistened wetly on the hard-packed sand at the edge of the sea, and little waves curled and frothed about it. Some seaweed had caught on its tail, and as each wave licked up and away, the long green streamer coiled waveringly. Our yardman Ogata and others from along the beach stood around, talking excitedly.

A *baby*? I thought it must be dead until I saw the small dark eye, which seemed to be looking at me beseechingly.

"Get it back into the water!" I shouted.

"It got itself out, silly," Wobert said. His brown eyes were shining, his pale hair stood on end—no time for a hairbrush on a morning like this.

"How could it?" I demanded indignantly. "Tell them," I begged Holly. "Tell them to roll it back in."

"Did it really get on the beach by itself?" she asked. "Poor thing! Get them to push it back in, Boy." Her hair too was in disarray, hanging in tousled brown locks about her anxious face.

Wobert shrugged his shoulders. "How would it get back over the reef? It would just die anyway."

"The same way it came," said Holly. "At high tide."

Far out, above the sea, the reef showed in a long curving ridge of coral. Its mother would be looking for it. Perhaps even now she swam back and forth out there, searching. Since seeing the look in the whale's eye, I could almost believe it was a baby in spite of the great hulking body.

"Hifteen heet!" Ogata was saying. "Hifteen heet, sure." He held out his arms, measuring.

"Maw," said the yardman from next door. "Maw den hifteen."

My mother and June were coming along the beach, and Holly and I ran to meet them.

"Mother, get them to put it back in the water!" Holly cried.

"It will die," I said. "Tell them!"

"It looks dead already," Munna said.

"No! Look at its eye."

June took my hand and said, "Come, honey, let's go in."

"Yes, it's breakfast time," Munna said.

"No!" I wrenched my hand from June's. June was one of my mother's prettiest friends, with soft brown hair and laughing eyes. But I couldn't let her lure me in now, treat me like a baby.

A baby . . . "Is it really a baby?" I asked wonderingly, and knew that it was.

The brightness of sun on yellow sand, on little ripply pale blue waves, hurt my eyes. The men were not going to put the whale back into the ocean. I turned away with June.

Neither Holly nor I wanted breakfast. We pretended to eat some papaya and puffed rice.

It was so strange, being here on Maui, and at the beach. I couldn't quite take it in that we had moved away from Brookside. Weren't we ever going back? And where was Kirey? At Cottage Grove, I knew that. But why not here, where we were? It was because of Miss Melbehn. She was here—and Kirey was at Cottage Grove. It was all wrong.

I pushed back my chair from the table.

"Remember to fold your napkin," said Miss Melbehn. "And say, 'Excuse me,' when you leave the table."

I folded the napkin and shoved it into its ring. "Try again. You can do it more neatly than that."

I didn't go back to the beach until late morning. The tide had ebbed, leaving the whale more stranded looking than before. The sand under it was drying, and a lighter shade than it had been earlier. The body looked different, too; sun had parched the tough gray skin, and it was dull rather than glistening. The eye was still open but there was no life in it. I walked round the head to where water swished gently over my feet, and looked into the other eye. Remembering how the beachward one had seemed to plead with me, I realized that the whale was dead.

A momentary picture was startlingly clear in my mind: the mother, at the other side of the reef. Swimming to and fro, to and fro. Unconsciously I used Kirey's phrase instead of "back and forth."

My father, home for lunch, came out to the beach with his Kodak and said, "Come along, kids, jump onto its back."

I hesitated, then followed the others: Wobert, Holly, and our cousins who lived next door. The dark skin was rough under my feet, not slippery as I felt it should be. When my father said, "All ready?" I smiled into the camera. Only a mass of dried-out flesh; a dead whale on our beach.

In the afternoon, Ogata and some other men cut it up. I watched from a bank above the beach, wearing my sunbonnet. The sun was on its lowering course, toward the West Maui Mountains that lay now across an expanse of gold-topped ocean waves. Kirey had made it for me, the sunbonnet that shaded my eyes.

It was as if we were Eskimos, I thought, waiting for our share of a slain bear. Or whale—they killed whales, too. The meat was dark, not like fish at all.

"A whale isn't a fish," said Holly. "It's a mammal."

"What's a mammal?"

"Like people."

She seemed serious, but of course she was trying to tease me. Besides, I didn't think people looked dark inside. Holly's hair swung now in its usual long curls, having been deftly twisted about Otoru's slim fingers, and brushed and brushed. She looked more natural.

"That's blubber right under the skin," she said. I remembered that Grandpa had told us about blubber, at the Museum.

Mori, in the kitchen, looked the steaks over with an expert eye and said, "I fry." Then he shooed us out. Mori was tall for a

Japanese and he had a stern face. He was an excellent cook, perhaps because he didn't let us bother him. Men cooks were like that, in my experience. But Mori was a great improvement over Ah Loi. He didn't really seem to mind us too much.

Usually the three of us had dinner early with Miss Melbehn, but tonight we were allowed to have it with the grown-ups because June was there.

At the table, Munna, June, and Holly said, "No, thank you," to whale steak and had some left-over cold meat. Daddy had whale, and Wobert said to us, "What's the matter with you? It will be good." I nodded, and took some from Otoru as she passed it.

"Use your right hand to eat with," Miss Melbehn said, and I switched my fork over.

But then, with my mouth full, I realized that I didn't want to eat any of the whale. I spit out what I had been chewing, and ran and was sick.

If Kirey had been there, she would have read to us at bedtime. Would June read to me, perhaps? But after dinner, she went right into the guest room and my father and mother went upstairs. I followed them and sat in what Munna called her "boudoir."

While she sat at the dressing table, I picked up her orangestick. These always made me think of Kirey. "Brush your nails well, then use the orangestick, child."

Holding it in my hand, I looked round the little room. It was very nice; I loved the wallpaper. Describing it to one of her friends, Munna had said, "White satin background with a strip of pink roses every foot or so. It's pretty enough to eat."

After a while, it occurred to me that she was dressing for a party. Were they going *out*? I felt dismayed, cheated! I needed to have them at home, needed Munna or June to read to me.

I rushed downstairs. It was true. June was in the living room now, wearing pink satin, her hair puffed out over the "rats" that she and my mother wore when they dressed up. She looked so beautiful that I could scarcely breathe. It was what a lady should wear, a pink, shiny dress like June's.

While waiting for Munna and Daddy, she went to the Victrola and put on a record, and waltzed around the room singing, " 'It's three o'clock in the morning—we've danced the whole night through' . . . That's what it will be when we come home, little lamb." She bent to take my face between her hands. How delicious she smelled. "Three o'clock!" She held out her hands to me, and swayed with the music. I could picture her dancing with some man, while I was here at the beach, wanting her near. "Just one more waltz with you," she sang, and took my hands in hers.

"No!" I shrieked. "No, no!" I pulled away and then dived at her, wanting to hold her there and not let her go away. My hands ripped at her dress, tore a great slash right down the front of it. I threw myself on the floor, and kicked and screamed.

The grown-ups were late leaving for their party, because Munna had to lend June a dress. I thought Munna might spank me, but she didn't. She kissed my teary, swollen face and turned me over to Otoru to be put to bed. If it had been Miss Melbehn, I couldn't have stood it.

Otoru, in her gay butterflied kimono, sat by my bed until the sounds of departure had stilled. I thought Holly, in the other bed, was asleep until she said, "I dreamed last night that Boy was made into boy salad."

Boy salad! Now I'd never be able to call him Boy, as Holly and Munna did sometimes.

I could barely see Otoru in the pencil of light from the bathroom door, but I liked having her there. Holly did go to sleep soon, and I lay without moving, hugging Teddybear and willing Otoru to stay. I didn't dare speak because Miss Melbehn was in the room beyond the bathroom, and I didn't want her to come in.

After a while, Otoru went softly out.

The eye of the whale haunted me. When I closed my eyes,

that was what I saw. The mother might be swimming in the dark, cold water, still searching.

Would it really be three o'clock when they got home from the party? Exhaustion pressed down on me, and I felt hollow. But I couldn't sleep. Kirey had said my guardian angel would watch over me. I lay thinking of the angel, and of Kirey. Oh, why wasn't it she who was in the next room? Why weren't we at Brookside?

I got up at last, quietly, quietly, so Miss Melbehn wouldn't hear me. Clutching Teddybear, I tiptoed across the living room to the guest room and opened the door. Leaving it ajar, I climbed into June's bed, and laid Teddybear on the pillow beside me. Light streamed in over the chair on which lay the ruined pink dress.

Noises, voices saying good night, then June switching on the light. Seeing me, she turned it off and lit a dim lamp instead, and came and stood beside the bed.

"I'm sorry, June."

"You didn't mean to. Not really."

I shook my head. "Is it three o'clock?"

"No, it's earlier. Go to sleep, now."

"Here?"

"Mhm. You and Teddybear stay with me tonight."

I lay for a minute longer looking up at her. She seemed taller than usual, standing there above me. "You're taller than Munna, aren't you?" I asked, wondering whether I quite liked that.

"A little." She leaned down and said, hugging me, "But she's older than I am."

"Oh." That made it all right. I snuggled down among the pillows that smelt faintly of the lovely, pink-satin-lady fragrance of June, and was asleep before she came to bed.

The Beautiful 5

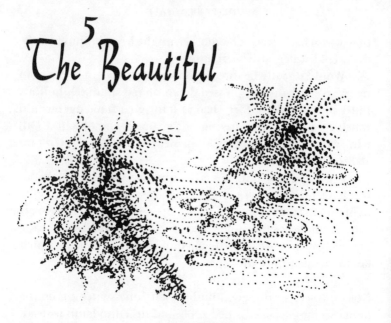

Kirey said: "Jack Frost has been here."

I jumped out of bed and ran to stand beside her at the window. A shimmer lay on the grass, pale, shining, spread over all of it from the lilies to the climb-up-the-outside trees. I thought of the fairies Holly had told me lived in the lilies, and wondered if they had seen Jack Frost.

"Does he come in the night? When it's dark?"

"Just before it gets light, I always think."

I'd like to see him, frosty and white, running over the grass and scattering sheen upon it.

From a window in the other wall I saw that the shimmery veil was on that side, too. Past the sweet pea arbor, across the croquet lawn, right up to the dark branches that swept the ground. Air coming in at the window was cold, delicious, mountainy; it made the scent of roses that clambered to the sill a cold scent. They grew in clusters, tiny pink ones, and there was dew on them.

Kirey and I were staying at Olinda for a few weeks, with my uncle, aunt, and cousin, while the Ranch House was being

38

finished. The rest of the family was at the beach. Olinda was higher on the mountain Haleakala than where the Ranch House was being built. A narrow, winding dirt road, lined by rows and groves of eucalyptus trees, led up to it. Above were pastures of the Ranch.

Kirey and I were in the blue room upstairs, a light room with all white furniture. The sun came in early at the lily-side windows, making patterns on the floor and wall. I usually lay watching them from my bed in the corner when I woke. The other windows looked toward the ocean, though you could see only a far line of it over the tops of the garden trees and the eucalyptus at the bottom of the Olinda horse paddock.

"Get dressed now, child. And your warm sweater!"

Kirey was already partly dressed, with her kimono back on: her corsets and the corset cover edged with tatting, her combinations, and long cotton petticoat from the waist. For dinner, under the church dresses that she wore at night, she had petticoats that rustled.

I tugged at her skirt and said, "I don't have to wear as many clothes as you—I'll be dressed first!"

"Mischief!" said Kirey. When she called me that, she pronounced it "Mischeef."

I hurried into my panty-waist and buttoned the panties to it all the way around, then my yellow bloomer suit and socks and sandals, and was ready by the time she was fastening her high black shoes with the buttonhook. She was wearing a lavender and white checked dress this morning. Her Overseas pin, the white circle with a red "S" in it, was on her bosom, and the initialed gold case with eyeglasses attached. The blue pin with "N.Z.R.N." on it, for "New Zealand Registered Nurse," was in her ivory jewel box.

I took Teddybear out of my bed and sat him on a small chair, and we went into the dark hall and down the stairway with its landing, for breakfast in the room facing the mountain. A fire cracked in the corner fireplace. I loved this room with its blue wallpaper and the high shelf for beer mugs that Uncle Henry had collected.

Uncle Henry had had his breakfast very early, as usual, and Diane wasn't down yet, also as usual on Saturday. "Big girls do sleep late, for some reason," Kirey had said. "When it's not a school morning."

Aunt Ella smiled at us from her place and said, "What a chilly morning—autumn is here! Come and sit down, you two, and we'll have Kirey's teapot here in a jiffy. Some hot chocolate, too." Aunt Ella was my mother's sister, which made her easy to know. She was quite like Munna, only bigger. "I love being at the mountain house at this time of year."

As Kirey poured, steam rising from her teacup looked especially inviting.

"Diane put a glass of water on the kitchen steps last night, hopefully. It's *almost* cold enough for it to be coated with ice, this morning."

I craned my neck, trying to see the steps at the far side of the pergola grown with wisteria and big white roses.

"We'll go out there after breakfast," Kirey said. "Eat your porridge, now."

No film of ice on the water in the glass, but it was very cold. I stuck my finger in and it nearly froze. We stood for a minute looking up at the horses in the paddock above. The air seemed still, yet sunlight danced over the leaves of eucalyptus trees at either side of the hill. Beyond the grassy knoll, the mountain rose to a peak, sharp and free against the sky.

We walked round the house, going under the porte-cochere. "Let's stay on the driveway so we won't mark up Jack Frost's grass," Kirey said.

The house was surrounded by flowers. Fuchsia, heliotrope, geraniums were bright splashes on the red-brown walls, and trellised roses were everywhere, climbing to the roof. Their fragrances mingled with those of the climb-up trees and of eucalyptus.

"Olinda flowers are the loveliest of all!" Kirey exclaimed. "So many still blooming." Then, as we reached the edge of

Jack Frost's grass, "This won't last long, I'm afraid."

"Will it really go away?"

"When the sun is higher. By the time it's over the treetops."

"Kirey." A thought came to me, at the same moment, it seemed, when I was considering the fleeting quality of that lovely frostiness.

"What is it, child?"

"Last night, in the night—who was that man sitting on your bed?"

The hand holding mine tightened. Her face under its brimmed hat looked shaken; I had never seen Kirey like that.

I stood with my face turned up to her, and after a minute she said, "I dreamed last night of someone, a man I knew in New Zealand. Someone I loved very much."

"But you don't now?"

"I do," she said softly. Then, to herself not to me, "Those many years ago."

I waited, still wanting to know who had sat at the edge of her bed.

"There was no one there," she said at last. "I was dreaming, that was all."

"He had a beard," I said doubtfully. "A short beard."

"Was it so light that you could see him?"

I thought about this. "The moon was shining through the windows. It wasn't very light, but I could see him."

Already little patches of shimmer were beginning to go from the grass, and the yardman Fuji was walking across the far end of it. I didn't want to see his footsteps on it, and turned away. "Let's go down the flower road."

Below the long driveway, sloping nearly beside it, was what seemed to be an older road, and along it Aunt Ella had planted golden poppies, lilacs, chrysanthemums, cosmos, all sorts of flowering plants. Kirey and I often did some gardening there, pulling up weeds, loosening earth, cutting off dead blossoms and leaves, watering, she holding the hose and I with a watering can. This morning we walked slowly down the road, feeling the first real warmth of the sun on our backs, with crispness still on our faces, hands, and my bare legs.

It was a miracle that Kirey had come to Maui and that she and I were together at Olinda. "A few weeks" sounded like a wonderfully long time, and I needn't think of any future when she would be back in Honolulu and we still on Maui.

I loved the familiar dresses she wore, mostly in light gardeny colors: shades of blue, sometimes a pale rose, or green. One was white with a filmy design of black, like spider webs.

She said, "Would you like to know the Lord's Prayer?" She said it through as we walked along, then, "Say after me, 'Our Father, who art in Heaven, Hallowed be thy Name.'"

"Shouldn't we be kneeling?"

"Not while you're learning it. When we say it at night, we'll kneel. And put our hands together, like this." She placed her palms together, fingers upward, as she had taught me to do during my prayers. "We'll walk to and fro, while you learn it."

When I could say with her through the line: "On earth as it is in Heaven," we went on down the driveway's incline to where it curved and leveled going toward the gate.

A path of log steps and gravel went up quite steeply just there, through the eucalyptus trees, with the Japanese Tea House about halfway up the slope. Here we stopped to sit for a while on the bench that went round the inside, and to look out through the trees to the gulch with its fallen-log bridge. The sound of water flowing down the streambed reminded me of the brook. But with Kirey there, the despairing longing became a memory of days she and I had been there together, days so numerous that they blended into remembrance of a loved place. For the first time since we had left Brookside, my mind was able to look back to the brook without a churning sickness of spirit in me. Perhaps, even, we *would* go back there some day.

As we walked on up the path, voices came to us from the stable at the top. Here we were on the level of the house again, across the lawn from it. We rounded a wisteria vine on a latticed frame, where raspberries grew too, and saw Uncle Henry and Fuji sitting on their heels beside the gray mare Hina. Their expressions of angry distress were identical.

Fuji shook his head worriedly. "'At's the way I find 'um. How he do, no can say."

They had been doctoring a gash in the mare's belly, a round hole that dripped red.

Kirey went quickly and bent to look at the wound.

"What do you say, Miss Kire?" asked Uncle Henry. "Anything else we can do right now?"

Kirey pulled her glasses out on their chain and put them on, and felt round the dreadful hole with gentle, sensitive fingers.

"It's draining nicely," she said. "One is always afraid of infection. It looks as if she had landed right on a jagged sapling stump. How can she have done it?"

"Put horse iodine already," Fuji volunteered, holding up the bottle. "Better doctor come, I think."

Uncle Henry stood up. "Yes, I'm going in to try to get hold of him."

Uncle Henry was a nice, not too scary man with eyes that smiled often. My father's brother, but he didn't look much like Daddy, maybe because of the moustache.

We walked toward the house with him, and he said, "I only hope it doesn't take me a week to get hold of Doctor Fitz and get him way up here."

"The telephone is a wonderful instrument, isn't it?" said Kirey.

"When it's working, and you can hear over it!"

"How long is a week?" I asked.

Uncle Henry said, "Seven days," looking at me gravely.

Seven days! How could it possibly take Doctor Fitz seven days to get here? I saw then that Uncle Henry's eyes were smiling. Often I didn't know when he was joking, which could be puzzling.

Seven days in a week . . . and Kirey and I were to be at Olinda for a few weeks. It seemed forever. I took hold of her hand.

One morning I sat at the very top of a tree, watching for Grandpa. Aunt Ella had told me it was too early. After getting in on the *Claudine* from Honolulu, he would have breakfast at the beach house, and stop to see my cousins Lorry, Cathy, and Bubbles on the way up the mountain. Bubbles was the baby. He didn't have any real name yet so we called him that.

Uncle Henry had driven the car down for Grandpa quite a while before, so maybe he'd come sooner than Aunt Ella thought. And I didn't want to miss seeing the car come up the drive. Kirey had helped me over the tree's bottom branches, the ones that touched the grass, and after that it was easy. Right up the outside—I'd never seen a tree like this. The top was round and made a lovely place to sit cross-legged.

The branches smelled good. They were a dark green with lots and lots of tiny leaves—needles, Kirey said—and small brown nuts, something like the ones the eucalyptus fairies lived in. I wondered if fairies lived in these.

After a while, Diane climbed up and sat by me. She had stayed home from school because Grandpa was coming. Usually she went early with Uncle Henry, when he drove down to the plantation.

"We'll be able to hear the car coming up the road," she said.

Diane was nice, the nicest big girl I knew. It was hard to get used to her with her hair up, though. She was in high school this year, and could put it up.

"I love to have Grandpa come," she said. "Do you?"

I considered. "I've never had him come *here*. Once to the beach house, and Grandma too. Mostly we've lived across Bates Street from them." I was on the edge of the ache that thinking about Brookside made in me. But Kirey was in the flower road, digging with a trowel. She was wearing her gardening smock over her dress today. And Grandpa was coming!

"I love to stay with them in Honolulu," Diane said. "Have you ever gone to Grandpa's office with him?"

"No."

"He used to take me on the streetcar sometimes, before they had an auto and Taka to drive them. He'd let me play with things on his desk, like paper weights. As long as I didn't upset his inkwell! Or when I didn't go and he was at the office all day, I sat on the cement wall on Nuuanu Avenue, waiting for his streetcar. If I wasn't there he'd whistle, and I'd go flying down the black sand driveway. Now sometimes I go there with him and Taka, or to the Bishop Museum to see the whale and the Hawaiian feather capes and other exhibits, or the Insane Asylum when he takes fruit and things to the people there . . . When I was small, he carried me upstairs to bed on his back."

"I love to have him come in the door and whistle for us," I said. We both sat thinking about him.

"Did you know I'm your double cousin?" asked Diane.

"What's that?"

"It's because our fathers are brothers and our mothers are sisters."

That was so, but I'd never realized it made us any different kind of cousins.

"It's as though you were my little sister. Almost."

I looked at her. "Oh."

"Do you mind?"

"No." I really liked the idea very much but didn't want to say so, or didn't know how. "How's Hina?" I asked instead.

Doctor Fitz had come the same day she had been hurt, now a long time ago, and I knew she was much better. But it was good to have Diane say so, too. Poor Hina. We couldn't ride her, of course. But Diane took me riding on Blackie quite often.

"Listen!" She cocked her head.

I could hear the engine, too!

"It's still way down the road," she said. "Coming out of the trees. Now it's turning the big bend . . . coming along toward the next bend."

"Coming up the straight road now!"

"Almost to the gate . . . slowing up, turning in." She stood up, looking down the driveway.

While I was trying to stand up too, she said, "There it is!" and was off down the tree.

By the time I had scrambled, slipped, and slid my way down, Grandpa was out and hugging Diane, his cane against the car door. Kirey was hurrying from the flower road, wiping her hands on a big handkerchief.

I hurled myself on Grandpa, and he lifted me high. "Merry Sunshine! Don't tell me *you're* here!" He looked amazed.

I laughed and put my arms around his neck and let his moustache tickle my cheek and ear. "Grandpa, you *knew* I'd be here!"

"Well, isn't it lucky that I just happened to bring some molasses cookies." Grandpa always brought a long, long box full of big round brown molasses cookies from the Young Bakery, the best in the world. "And here's Miss Kire!"

He set me down and took both of Kirey's hands. Then Aunt Ella came running out of the house, and we were all around him as if we were playing Ring Around a Rosy.

When Kirey and I went toward the living room before dinner, from the stairs we could hear Harry Lauder singing: "Roamin' in the gloamin' on the bonnie banks of Clyde, Roamin' in the gloamin' with my lassie by my side." Diane was always playing records on the Victrola, with the big megaphone and a picture of a dog with "His Master's Voice" written below it.

"Come along in!" said Aunt Ella. "We're hearing all the Honolulu news from Papa."

Grandpa made room for me next to him. Kerosene lamps and the fire threw a wavering light over where we were sitting, leaving the corners shadowy. The room was full of the smell of burning eucalyptus, and the snapping of its dried leaves and twigs. The flames were lovely and warm. Over the mantelpiece hung a sign reading:

> *"As a rule a man's a fool,*
> *When it's hot he wants it cool.*
> *When it's cool he wants it hot—*
> *Always wanting what is not."*

Often I sat by the fire on the round velvety footstool, but tonight Grandpa had one leg stretched out on it. The paneling of this room was dark, and bookshelves nearly reached the ceiling at the sides of the fireplace. On one of them was a stuffed mongoose. On a low shelf, *The Slant Book* and *The Hole Book*. Kirey or Diane read these to me, or I looked at the pictures and made out the words. I knew them both by heart.

Grandpa said: "Mama and Mutie wanted to come, too. But Mama is having a bout with rheumatism, so Mutie is tending her and keeping her company. Usually they're busy enough looking after my welfare. Blessed is he who has the loving care of a sanctified, well-seasoned woman of advancing years—and I've got two!"

"What a shame they couldn't come," said Aunt Ella. "Is Mama feeling quite poorly?"

"Physically, her vigor is rather low and she has to favor herself. But she and Mutie are both in excellent vocal vigor. I, as you know, am always gentle and patient."

"You wrote us of your fall not long ago, Papa. Have you really quite recovered? Tell us more about it."

"There isn't much to tell, except for the effect on your devoted mother and the beneficent Mutie. While I was walking hastily along the sidewalk on Hotel Street, near Benson Smith's, my foot slipped and I fell, spreading all over the pavement. My knee and ankle were bruised, and the ever-present walking stick clattered off with great noise."

"Oh, Papa! How awful."

"When I told the doting elderly women at home about it, they, poor creatures, laughed with great glee."

"Naughty things."

"Come to think of it, when those two ancient suffragettes

are unusually hilarious, it indicates a pretty good state of health. I wonder just how bad that rheumatism is!" He looked at me and added, "The bliss of little children is always inspiring, and is second only to the delight of old ladies when they are joyous."

Their house and Brookside seemed, that night, like part of a dream world. Some protective instinct bade me not think too hard of them. It was enough, for now, that Kirey and Grandpa were here at Olinda.

Kirey took out her tatting and the shuttle she worked it with. But after a minute she said, "Bother!" and Aunt Ella said, "This light is really too uncertain for needlework."

"Grandpa," I said, "what's black and white and red all over?"

"Good gracious! How can I possibly guess that?"

"A newspaper!"

He was so astonished that he nearly fell out of his chair.

Kirey put away her tatting and, as Diane took *Foolish Questions* off the Victrola and wound it up, she asked her if she would play *Tales from the Vienna Woods*. Kirey's face looked faraway and sad as she listened, and something made me think of the man with the beard who had sat on her bed. It was the kind of music June had danced to, that night at the beach. A waltz. Had Kirey ever waltzed? I looked at her, wondering.

"Will you play with the medicine ball with me tomorrow?" I asked Grandpa.

"That's just what I need—a medicine ball to cure my aches and pains."

It was the biggest ball I had ever seen or could imagine. I could lie on it and let it roll me over. While the grown-up talk went on, I sat thinking about it, and about the hammock on the side lanai, and the gaily colored croquet mallets that were kept there.

I waited for a chance to ask Grandpa if he'd play croquet with Diane and me.

"Do you mean that young person with her hair up? I've

noticed her around. Her hair up! What will they be doing next?"

"I don't know. But Grandpa—what about croquet?"

"I'm going to have an athletic time of it, I can see that," he said. "Venerable ancestor though I may be."

On a morning when Kirey was helping Aunt Ella to rearrange the pantry shelves and Grandpa had gone to the plantation with Uncle Henry, I took Teddybear off my bed and we went outside by ourselves. For a while I had watched the shifting of blue and white willowware plates and bowls and tureens, and delicate tumblers with stars on the sides. Aunt Ella said, "I like to do this kind of job myself. Sumiko is a whiz in the kitchen, a wonderful cook and she keeps things spic-and-span as far as cleanliness goes. But I like things put away in apple pie order."

Outside the Dutch door, Teddybear and I looked around and then went down the steps in the direction of the hill where Hina and Blackie grazed. There was a flight of steps at either end of the porch here.

We went between tall totem poles that Uncle Henry had brought from Alaska, up through the gate to the paddock, and sat near the horses for a while. I fed them some tufts of grass, then climbed over the gate at the water trough beside the stable, and walked down the path that led from here to the Japanese Tea House. It was a nice place to sit, with Teddybear propped on the bench next to me. We looked at the tree trunks grown with orange moss, and listened to the leaves rustling. But the murmur of water running down the gulch disturbed me today. I picked Teddybear up and walked down the rest of the path to the driveway, and along it past rhododendron bushes to the gate. It was open, as always when the family was staying up here at Olinda, and I swung on one of the halves that met in the middle.

It was a wonderful yard to wander round, but something made me restless and, walking back, I was delighted to see

Diane and her friend Nora sitting on the ground in the wood. There was a picnic basket near them. Maybe they'd ask me to have a picnic lunch with them!

Hurrying in their direction, I could hear Nora saying, "You know that new boy, Eddie? I think he's cute."

"Who doesn't!" said Diane. "He likes you, I think."

"Oh, no, I don't think so!" Then after a bit, "Do you *really?*"

Diane started to say something, but caught sight of me and called instead, "Baba, what are you doing here?"

"I saw you so I came over to talk to you and Nora."

She frowned slightly, and after a minute said, "Why don't you go and find Kirey?"

"She's helping Aunt Ella in the pantry."

"Go see the horses then."

"I already have. Hina's lots better. When do you think we can ride her?"

"I don't know," said Diane crossly. "Oh, for Heaven's sake—go climb a tree!"

I stared at her. What was the matter with Diane? Usually she climbed trees *with* me.

She waved me away with both hands, saying, "Scoot! If you can't think of anything else to do, go stick your head in the grass."

I stumbled off, hearing them laughing and then go on talking. Diane, acting like other big girls who didn't want you around!

At the top of the driveway I felt suddenly very tired, but Kirey was just coming out of the door with her wide-brimmed hat on, and I ran to meet her.

I didn't tell her about Diane, but there was something else I'd been wanting to talk about.

As we walked along, I said, "Miss Melbehn makes me use my right hand to eat with and when I write."

"I noticed that you'd been doing that. Is it hard?"

"It's much *too* hard. I hate it. She makes us all eat a raw egg, and I have to have something terrible called beef juice. And we can only have ice cream on Sunday!"

Kirey clucked sympathetically but didn't say anything for a minute. Then, "She wants you to do what's right for you, you know."

"' For your own good!'" I mimicked. "She says that all the time. She won't let us drink milk."

"Milk!" Kirey was startled.

"And we have to take *cold plunges* in the morning, in the bathtub."

Kirey said nothing.

"We can't look at the funny papers, even. Not the Katzenjammer Kids, or anything." I kicked at a stone with the toe of my sandal. "I hate her finger nails."

"Her finger nails!"

"Yes. They look like—like—they don't look like yours." Kirey had slender, well-shaped, strong hands. "Strong hands and wrists," she would say, "from having nursed for so long." She wore a ring set with a small diamond, always except when digging in the garden. I loved seeing the diamond flash as her hand moved.

"You know, dear, she's trying to do what's best. And she's far from home. She may get homesick sometimes. Did you ever think of that?"

"No!" A faint memory stirred, of Grandpa's having said something like that, but I couldn't be bothered with it now. "She says, 'Let me see if your tongue is coated.'"

A car was coming up the driveway, and all at once Grandpa and Uncle Henry were there, home for lunch.

Uncle Henry said, "A letter for you, Miss Kire. From New Zealand!" He searched among the letters in the mail he held, and gave one to her. It had a different-looking kind of stamp.

Kirey's face was alight with pleasure. "Oh, thank you!" and to me, "I'll just take this indoors to read."

I followed her to the door of the upstairs lanai, which faced down the mountain. But I'd better give her time to read her letter. I went into our room and put Teddybear on his chair, and strolled around the room. It was good to see Kirey's ivory things on the dressing table, her brush and comb and mirror, clothes brush, and the carved jewel box. The hairbrush had a silver "K" on its back.

Then I thought I'd write a letter to my father, from Teddybear. I sat at the little white desk to do this, remembering to change the pencil to my right hand.

Kirey must have finished reading her New Zealand letter by now! I looked through the lanai door to where she sat. The letter was on her lap, and at first I thought she was looking up through the screen of the windows. But her eyes were closed. As I stood there, she began saying the Twenty-third Psalm in a low voice, the Scottish version she loved:

> "The Lord's my Shepherd;
> I'll not want. He makes me down to lie
> In pastures green; He leadeth me
> The quiet waters by.
> Yea, though I walk in Death's dark vale,
> Yet will I fear none ill;
> For Thou art with me, and Thy rod and staff me
> comfort still.
> Goodness and Mercy all my days
> Shall surely follow me;
> And in God's House for evermore
> My dwelling place shall be."

At lunch, Grandpa said: "Where's Miss Kire?"

"I'm sending her up a pot of tea and some bread-and-butter," Aunt Ella said. "It's all she wants."

Uncle Henry asked, "Is she not feeling well?" and Aunt Ella hesitated, and said, "She'd like to be quiet for the afternoon."

When lunch was over I went upstairs, but the lanai door there was closed now, so I got Teddybear again and went outside.

Uncle Henry was at the stable, talking with Fuji. He stood at the saddle room door, saying, "No forget, sweep insi' here, polish saddle."

"Yeah, yeah. Excuse for me, please."

When Uncle Henry started back toward the house, I went with him. He smiled and said, "Are you having a good time at Olinda?"

"Yes. It's nice here."

"I love it, too."

"What does Olinda mean?"

"It means 'The Beautiful.'"

"Oh!"

"An uncle of mine—your great-uncle—built the first house here, right where this house is. He named the place Olinda."

"What happened to the house?"

"It went down the hill on rollers, down through the horse paddock. You can just see it, there through the trees."

Yes, I could, with its veranda round it.

Diane came along then. Nora had gone home.

"How's Teddybear?" she asked, smiling. She seemed just as usual, as though she hadn't told me to go stick my head in the grass.

I couldn't help smiling back. She was so nice, and so pretty, and she was Diane again. My double cousin. "Teddybear's fine," I said. "He gets tired of being alone upstairs, so I take him around the yard."

"I should think he *would* get bored. Let's take him up to the top of one of the trees."

I squeezed Teddybear. He'd love that!

Late in the afternoon, I went up the stairs to see if Kirey was still on the lanai. She wasn't.

I loved this lanai. If you looked sideways and backwards through the screen at the end, you could see a slope of Haleakala beyond a rift in the trees—I showed it to

Teddybear—and looking downward, there was the ocean at the horizon line, and the tip of the West Maui Mountains. Closer were the tops of the trees in the garden, and in the paddock. I lay back in a wicker chaise longue, with Teddybear beside me.

After a while, Grandpa came to the doorway. "Little Jumping Joan, when nobody's with me, I'm always alone."

I held Teddybear up to show him I wasn't alone. He came and sat down near me, leaning his cane against the arm of his chair.

"It's nice out here, isn't it?"

I nodded, and after a bit he said, "Are you thinking?"

I shook my head. "Looking at the mountain, looking at the sea."

"That's a good thing to be doing . . . You know, Kirey is feeling very sad."

I looked at him, waiting.

"She had news in her letter from New Zealand. Someone she loved very much has died."

Poor Kirey. So that was it.

"We must all be especially kind to her. You'll be a good girl, won't you?"

"I'll try."

I thought about dying when Grandpa had gone. I never would, or Kirey, or Grandpa. But it was sad when people did die.

I was still there when Kirey came, later.

"You and I are going to have supper up here, in a little while. Won't that be nice?"

"Kirey . . . "

"Grandpa told you, didn't he? About my letter."

"Yes."

She sat down beside me, and said, "See, there's the Evening Star."

What a big star it was. Not twinkling, like most. It shone brighter and brighter.

"Kirey."

"Yes, child?"

"Was it the man with the beard?"

She drew her breath in, and said softly, "Yes."

"The night he was here, he was going to die, wasn't he?"

She was quiet for so long that I thought she wouldn't answer. Then she said, "That was the night he died. The night I dreamed of him—and you saw him."

We sat there watching the sky darken, and the garden below it. The Evening Star was over the tree Diane and I had been on, the day Grandpa came.

Kirey said, "He's found his star," and for a second I thought she meant Grandpa.

"You mean—"

She put her hand on mine. "I like to think that when someone I love dies, he has found his star."

"And lives there?"

We sat without speaking until the sky was dark, dark, and the Evening Star shone so bright that it seemed very near.

6
The Picnic

"You don't have to wear shoes in Hawaii," I said. "Not in summertime, anyway. Take off your kamiks and you'll see how much nicer it is to walk on the grass with bare feet. I'll bet you don't even know what grass is!"

"Who are you talking to?" called my mother from the lanai, where she sat talking with Brownsey.

"Menie and Monnie."

She looked around and asked, "Who are they? And where are they?"

"The Eskimo Twins. They're staying with me," I explained.

"Silly girl," Munna said, laughing toward Brownsey.

Brownsey smiled her nice smile and waved at me. "What time is it, Baba?" she asked.

I took my new round Big Ben watch out of its special little pocket and said, "Fifteen minutes after ten." Brownsey was always wanting to know what time it was, it seemed to me.

I went over to the kukui tree, farther from the house. It had a low, wide crotch with room for the three of us, if we just

56

squeezed a little. And Teddybear. There had to be room for Teddybear. The large light green leaves sheltered us; they made a rustling sound in the gentle trade wind.

"You know what a teddy bear is, anyway," I said to the Twins. "Tell me again about when your father killed the bear." I shivered, listening, and held Teddybear very tight. You're safe, I told him silently. Nothing like that is going to happen to *you*.

It was fun having the Twins there. They were so amazed by all they saw, like trees and flowers, and houses with steep roofs and lanais instead of igloos, and the horses and cattle in the Ranch pastures.

"Do you have mountains, like the one we live on?" I asked. "I know there's a hill you slide down."

They told me about their sled made of driftwood, the only kind of wood they had, and about fishing through a hole in the ice, and wearing fur clothes. They had these on.

"You'd better take those hot things off," I said. "Shall I lend you some clothes?"

But underneath they had on something like my overalls. I knew already, of course, from reading about them, that Monnie wanted to look like a boy, just as I did. In their fur suits, she and Menie looked exactly alike.

We were living at the Ranch House now. It was a big, brown-shingled house, not tall and square like Brookside, but longer. The lanai where Munna and Brownsey were sitting was only a shallow step up from the brick terrace. The yard had lots of trees in it, big old eucalyptus, a Christmas berry, and a camphor tree that was right in front of the house.

I liked the new house, and my bright room at the back, and everything was still almost as new to me as it was to the Twins. But there were times when I longed and longed to be at Brookside, and with Kirey. Kirey had said she would come and stay with us at the Ranch House sometimes.

At dinner time, I pulled up a chair at either side of mine.

Teddybear wasn't allowed at the table, but the Twins were people. Menie's chair was shoved in very close to Brownsey's but she said she didn't mind.

Munna looked as if she were going to object, until Brownsey said, "Perhaps Menie and Monnie would like to have a little reindeer meat."

I shook my head. "No, they want to try our kind."

Wobert and a cousin of ours, Monty, were sitting across the table. Monty had about a hundred freckles, probably more. They just sat there and giggled and made jokes about Menie and Monnie, until my mother asked them to be quieter. Holly had the flu and was in bed.

Brownsey gave a little sort of half-chuckle and said to me, across Menie, "She opened the window, and in flew Enza."

She was always saying things that were so funny they made you laugh until you hurt. Brownsey was Irish, and came from somewhere far away, in the States. She had black, black hair, and the bluest eyes of anyone. She lived on Maui now, not far from us, and came to our house often.

While I was explaining about Enza to the Twins, I heard my mother saying, "I thought we might go on a picnic tomorrow night. A riding picnic."

I bounced in my chair, and cried, "The Green Tanks Pasture!"

Munna smiled at me. "What do you think, Dan?" she asked Daddy. "Our flu girl wouldn't be able to go, of course."

"I should be glad to stay at home with Holly," Miss Melbehn said. "As you know, I haven't learned to ride very well yet, in any case." She sometimes rode Merry Legs, who was twenty-six.

"It's a good idea," Daddy said. "We'll ride up in time for the sunset."

When Brownsey stayed with us, she always came in with Munna to say good night to me.

Munna said, "Why are you and Teddybear scrooged so far

over at the side of your bed?''

"They had to make room for Menie and Monnie,''
Brownsey said, with the smiling twist to her voice that made
everything she said fun to hear.

I nodded. They both kissed me, and Brownsey said, "Sweet
dreams, darlin'." She didn't say exactly "darlin'," but it wasn't
quite "darling," either.

As they went out of the room, I began to tell the Twins
about the Green Tanks. "There's a fig tree we can climb," I
said sleepily.

The next morning, as I lay half-dreaming of the picnic and of
Bessie, my Shetland pony, Brownsey began to sing under my
windows.

> *"You'll hear me calling, 'Yoo-hoo!'*
> *By your window, some sweet day."*

My room jutted out from the back of the house, and in the
mornings it was filled with sunshine. The sunshine that day
seemed a part of Brownsey's voice. I leapt from bed and ran to
the window, and listened to the lovely sound of Brownsey
singing.

She ended with:

> *" . . . means 'I love you.' "*

Brownsey was wearing a blue skirt with a white shirtwaist.
Her eyes were blue, blue, and I stood grinning down at her.
The ground fell away at the back of the house so that I was
above the top of her head.

"Good morning, Merry Sunshine," she sang up to me.
"How did you wake so soon?"

"That's what Grandpa calls me," I said. "He doesn't sing
that little song, though."

"You must teach it to him."

"Yes."

I leaned on the bookcase at the window, looking down at

her, and wondered what had bothered me a little about the
song as Brownsey had sung it. There was something not quite
right—but what?

When we first knew Brownsey, there had been Mr. Brown.
He was tall and thin with an un-smiley face, and we were glad
when he went away. You couldn't picture her singing "Yoo-
hoo" to *him*.

I stood there with my elbows on the low bookcase,
frowning a little but thinking how nice she looked standing by
the summer lilac bush. She smiled up at me for a moment
longer, as if she had been going to say something, then blew
me a kiss and walked on.

Bessie was a pinto, brown and white. Daddy had got her for me
from a man at the Maui County Fair. I was going to ride her in
the next Fair, on the race track, when the horses were judged.

I held the reins in my left hand, as my father had taught
me, and with my right arm balanced Teddybear back of the
pommel. The picnic things were distributed among the
saddles, but Bessie couldn't take any because of the Twins.
They both sat behind me. Bessie was small, but very strong, so
she could carry the three of us.

As we rode slowly up through the pastures, Brownsey
sang. The rest of us were quiet, listening to that voice that
made whatever place one was in seem more alive. As she sang,
a skylark trilled far overhead—surely in answer.

Though we were in sunlight, rain in a misty, luminous
curtain slanted across the slope of the mountain above us, and
there was a rainbow, whose end fell on the Green Tanks and
the fig tree just beside them. The bands of color were so distinct
that you could imagine the rainbow fairies dancing down the
curve, each on her own color. Brownsey's song was a song of
the rainbow, and the fairies, and the skylark, all together—just
as that morning it had been of the sun in my room.

When she had stopped singing, my father said, "It's only a
shower. It will blow over."

It was so; as we rode toward it, the rain swept on, and when we had reached the tanks it was gone. My father said that he and the boys would have more of a ride, and go on up into the next pasture. "You girls can be getting supper ready," he said, smiling at Munna, Brownsey, and me.

I said that Menie and Monnie wanted to go, too.

"I think this has been enough of a ride for you," Munna said. "We've come up through three pastures. And there will be the ride back, you know."

"Why don't you and the Twins go for a little walk?" Brownsey suggested. "They're not very used to riding."

"Well—all right."

I tied Bessie to a fence post, showing the Twins how to make a cowboy knot and to loosen the saddle girth, and we walked and ran in the field nearby, jumping hillocks of grass. White-faced cattle were grazing in the pasture.

There were great splashes of gold in the sky above West Maui and the island of Lanai. Seeing them, I thought of the pot of gold. It must be at the Green Tanks, where I had seen the rainbow's end!

"Let's go see!" I shouted, and the three of us ran across to the tanks.

Munna and Brownsey had the picnic things out on a cloth, and they were sitting under the tree in their riding habits and pulled-down hats. They sat on a saddle slicker because it had rained, though the grass was barely damp. Both of them were leaning against the trunk, with their backs to me. They must be watching that lovely sunset, I thought. The branches of the fig tree, gnarled and twisting, beckoned me. But first the pot of gold! Could it be inside one of the tanks?

I sat Teddybear carefully at the bottom of the ladder of the nearest one, and climbed up to see. Menie and Monnie were right behind me.

Brightness filmed the surface of the water. The gold! I had known it would be there. I turned excitedly to tell my mother and Brownsey.

Munna was saying, "I simply cannot accept a faith that forbids you to marry again, I don't care what you say."

There was a short silence, then Brownsey replied, dryly for her, "My husband is still living."

"Yes! And *he's* married again . . . You know, it seems to me that a religion like that could force you to wish for another's death. Surely *that* is not a good thing?" My mother's voice had risen; it was shrill, unlike her.

Brownsey said sharply, "If one believed in one's religion, that wouldn't be possible."

"Without your quite realizing it, it might!" Munna retorted.

"You won't even *try* to understand!" cried Brownsey.

Grown-ups didn't say those things to each other, did they? Quarreling things, in those voices. My mother must be right. But Brownsey . . .

I loved Brownsey best of all my mother's friends. She understood things like—well, like Menie and Monnie. And she said things like, when I had a cold, "Why do you remind me of Bessie? Because you're a little hoarse."

I gripped the top rung of the ladder, and stared into the gleaming water while the voices went on and on.

When Daddy and the boys came back, I went down the ladder and we had supper. The picnic was good, but I wasn't hungry. And I didn't feel like climbing the tree, after all.

As we rode homeward, the sky over the ocean was a pale gold in the afterglow. Munna and Brownsey rode together, talking lightly of something. But the knowledge of what they had said, and the tones of their voices, was heavy in me, and the far radiance in the sky only made it more of a burden.

Getting into bed, I realized that Teddybear was still at the foot of the ladder. Shock and grief numbed me for a moment, then I began to ache—especially my arms. Teddybear! I would never have believed that anything could make me forget him.

My mother and Brownsey came in, and Munna said, "Where's Teddybear?" She had had a bath and was wearing a pink kimono, and her hair was down. She looked and smelled very nice.

I just shook my head. She seemed in a hurry tonight and I couldn't tell her.

"And right in the middle of the bed!" she said gaily. "What about those poor Twins?"

She seemed to have forgotten her dispute with Brownsey. I looked at her wonderingly. Was that the way grown-ups were? Did they forget so soon? She kissed me and went out.

"Brownsey . . ." I hoped she would stay, at least for a minute.

"Yes, darlin'?"

"Menie and Monnie have gone home."

She stood smiling down at me. "It was fun having them, wasn't it?"

I nodded, wanting to tell her about Teddybear. Looking up at her, I remembered the rainbow. Teddybear was where the gold was. But it was dark now . . . the rainbow would be gone.

I knew, anyway, that the gold was not really there.

"Brownsey . . ." I choked.

"Sweet dreams, darlin'," she said softly, as she bent to kiss me. There was something about her tonight that was not quite the same as usual; something a little sad. Perhaps she did remember that she and Munna had quarreled. Or perhaps— perhaps the real reason was what the quarrel had been about.

I thought of what I had felt that morning, that she would never sing a song like "Yoo-hoo" to Mr. Brown. Was that why she seemed sad now? That it was a love song, and she had sung it to me instead of to a man she might marry.

I put my arms around her neck, and hugged her and hugged her.

"Brownsey," I whispered. "It's fun having *you*." When I had stopped hugging her, my arms didn't ache quite so much.

7

Wobert and Wandy

As we sat at lunch in the big, high-ceilinged dining room at Brookside, an unmistakable scent drifted in through the windows: burning wood. My father sprang up and ran out by way of the pantry, across the back porch and down the steps, all of us following him.

"I know where it is!" I yelled, inspired. "In the bathtub!"

Like many of the old houses in Honolulu, Brookside was built high off the ground. At the foot of the steep back steps, a double doorway led to "under the house"—a fascinating region. First came the fairly well lighted part where garden equipment was kept, and from there the "rooms" went on and on, lit by an unearthly glow that filtered through the latticed and wired sides of the house. The best room of all was at one side, and contained a large oblong bathtub. I never wondered why this should be; it was just there.

The fire had been carefully laid, and it was in the tub. Daddy put it out with an extinguisher and turned to Wobert. My father was a mild-mannered man, so his expression was all the more frightening.

64

"Robert." He didn't raise his voice, but there was an unaccustomed note in it. "What do you know about this?"

"I don't know anything about it, Daddy," Wobert protested.

As we trooped out through the wide doorway, Holly said, "There's Randy," and we saw him peering from behind the thick monkey-pod trunk nearby.

"Come, children," Munna said briskly. "We'll go back to the table."

My father was striding purposefully toward the tree. "Randy," we could hear him saying, and I was glad he was not speaking to me.

We were back at Brookside! Holly told me that we always had been going to come back, for most of the school years, with Daddy coming for weekends when Munna wasn't at the Ranch with him. "That's why we have Miss Melbehn," Holly said, "so Mother can come and go. What a dummy you are not to have known this!" Dummy or not, here we were, and it was wonderful.

The day of the fire was the first occasion when it occurred to me that Wandy would go to prison when he grew up. Other reasons followed: the three tires that blew out as Daddy started up the Hupmobile to take us for a Sunday drive; the airplane made from a dress box and a bicycle; and the falling of Mademoiselle from the plank bridge into the brook.

Wandy was my friend and I felt concern that he should be going to prison, but began really to worry about it upon suspecting that he would take Wobert with him. Wobert and I liked to do the same things and we and Wandy were together much of the day out of school: catching 'opae in the brook, playing marbles, building a tree house. I always dumped my 'opae out of the net and the boys said, "Just like a girl!" but let me go on playing with them.

After the fire, though, Wandy didn't come back to play with us for at least a week. For a while, we were afraid he wasn't going to come at all. But we heard Munna and his mother asking Daddy please to let him.

"He wasn't going to let the fire keep on *burning*," Wandy's mother said.

"Of course not," Munna agreed. "He was there, watching—you saw him. Children *are* such a handful!" she added, sighing. "Some days I don't know which way to turn." Wandy's mother, who had only him, looked thoughtful.

It was a long week. Wandy lived not far away, up Nuuanu Avenue, and we were used to having him play with us—and everything was more fun when he was there. In the end, he came one afternoon as Wobert and I were playing Fish on the cement under the wiliwili tree near our back door.

We both looked up, pleased. Wandy had brown hair that never looked really untidy, very smooth, fair skin, and usually the sort of expression that made my mother's friends say, "What a dear little boy!" Right now, he looked scornful.

"Playing *marbles*," he said.

Wobert looked startled. Wandy was carrying a red and white top, its cord coiled. He flicked it down and it spun into our game, sending the marbles flying.

"Wandy!" I shrieked.

But Wobert was regarding him silently.

"Don't you even know that it's top season?" Wandy asked.

He didn't go to Lanai, but to the Valley School, which was almost across Nuuanu Avenue from our house. One terrifying day, two big boys had chased him into our yard and dragged him back to school—terrifying because we were left to imagine what he could have done, and what was going to happen to him.

"How do you know it's top season?" I said crossly.

"You just know, that's all. You just feel like spinning tops, and everybody at school starts doing it."

"Yeah, you just know," Wobert said. "Pick up the marbles, Bobora." He stood up, while I still squatted beside the ruined game.

"Bobora Atama," Wandy said tauntingly. "That's a good

name for you, all right. You can't even say our names right."

I was puzzled by this onslaught from Wandy, and stared up at him.

"Don't think I didn't hear you tell your father where the fire was! Spying on me, weren't you?"

"I wasn't!" I said indignantly. But how to explain that I had simply known the fire was in the tub? It couldn't be done convincingly.

Wobert was looking at me uncertainly.

"Wobert!" I said. Surely he didn't think—?

"Wobert!" mimicked Wandy. "What a Bobora Atama."

"Yah!" agreed Wobert. "Can't even say our names. Come on, Ran, I wanta show ya something."

Miserably, I sorted the marbles, Wobert's in one group and mine in another. As a rule, I loved handling the different colored ones, but now even our most prized agates meant nothing. A few red wiliwili seeds had fallen amongst them, and these I tossed aside impatiently. My nickname, Japanese for "Pumpkin Head," had never bothered me before, but the way Wandy had said it had been infuriating. Of course, I'd have told there was a fire if I'd known it, but would have tried to protect him. More than anything, though, my misery was due to Wobert's desertion.

Upstairs, the hall smelled of Japanese matting. This covered all of the upstairs floors except those of the bathrooms and the sleeping porch, but its essence seemed to be concentrated in the inner hall. A clean, somehow exciting smell; exciting now, anyway, because of the toys and boxes of games that had been stored on the nursery closet shelf while we had been away. When we had come from the Ranch on Maui in time for school, they were taken down, and were far more interesting than brand-new toys because of their being at once familiar and half-forgotten.

We had rooms of our own now, instead of being on the sleeping porch. I had asked for Kirey's old room, hardly daring to hope—but it *was* mine now! It overlooked the drive lined with royal palms that came in from Nuuanu Avenue and, through the other windows, the long slope of land to monkeypods and the brook.

A ray of late sunlight glittered across the top of a palm and slanted over the sill to lie in a window-paned splash on the matting. I stood looking at it, my hand still on the door knob, then went back down the hall to Wobert's room and picked up one of his tops, a bright blue one. He hadn't minded, during last top season, when I had borrowed one from time to time. But I coiled the cord slowly, wondering if today he would mind. This one was his favorite.

I knew it was impossible for me to spin a top, and it was silly to try. Nevertheless, I stood there winding and hurling until Otoru called me for my bath.

The week when Wandy hadn't been there had seemed long, but Wobert had played with me as usual. The next days gave me my first experience of being an outcast. The boys simply went off about their affairs without me.

Once I ventured quite close, when they were wading in the brook.

Surprisingly, Wandy turned with his sweet smile. "Did you ever catch a mynah bird, Bobora?"

I shook my head.

"Good fun. You oughta try it."

Wobert frowned at me, as if he were going to say something, but Wandy went on: "You can teach them to talk. All you have to do is put salt on one's tail, and you got him."

As easy as that! I sped up the hill. There was an old bird cage under the house. I could keep him in that—right by my bed.

I stalked mynah birds the rest of the afternoon. It was only as Wandy was going home and called teasingly, "How many did you get, Bobora?" that I realized he had been getting rid of me.

A few days after the Hupmobile tires had exploded, Wobert came into the house and asked Munna for a dress box. She was busy writing a list, or something, and found him one absently. I sat at the top of the back steps as Wobert, under Wandy's direction, attached the halves of the box to either side of his bicycle.

"Now let's get a ladder," Wandy said.

They went under the house and dragged out the ladder. Wobert had a determined air, which showed in the set of his shoulders and the lift of his sandy-white head. Whatever he did was worth doing seriously.

With great exertion on his part, and a little on Wandy's, the ladder was placed against the trunk of the monkey-pod tree and the airplane carried up it. Boys and plane balanced somehow in the high crotch, and Wandy said, "You can have first ride."

Wobert looked surprised. His hair stood on end and there were smudges of bicycle grease on his face and overalls. Wandy was crisp and immaculate.

Perhaps if Wobert hadn't looked surprised, it wouldn't have seemed so imperative. I ran into the house screaming for Munna.

My mother could move with astonishing speed, and she had a curiously ringing voice for a person so small. "Robert!" she cried from the back steps. "Randy! Come down this instant."

When she had gone and boys and bicycle (no longer airplane) were on the ground, Wandy said, "Yah, Bobora. Always have to butt in, don't you?"

"Yah!" echoed Wobert. "Where's your top, Ran? Let's go spin."

Mademoiselle lived in the cottage at the far side of the brook, where she gave us French lessons on Saturday afternoons. Munna always had someone staying in that cottage, someone she wanted to "take under her wing," she would explain.

The day Mademoiselle fell into the brook was a Saturday, and when we presented ourselves at her door later, she spoke to us sharply in French and swept by us down the steps. She wore a long white garment that flowed about her, and the end of a scarf brushed me in passing. Her shoes were pointed and had buckles, rather like a witch's shoes.

Wobert asked, "What did she say?" He looked worried.

We watched as she hurried down the path, went through her little gate and turned up Nuuanu Avenue toward the entrance of our drive. No short cut by way of the brook this time.

"What did she say?" Wobert repeated as we walked down the slope toward the brook.

"Something about no lesson today, I think," said Holly. "And more, but I don't know what." On the bridge, she asked, "What are those piled-up stones in the brook, Boy?"

Wobert glanced casually at the piled stones and then away, but not at Holly. I had seen him and Wandy making the dam that morning, just above the bridge, but hadn't gone too near for fear of a rebuff. They had made a place deep enough to swim in, but now some of the stones were pushed aside and the pool was no longer there.

Holly turned to face him. "Rob! Did you and Randy have anything to do with you-know-what?" she asked severely.

Even then he wouldn't look at her. A stillness touched me, and I thought, Oh Wobert, I don't want you to go to prison. I said, "They were only making a dam and breaking it up and if Mademoiselle walked by and fell in, how could *they* help it?"

Holly just looked at us, and marched up the hill toward the house, her long curls swinging. We knew she wouldn't tell—but it didn't make much difference, as Mademoiselle was at that moment walking up the drive.

I wanted to stay back and tell Wobert that he must say *no* when Wandy suggested these things. But I couldn't speak, when he and Wandy had been ignoring me. I walked slowly up the slope behind Holly.

In the hallway, she and I could hear Mademoiselle's voice in a torrent of half-French, half-English, and Munna's low but carrying tones in response.

She said, "I'm very sorry indeed that this has happened, Mademoiselle, and the boys will certainly be punished. Randy is an only child, you know, and mischievous—and Robert is full of high spirits and can be naughty. But of course, if you really feel you must go because of it . . . "

Later, I heard her say to Daddy that she was sorry about it all, but it was better not to try to persuade Mademoiselle to stay if she was determined to go. And Munna had met a most interesting retired teacher recently, who was a student of numerology . . . "You'll have to speak to Rob, I'm afraid," she added.

So one of those incidents I dreaded took place in the guest room, when my father "spoke to" Wobert. I could hear the whacks, and Wobert's cries, and felt a freezing at the pit of my stomach.

Afterwards, Wobert came to my room. He stood there for a minute as if not knowing exactly what to do, then asked abruptly, "How did you know about the dam? Were you watching?"

I nodded. "At first. I didn't see her fall in, but when we were coming home this afternoon I knew how it must have happened."

"It was so funny," he said, laughing. "She came along, talking that cockeyed way. Ran just looked at her and began to take the stones away, and I did too. She's disgusting! The water barely trickled over the bridge. She didn't have to fall in. We never thought she would—just get her feet wet. But she got scared."

"Yeah, she's disgusting, all right." A happy feeling began to well up inside me.

Wobert noticed the blue top where I had left it on the floor after my last unsuccessful bout.

"Can you spin it yet?"

I shook my head.

"Here, look." He wound the cord carefully. "You have to give a flick to your wrist, see?" We stood watching as it spun in wandering circles. "Try it," he said as it stopped and rolled over. "I'll wind it for you."

I watched the square brown hands. Wobert couldn't be going to prison; he just couldn't.

He handed the top to me, I flicked my wrist—and it spun. I gazed unbelieving, and he said, "Good spin. Say, Bobora." The name as he said it didn't sound at all as it had in Wandy's voice. "Would you like that top? I'll give it to you."

This was almost more than could be borne.

"Robert!" I said. "Oh, *Robert*."

8
The Clevelanders

"Who're coming?" demanded Rob.

"The Clevelanders."

"Who are *they*?"

Holly said pityingly, "Our cousins from the mainland, silly. From Cleveland. Don't you know *anything*? When I go away to boarding school in a few years, I'm going to visit them at vacation time."

"Visit them! Visit them!" Rob mimicked. "You sound so ho'okano. Why can't you say you're going to stay with them?"

Holly ignored him, and he muttered, "Fancy talk," and after a minute, because he really wanted to know, "Where's Cleveland, and how did they get there?"

"It's almost across the States, and they got there by being born there. Dimwit!" Relenting, she went on, "When Daddy's brother Uncle Douglas married Aunt Rae, he stayed there to live and they've got six children and they're all coming to spend the summer on Maui, with Grandma."

Rob grunted. "Sissy kids from the States! And I s'pose they'll be wanting *us* to show them around, and do things with them. Well, catch me letting them ride Jack. Bet they don't even know *how* to ride.''

Jack was Rob's chestnut pony, half Shetland. He was a wonderful horse, much better than mine. I loved riding Jack. Once in a while, Rob let me ride him instead of Wiwi. (You spelled her name like that, but called her 'Veevee.') She was very high and so skinny that I couldn't ride her bareback. That was what her name meant—skinny. What a backbone! Sometimes I still rode the Shetland pony Bessie, but she seemed awfully small now.

"They won't have to ride Jack," Holly said. "Grandma's got horses in for all of them, at Maluhia. Sadie's your age, Rob. Eight. Zander's mine. He looks nice. I saw a picture of them all.''

"What about me?" I asked. "Aren't any of them seven?"

"Lee's the youngest. But no, he's six. The other three are older than any of us. Henley goes to college.''

Rob and I more or less forgot about the impending visit. On many days Rob "went out with the cowboys," but I wasn't allowed to. Or to ride anywhere by myself except in the gulch pasture and yard, down to the Dairy, or along the road to our cousins', the Knapps.

Sometimes Holly rode with me, and then we went into the Home Paddock beyond the gulch, or the pastures above the house. But she was very interested in birds, and often wandered all over the gulch and yard looking for them, and writing things about them in a composition book, and taking pictures with the new Brownie she'd just gotten for her tenth birthday. She didn't want to ride when she was in a bird-hunting frame of mind.

There was a baby at our house now, Keiki. She was the cutest baby there had ever been, and of course we all played with her. I used to look over her tiny clothes and ask Munna if she could wear the blue sweater, or the pink sacque, or the booties with yellow pompoms of yarn on their toes. But you couldn't play with a baby for very long at a time, so when I wasn't riding I was usually at the stable, helping Masa. Masa was in charge of the riding horses and all of the stable, which included the warehouse. The saddle room had two long hanging racks of saddles running down the length of it, and pegs for bridles around the walls, and blankets, and a huge bin of feed near the door. Masa let us eat some of it now and then. It was whitish and sweet-smelling, and tasted awfully good. He did the leather work for the Ranch, too, and was always mending a broken saddle strap or girth or stirrup, or some band of a bridle. He wore light-colored overalls that had all sizes of pockets in them for his different tools.

The best times were when Rob rode with me and we went quite far in the pastures. Or no—the very best, the super days were when he let me ride Jack.

Jack was very tame, so that you could even get on from the wrong side if you wanted to. But he was always ready to go, nothing lazy about *him*. He held his head up, and jogged right along. We mostly rode him bareback, except Rob on his cowboy days.

Jack was a pony because of his being part Shetland, but still he was much bigger than Bessie. He had a diamond-shaped star on his forehead, and his chestnut coat shone, and when I was alone with him, I hugged him around his neck and thrust my nose into its warmth. That most delicious of smells! Sometimes he would turn his head and look at me, and I thought, He knows I love him. He wore his mane on the left, because Masa said that was the thing for boy horses. Girl horses wore theirs on the right.

One day when I had been riding, and had tied up at the hitching rail and gone in to lunch, Munna said as we sat down at the table, "Well, tomorrow's the big day!"

"What big day?" asked Rob through a mouthful of bread. There was always a slice of it already on the table, on each butter plate.

"Don't talk with your mouth full, Robby. And wait until we're all served and I've lifted my fork. The Clevelanders are coming in on the *Claudine* in the morning. They're in Honolulu now, staying with Aunt May."

Tomorrow! They became real people, about to arrive on Maui.

"Do we have to see them?" I asked hopelessly. Such a lot of strange relatives. . . . .

"We're anxious to see them, of course! They'll be tired after their long trip, first the train across the continent, and then the *Wilhelmina* from San Francisco. So we'll wait till afternoon to go over to Maluhia."

Grandma's house had steps going up to the lanai in front but we always drove around to the back, where there was a porch just beyond the kitchen door. This was the family entrance. The ground sloped under the house so that it was only two steps up. Maluhia meant "Peace." It was a good name for the place. Usually—maybe not today!

We went through the dining room door as always, and could hear a clatter of voices from Grandma's sitting room beyond. My knees quaked, and I grabbed for Munna's hand.

A man came to the archway between sitting room and dining room, and for a minute I thought I was seeing things. He looked so much like my father, only older. Not so handsome, of course, but tall and thin and with twinkly blue eyes. He kissed Munna, and shook hands with Daddy and said, "Well, well! Isn't this wonderful!" When Munna had each of us shake hands with him, it wasn't too bad.

The room ahead was a different thing.

Grandma got up from her rocker, a laugh in her voice. "Come in, come in, my dears!" Her voice always had a special sound. It was part music, part her being glad to see you. Today there was an extra happiness in it. I hung on to her when it was my turn to kiss her—I hadn't even looked yet at all those people behind her.

Munna and Daddy were saying hello to everybody, and there was lots of kissing, and what an uproar! There were so many of them! The room seemed to be full of Clevelanders. At last we had to meet them all, and I could see that even Holly was shrinking back.

I knew Lee because he was the smallest. He was wearing a sailor suit with long sleeves and a white cord instead of a tie. Sadie had long brown hair like Holly's, but she wore it thick and loose down her back, not in curls. She was little for her age and all smiley. Not shy a bit. She was talking away to Holly and Rob already. He looked the way I felt, and didn't say anything.

Grandma made me sit on a bench with Lee. He had an alert, wide-eyed expression—impish, if I had thought of the word—and he was more talkative and much more question-asking than my Island cousins. He wanted to know all kinds of things, everything about Maui, like how much sugar cane there was in a field, how many horses and cattle we had on the Ranch, how deep was the ocean where we swam, and what kinds of fish were in it. I found this upsetting. How did I know all of those things? I'd seen fish when we swam, of course, and when the Hawaiian fishermen with their glass-bottomed boxes speared them, but how describe them? With relief, I remembered the name of one of them—manini—and that it was striped.

As we sat there, I looked around at the rest of them. I could tell Zander, the one who was Holly's age. He was darker than the others, and had short, thick curly hair. There were two bigger boys and a big girl. Not really big, she was small like Sadie, but older. She looked like Sadie, and I thought she wouldn't be so scary as the others.

Our bench was by the cabinet of shells like those we found on the sand and in the shallow water, and lots of others that were bigger and strange looking. I was able to tell Lee which ones we picked up on our beach, and the names of a couple of them.

He began looking around at the photographs that covered
the walls. They were above the doors, between windows,
everywhere. Each family was grouped together, and there was a
picture of every single person.

"Why weren't you smiling for yours?"

I didn't want to tell him. It was because one of my teeth
had been out, right in front. Probably Lee's teeth never did fall
out! So I just kind of mumbled.

Kiku San brought in punch and cookies and passed them
round. Lee said they were super, and I guess they were good,
but I took some every time mainly so he wouldn't be talking to
me so much. Or at least, I wouldn't have to answer right away.

Grandma was saying, "We'll have to have a family
reunion this summer, one Sunday, and have photographs
taken. When May can come from Honolulu with her family.
All of us here together!"

"How many grandchildren now, Mother?" asked the man
who looked like Daddy.

"Twenty-five, with little May and Keiki. Isn't that a lovely
family?"

Keiki would be the youngest one. Five months.

Grandma said, "I'd like to hold her, the littlest one, for the
photos."

When it was time to go, one of the biggest boys came up to
Lee and me. He had curly brown hair that he had slicked
down, and eyes just the same color, and a wide smile in his thin
face.

He said, "It's going to be fun, isn't it, this summer?" and
put a hand on my shoulder. There was something in him that
was familiar to me, and I thought, These are my *cousins*.
They're not just anybody, that I have to be scared of.

I smiled up into his friendly face, a somewhat trembly
smile perhaps, and said, "Yes! It *is* going to be fun."

On the way home, Rob said carelessly, "Sadie's coming on the
drive of Pa Lakea tomorrow."

"Sadie!" How startling.

My father said from the driver's seat, "So is Lee, and so is Zander, and so is your Uncle Douglas."

My goodness! Did I want to go, then? Oh, *yes*. I couldn't miss a cattle drive because of other people who were going on it. And Sadie was cute, really. Lee . . . all that talk bothered me, but I could keep from riding with him. I remembered the big boy with the friendly brown eyes, and even though he wasn't coming on this small drive, it didn't seem so bad that the others were.

Daddy was going on, "In August we'll be driving the Mountain Pasture, and Zander can come then, too, along with the older Clevelanders. Rob—don't you think it's about time you spent a night at Ukulele?"

Ukulele! Was Daddy really going to take Rob on that drive? The mountain drive was the biggest one of the summer, starting inside the crater that was up at the top, and all the way down to the Olinda branding pens. Everyone spent two nights at Ukulele, far up the mountain, where there were three old red cabins in a grove of giant eucalyptus. Huge holly trees, too, and calla lilies growing wild everywhere. I'd been there on a picnic, and longed for the day when I'd be old enough to stay there for a drive. Now Rob was going. He sat smiling to himself, and I knew how he was feeling.

The first thing I heard on cattle drive mornings was my father's booted footsteps, as he approached my door as quietly as he could. I was always awake and out of bed, with the light switched on, by the time his gentle knock came.

Clothes laid out the night before: khaki breeches, blue-checked palaka shirt, bandana with its kukui nut slide (made by Rob), socks and heavy shoes, and leather leggings that strapped on at the sides, their tops covering my knees. A jacket too, that I never wanted. As if I could feel cold on a morning like this!

On drive mornings, we had breakfast in the pantry, not

much smaller than the kitchen on one side and the dining room on the other. We were gathering there—Daddy, Holly, Rob, and I—and saying good morning to Otoru and Misao, who looked sleepy (we knew Mori was in there at his wood stove, but didn't dare speak to him at this hour), when there was a commotion of chatter at the front door. It was surprising, even alarming; quiet was instinctive with all of us on these early starts.

Daddy went to the entrance to meet them, and the three youngest Clevelanders burst into the room. Uncle Douglas followed with Daddy. Their resemblance was heightened this morning by their nearly identical dress: long-sleeved white shirts and dark ties, sweater-jackets, and khaki breeches with English boots. Daddy often wore leggings, but these were really more for drives in the panini pastures, where cactus thorns could stick you.

Breakfast was papaya, two poached eggs on rice, bacon, toast and guava jam, chocolate for us, and coffee for grown-ups. I attacked mine, letting talk swirl around me, leaving it to Holly to do the answering.

When we reached the stable, it was getting light. Masa's kerosene lantern hung from its hook beside the saddle room door, but its beam was growing faint, just a flicker, as the sky lightened and the last stars disappeared, one by one, as if they had been blown out. The trees around the blacksmith shop could be seen separately, no longer a dark mass.

The Clevelanders had ridden their four horses over from Maluhia late the day before, and they stood saddled and tied with ours. There wasn't room for all in the hitching shed, so five were tied to iron rings on the eucalyptus and silky oak trees in front of the Ranch office. There was a stump that Munna stood on to mount when she rode, she was such a small lady, and I had to use it too for any horse as tall as Wiwi.

The cowboys joined us from their stable around the curve of the road as we went by, and we strung out, winding through a gulch with eucalyptus groves on either side. The hoofbeats were a good sound on the hard dirt surface, and the jingling of spurs. There was a smell of horses and saddle leather in the cool early air, and sometimes of cigarette smoke. One of the men's faces would be lit for a moment by a match, in the pale light before the sun rose.

Lee rode beside me and asked, "Who's that riding up in front with Daddy and Uncle Dan? Is he a Hawaiian?"

"That's Joe Francis, the cowboy foreman. He's Portuguese."

"What's the name of the place where we're going?"

"Pa Lakea. That means 'White-faced cattle pasture.' " He'd ask me, so I might as well tell him the meaning right away.

"Why? Aren't there white-faced cattle in any other pasture?"

"Yes, the whole Ranch has them."

"Then why?"

In the steepness of the pasture, Wiwi was falling back and Lee, whose little horse was frisky and looked just right for him, rode on ahead. I found Sadie beside me, on Maka Beauty. Maka Beauty was old and almost blind in one eye and her name meant Beautiful Eyes! She was slow, too, so Sadie and I rode together, following the trail in the tall grass. Frankly, Sadie was a relief to me. I liked Lee—you couldn't help liking him— but he made you answer questions all the time. I'd been saved this time because his horse was faster than mine. I'd never have known what to tell him, anyway.

We were riding up through Pa Poepoe, and near the edge of a gulch grown with trees, I said "Come over this way," to Sadie. Not far off, built into a hillside of the open pasture, was an underground room that had once been a dairy. We got off and one at a time, the other holding both horses' reins, went along the steep-sided little path to the old door, and into the room. There was an opening in the top at the other end, but of course no windows. It was cold and dank, and smelled funny but exciting.

"We ride up here often," I told Sadie.

"We could have a club here! Wouldn't that be fun?"

It *would* be fun. What a wonderful idea!

I had to get Wiwi into the beginning of the passage, to stand on the high ground to get on, and when we started up the hillside again we were quite far behind.

"It's all right, they'll be waiting at the top of Lakea," I said. "We'll all have to spread out across it, to drive the cattle down."

We passed groups of Herefords, placidly grazing, cows, and lots of quite big calves. The sun was up now, just over the rim of Haleakala, and it made the red backs shine.

"That's what this drive is for," I said. "To separate those calves from the cows in these two pastures, and wean them."

"Where will the separating be?"

"Back near the stable and Ranch office. There's a kind of platform on a high stone wall, where we can sit to watch it."

"Poor things!" said Sadie. "They have no idea what's going to happen to them. Will the cows ever get their calves back?"

I shook my head. "Not after they're weaned. They cry for their babies for a couple of days afterward, and the calves cry, too."

"Poor things," said Sadie again.

I was sorry for them, but it was what you had to do on a ranch.

If we had worried about the Clevelanders being able to ride, we needn't have. Besides living in the city, they had a farm, and lots of horses. Sadie told me all about it, and about a path through a wood that they called the Snake Trail.

"It twists and turns all the way," she said, "and there are fallen logs across it that your horse has to jump. We always take people on it, just gallop in and they don't know where they're going."

She told me about the winters too, with snow on the ground and on the trees—"Evergreens, you know, like the pine trees you have here"—and about Toboggan Hill. You went either alone on a sled, or with three or four on a toboggan, and flew like the wind down a long, steep hill that had an icy pond at the bottom. They liked to creep up behind someone and send him hurtling, before he knew it.

"You'll see," Sadie said. "When you're bigger and go away to school, you'll come and stay with us for Christmas and Easter. Mother said so."

I, go away to school! Leave the Ranch, and Brookside. No, never. Holly would go someday. But *I*? I couldn't.

"I'm not going away to school," I said. "I'm always going to stay here, and at Brookside."

Sadie looked at me sideways. "Wouldn't you like to ride on the Snake Trail? And fly down the hill on a toboggan?"

Those things would be fun, of course. But I could never go so far away.

"It won't be for ages yet," said Sadie. "Years."

Years! Well, that was different. You didn't have to worry about things that were that far ahead. *Years*.

We got even farther behind in the next pasture. The last hill of Pa Lakea was very steep. But at last I said, "Look! We're almost at the top."

The riders were spacing themselves out along the fence line.

"What are those bright things on lots of the cowboys' hats?" Sadie asked.

"Hat leis. Made of 'akulikuli flowers."

"I thought you wore leis around your neck!"

"Not only."

"Who makes them?"

Rob on Jack was there beside us, and he answered. "Their wives make 'em."

"Oh, I wish I had one!" cried Sadie. "Aren't they pretty? Do you suppose one of them would—"

Rob looked shocked. "You couldn't *ask* them."

"No, of course not." Sadie looked thoughtful. She was

wearing a lau hala hat shaped rather like the cowboys' felt sombreros. A lei would look all right on it. Not on Rob's and my Haleakala Ranch hats!

At Masa's store at the warehouse, he sold round brown hats with brims all around, that we all wore, even Daddy. Some of the cowboys, too, and their children. I saw that Daddy had got Uncle Douglas to wear one of them.

On horseback, the two looked even more alike, because they rode the same way. Sitting straight, but not stiff.

Daddy came up to us. "How are you kids? I'd better check your saddles. Get off for a minute, OK?"

He swung off Maneli, his huge dark chestnut, and with the reins over his arm he adjusted first Maka Beauty's saddle and tightened its girth, and then Wiwi's. They had both slipped a bit on the uphill ride. Rob attended to Jack's saddle.

When I was back on Wiwi, Daddy grinned up at me and I grinned back. His face was much browner than when we had lived all the time in Honolulu. It made his eyes bluer than ever. He looks happy, I thought. I am, too! It was my first inkling that it was good to know it, when you were happy.

"Don't let the old girl run away with you," Daddy said, grinning even more and slapping Wiwi's flank.

I knew this was a joke, she was so lazy and slow.

It always made my heart beat faster to hear the cowboys' "hulu pipi yells" and the crack of their long whips, to start the cattle going. Rob had learned to crack a whip, and he uncoiled his from the saddle strap. There was a lasso on his saddle, too, held by its own strap below the pommel; a kaula 'ili, or hide rope. He was good at roping, too. I tried both, at home, but knew it was going to take practice!

Soon the cattle were trotting down the hills, prodded by the yells and whip-reports, calves staying near their mothers. Small groups joined to form larger, until they were red streams coursing over pale pasture grass; or tributaries bound for the river at the bottom of Lakea. Here they were herded through the gate between pastures.

Rob was riding near Sadie now, not seeming to pay her any heed, but cracking his whip with an expression on his face that I knew meant he hoped she was noticing. In between times, he trailed the length of it in the grass behind Jack, as the cowboys and my father did.

Holly and Zander had been riding together most of the morning. He didn't speak to me at all, but he and Holly seemed to be having fun together.

We passed a round stone wall near the bottom of Poepoe, and Sadie asked me what it was.

"A cistern. There's water inside, for the troughs. Come see."

We peered over the edge at the dark water. Near it was a big circular trough, with grass growing in the center. These two, the cistern and unusual water trough, made me wonder if they could be the cause of this being the Round Pasture, Pa Poepoe. I hoped Lee wouldn't ask me, though.

The cattle were in a single herd now, riders keeping them together, and chasing after one if it broke loose. Some of the cows drank at the trough, ringing it with white lowered faces.

We drove them along the road the way we had come in the early morning, and into one of the large rail-fenced pens across from the stable. Sadie, Lee, and I tied our horses to rings on the trees, loosened their girths, and climbed up to sit on the platform I had told Sadie about. Night-blooming cereus clambered up the stones of the wall, and you had to be careful not to be pricked. The platform was wide, a good place to sit, but it seemed very far from the ground.

Zander and Holly sat on a fence rail across the way. Rob was with the cowboys in the pen, on Jack.

The cows and calves milled around, their voices a constant rise and fall of sound, a murmur then a roar. The smell of dust, raised by restless hoofs, was in the air. Daddy sat on the fence at the end of a long chute, a cattle counter in each hand, with Uncle Douglas sitting beside him. Joe Francis stood on the

ground below. As cows and calves were driven through the
chute to be put in separate pens by means of a swinging gate,
Joe Francis called "Kane" or "Wahine" as the calves went by,
and my father clicked one counter or the other.

I explained to Sadie and Lee that kane meant boy, and
wahine meant girl, and my father kept track of the number of
each.

"How does he know?" asked Lee.

I was embarrassed, but Sadie answered, "Joe Francis looks
underneath, silly."

When the separating was done, it was lunch time. As we
walked out into the stableyard, a Hawaiian cowboy named
Mahi'ai rode past, and smiled at the three of us. On his hat was
a really splendid lei, purple and pink and white.

Sadie called to him, "Oh, your lei is just beautiful! Did
your wife make it?"

He reined in and said, "Yeah, the old lady, she always
making lei."

"Are they all the same colors?"

"No, sometimes red, any color."

"It's *gorgeous*."

Mahi'ai hesitated, took off his sombrero and looked at the
lei, and looked at Sadie. "You like this one?" he asked
diffidently.

"Oh, I'd love it!"

He took it off his hat and leaned over to hand it to her.
"Look nice on your hat, I think," he said, grinned at her
thanks, and trotted on.

So that was how it was done!

Grandma's koa dining table had all the boards in that day, so
that it nearly filled the room. There was a second "children's
table" in the living room. Thirty-seven of us, counting Miss
Temple with her ear trumpet sitting opposite Grandma, and
not counting Keiki, who was in the middle of a guest room
bed. Our oldest cousin was on his honeymoon, and the othe

baby, May, was sick, so instead of forty there would be thirty-seven in the photographs.

Sadie said, "Did you ever see so much family in one room!"

"Two rooms," I corrected, all for accuracy.

"Well, in one house, then."

I was sitting between her and Lee. Grandma always had one or two families for lunch after church, and we loved it when it was our turn to be there: seeing our cousins of various ages, dressed up so that they were slightly unfamiliar; listening to the grown-up talk, which was apt to be interesting; and eating Grandma's delicious lunch, predictably ending with large helpings of ice cream and either cookies or cake. This reunion Sunday was special and different, naturally. Seven families, all at once!

Grandma had had eight children, one of whom died in his early twenties. My father was the youngest, and because he was, she called him her poki'i. She told me that for sixteen years she nearly always had a cradle beside the high-backed, ornately carved walnut bed that she and Grandpa slept in. Grandpa wouldn't let her rock the cradle (at least, he told her she mustn't, it would spoil the babies), so when they cried at night, she very carefully put a foot out from under the covers to set it rocking. In the winters, she had a sock on the foot—Grandpa's!

Today, she was in wonderful spirits, which certainly was not unusual, but there must have been something very heart-warming in having very nearly her entire family there at Maluhia. I think she had the most serene face I have ever seen. It wasn't as if her world had held no storms, but as if she had weathered any that came her way. With serenity went amusement, interest in anyone of any age who happened to be near her, and a gentle wit that was peculiarly her own.

She was dressed for the reunion in black, with a little white at the collar, and of course her velvet neckband.

Luckily, though Lee was next to me, he had Rob on his other side, so Rob got some of the conversation. Lee really looked cute in his sailor suit, and his eyes were brighter than ever on this day. Rob wore shorts with a long-sleeved shirt and tie, and knee-length socks. The medium-sized boys all wore coats and long black stockings that came over their knees to meet their knickerbockers.

Sadie said, "I wish we lived nearer all you cousins. You're lucky, you know."

"Why don't you move out here?"

"I wish we could! No, I don't, really. Cleveland's home, and the Farm. It will be fun when some of you nearer my age start coming for vacations. The biggest ones do already, like Em and Diane and Ned and Wilfred. But they go round with Lois and my big brothers. Just think, we'll have years and years of all of you coming to stay with us!"

"But not me for *ages*," I said quickly, with a funny, cold feeling inside. Not ever, I added to myself. But Sadie . . .

Sadie and I had been having so much fun together, all summer: riding, going to the beach, or up the mountain to Olinda—and we had our club in the old dairy room. We let Lee and Rob come too, so it could be a real club with four people instead of just two. I had been surprised when Rob had consented to join us. He went riding with us quite often, too. He seemed to like being around Sadie. And who could blame him! She was so much *fun*. When you were with her, you giggled a lot. Everything was new, and different, and entertaining to her. And she loved to play jokes on people, like putting a kikania burr on your saddle for you to sit on, or a spider down the collar of your shirt. Rob had let her ride Jack several times. That was the really amazing thing. And yet—was it amazing?

"Your dress is pretty," Sadie said. "Mmm! Taro cakes!" She put one, steaming, on her butter plate.

Holly and I were wearing our organdy dresses, with little flowers embroidered on the wide collars and the sleeves that turned up at the elbow. Holly's hair ribbon was yellow and shiny and extra perky. Every one of the girls, big and small was wearing white, and all had sleeves that ended near or at the elbow. One of the biggest girls, Em, had pinned a rose to the front of her dress, and it looked very nice.

"Sadie . . . I wish you didn't have to go home. Really."

She looked sad for a minute, and then Cho, on her other side, said something and she turned away. She knows Christmas and Easter vacations don't last, I thought, and how can she stand to live in a city! I never thought of Honolulu as a city. It was a place—mostly Brookside, and Lanai School, and Grandma and Grandpa and Kirey, and trees and flowers everywhere.

The Farm—that was a different thing from Cleveland. How strange it was, to have this whole new set of cousins here, telling about far-away places. Oh, Sadie! If only *you* could stay!

After lunch, the men went to sit in the koa rocking chairs on the lanai, and lit their cigars and pipes. They never smoked in Grandma's house.

Sadie, Lee, and I sat in the big living room, near the lanai door. We seldom sat in this room. At Christmas, Grandma's tree reaching to the high ceiling was in here, and Santa Claus came. But on ordinary days, we were in her sitting room. The living room had a good smell, probably from the koa paneling halfway up the walls, and the staircase in the corner.

We could hear one of the uncles telling a story. It was about a haole man calling a Hawaiian on the telephone. He said, "I want to speak to Huu." The answer was, "This Huu." Thinking he had been asked for his name, the haole gave it. Silence. Haole: "Where's Huu?" Hawaiian: "Huu here." Haole: "I told you who I am! Please call Huu." Hawaiian: "Huu." Haole: "Huu, dammit! I'm getting huhu!"

It was Uncle Francis, and he rocked harder and harder as he talked, until all at once the chair fell over backward. The three of us leapt to our feet and to the door, but Uncle Francis merely finished his story, and got two of his brothers to right the chair, with him still in it.

Another uncle said that a few days before, his Japanese stableman had dashed into his office shouting: "Cow kaukau cow kaukau, cow kaukau horse kaukau."

I thought this was hilarious, but Lee said, puzzled: "What's he talking about?"

"Kaukau means 'eat' and it means 'feed,' too," I explained. "You know, horse or cattle feed. And sounds like 'cow cow.'"

Uncle Douglas' story was the best. As a man drove his horse and wagon, with the coffin of his wife, down the road past the church, they went over a bump. The coffin lid raised and his wife sat up, alive. A year or so later he was again driving the coffin down the road, just as everyone came out of church. Going over the bump, he reached back to put a hand on the coffin lid and said, "Watchit, old Wahine!"

Grandma was calling us for the pictures, and we went outside. A Japanese photographer had his camera set up on three long legs, and a black cloth over his head as he looked into it. The site chosen was across the driveway from the front steps, with a white pergola in the background, and some shrubbery.

A number of photos were taken, with different groupings: Grandma with her seven children, again with their wives and husbands too, and finally the big event—the whole family.

Grandma sat in her rocking chair at the center, holding Keiki, with the aunts sitting at either side of her. The uncles and the big boys and three biggest girls stood back of them, and the rest of us sat on the grass, with one of the big Cleveland boys, the friendly one, kneeling behind us. The big boys were all in suits, or in navy blue coats and white flannels—those looked the nicest. Several of the aunts were wearing long necklaces, very stylish. These were apt to be of amber, the dark, glowing round beads that came from China.

"A day to remember!" said Munna as we drove home. "Thirty-seven of us gathered at Maluhia."

My father sighed, but said nothing.

"Didn't you think so, Dan? I thought it went splendidly."

"Yes. Yes, it did." After a minute he said, "I wish Father had been there."

The mountain drive came during the last week that the Clevelanders were on Maui. I hung around the stable all day for a couple of days beforehand. Masa and his young Portuguese assistant, Tony, were airing blankets, rolling saddle slickers, packing supplies. They let me help with some things, but not often, as I had no experience with these preparations.

After a while, Masa said, "Better you go look Wiwi. Maybe ride? He stay in pen."

"No, I want to watch you." Was he trying to chase me away? I sat on the big feed bin, making myself as scarce as possible. They wouldn't have to open this for horse feed; there was plenty of grass at Ukulele, nice wet grass. And the bin sloped, so they didn't need it as a packing surface. The two of them were in and out of the saddle room and the warehouse next door all the time, but I could see them through the open door by sitting sideways.

A voice from the stableyard said, "How are they going to take all that stuff?"

Lee and Sadie had ridden over, and I jumped down to go out to see them.

"They're all packing like mad over at Maluhia, too," Sadie said. "But only clothes and things."

"Masa does this all the time—he knows just how. For the crater, it's tents, too, and frying pans and things." These weren't needed for Ukulele, because of the red cabins. "All this goes on pack mules," I added to Lee. "Except the slickers, of course. The packs of clothes go on top of them, at the back of each person's saddle."

Sadie got off Maka Beauty and tied her up, and we sat on a patch of grass out of the way. Lee rode over near the Ranch office, where the blankets were hanging over the fence.

"You'd never think they'd need so much," Sadie marveled.

"I wish we could go." I sighed. "Next time you come, maybe." There was an empty feeling inside me, when I thought of their leaving next week.

Someone rode around the curve of the road on a sorrel horse, who arched his neck and jogged along with ears pointed. With amazement, I saw that it was Rob. He stopped beside us, grinning as if he couldn't contain some thrilling knowledge.

"What horse is it?" I asked eagerly, stroking the white blaze on his forehead.

"Let me introduce you to 'Ilima!" The grin became a laugh, such a happy laugh. "Daddy gave him to me, and I've been trying him out this morning. Gosh, what a great horse! I have to hold him in, he wants to go so much."

"*Gave* him to you! Oh, Rob. Are you riding him for the drive, then?"

"Yes. Daddy said it was too far for Jack."

"Poor Jack. He'd probably love to go."

"He'll have a good rest. Unless—" He glanced shyly at Sadie. "Would you like to ride Jack while we're gone?"

"Would I! Daddy said Lee and I could ride up for the branding. Could I go on Jack?"

"Sure!" said Rob magnanimously. "Ride him any place you like."

"You're coming for the branding, aren't you?" she said to me.

"Yes, of course. Only Daddy said I'd have to come home in the car, if I got tired. I won't, though."

The cattle would be driven down the mountain the first day, and the second day there would be branding at the Olinda pens. Quite a few people would be riding up for that, through the pastures, or driving up the curving road and then for a way along a car track in the pasture grass.

"It will be a cowboy lunch," I said. "Salt beef and pa'i'ai. And cold boiled potatoes. And watermelon!"

"What's pa'i'ai?" asked Lee, and then, "Why's he called 'Ilima?"

" 'Ilima is a flower," Rob said. "Yellow. You make leis of it."

"Golden-yellow," I added. "It's the flower of Oahu. He's called that because of his color."

"What's the Maui flower?"

"Lokelani. Or roselani. A rose."

"We've got to get back home for lunch," Sadie said. "Gee, Rob, thanks for letting me ride Jack!"

At the bend in the road, Lee turned around and yelled back, "You never told me what pa'i'ai is!"

The week flew. I couldn't even be too excited thinking about the cattle drive and all of them spending two nights at Ukulele, because of the hollow feeling I had about Sadie's leaving. All of them—what a glorious summer it had been! Just as my brown-eyed cousin had predicted, all those weeks ago. I wasn't a bit scared of him now. Or of Lois, either. She was pretty, like Sadie, and nice to us. The only ones I still felt strange with were Zander and Henley, the one who was at college. "Yale," Holly said. "Everybody goes to Yale."

"*Every*body?"

"Well, practically."

It didn't matter about the two big boys I was still shy with, because I hardly ever saw them. But Sadie and Lee. Yes, even Lee! I'd picture him jogging along on his frisky pony, and wish he were here, asking me the name of a hill, or why you said 'Veevee' when it wasn't spelled that way, or something.

There was lots about the week that was fun. The branding, especially, and seeing Sadie on Jack that day, and two other times.

We went to the beach house and swam, and watched the fishermen walking in the water, far out, with their boxes and spears. Once when one came in near the beach, he let us look through the glass bottom. The sand at the floor of the ocean was so clear, you wouldn't believe it. There were curving ridges in it, it wasn't flat.

"That's the tide," Sadie said. "The currents in the water."

"How do you know?" asked Lee.

"Daddy told me."

The streamers of seaweed were so green, green, and long and curly, swishing this way and that under the water, sometimes tangling around your legs. You could see crabs on the sand, and shells, and coral, some with seaweed caught on it and waving as if it were trying to get loose. Once in a while, a fish would swim by, or a school of minnows. Some of the fish were bright-colored, and the shades of the minnows even were so sharp that they might have been colored.

We rode across to a high, round hill called Pi'iholo—"A volcanic cone, grown over with grass and trees," said Uncle Douglas. There were mountain pools there, icy cold, where we swam.

One day we drove all the way to Lahaina, on the other side of the West Maui Mountains. I had never seen it in the daytime before, only in the middle of the night when we sometimes had to catch a steamer there for Honolulu, going out to it from the wharf in a scow.

We saw the banyan tree that Grandpa had planted, when he was a young man. (Grandpa *young*?) He said of this that he had hated seeing people stand about in the blazing hot sun, in this central square, many of them waiting to go into the Court House. So when a young banyan sapling was sent to his parents by missionary friends in India, he had asked permission to plant it there. By now, it was enormous!

Next we went to the house where my other grandfather, the Maui one, had been born and lived when he was growing up.

On then to the beach, where there were lots of kiawe trees. They had long yellow beans growing on them, and very sharp kuku's on the sand underneath. You had to wear shoes if you didn't want to get stuck.

The water was lovely, and you could look across it to other islands. I had only seen a sloping half of one and the jutting against the skyline of the other before, at either end of the West Maui Mountains.

We had a picnic lunch under the kiawe trees, on a canvas Aunt Rae had brought. The waves rolled toward the beach, one after another, curled, broke, and flattened out to sweep up within a few feet of us, swirling and frothing over the yellow sand. The rushing and receding of the blue water was soothing in its rhythm, the sea beyond was very blue, and Cleveland seemed of another world.

Then, one day, they were gone.

I didn't know what to do with myself. Riding made me think of Sadie and Lee, even the stable did. I went outside and lay under the camphor tree in front of the house, and looked up into the hundreds of little green and red leaves, tossing gently in the breeze. Thousands, maybe.

I could hear the sound of slow hoofbeats, coming to my ear through the ground, before turning my head and seeing Rob lead Jack around the end of the stone wall. I wondered idly why he wasn't riding him.

He led him right up to me. I was crying, but I didn't even feel ashamed about Rob seeing me.

Rob let Jack's neck rope fall to trail on the grass beside me.

"I thought—I thought maybe you'd like Jack," he said.

Any other day I'd have loved to ride Jack. But it was nice of Rob to think of it.

I shook my head, looking up at him through tears. "Thanks," I said. "But I can't ride today. Thanks anyway. Any other time—if you'll let me."

"I mean to keep." He put the end of the rope over onto my lap. "I'm giving him to you. I've got 'Ilima now." He turned and walked quickly away.

I stared at his back, and then up at Jack. To keep . . . Was that what Rob had said? Jack—to keep.

I flung myself up off the ground and put my arms around his neck, and cried into his mane. Jack, I thought, *Jack*. To keep. Mine. I put my lips to his ear and whispered his name, over and over.

9 The Tidal Wave

My father said, "Nani and Lei could have their kids any time now."

It was Friday afternoon, and Nagata had just brought me up for the weekend with Kirey at the Ranch House. We were spending this school year at the beach on Maui, with Melbie as governess. We called her that now instead of Miss Melbehn, and we really didn't mind her too much. In fact, we were growing to love her. Especially now, as far as I was concerned, when Kirey had come from Honolulu to stay for a month or two at the Ranch House, for a change of air.

Daddy drove up the mountain every day to work and he was about to leave now for the beach. As he got into his car, I said, "Gee, Daddy, do you s'pose Nani will have hers this weekend?"

"She could, and Lei too. Masa's going to keep an eye on them and you can do the same." He waved goodby and was off.

In the house, Kirey and I smiled at each other, looking forward to the two days.

"I'll go see Nani," I said. "And Lei."

96

"Unpack your things first, child. Then run along."

It was good to hear her voice. Something about our having the house to ourselves, and my being the only one of us children to roam the grounds, gave these weekends a quality of enchantment for me, a sense of freedom the more precious because it was bound by the limits of Friday to Sunday.

Kirey was in the room next to mine at the back of the house. Her long, crisp cotton dresses, gaily printed or checked, hung in her closet beside two or three church dresses. I put my church dress on a hanger in my closet and dumped everything else into a drawer. Already wearing overalls, I was ready to go.

Nani and Lei were in a small pasture on a slope above the house. They were fawn-colored, with surely the softest coats that goats ever had. Under their chins hung little fur-covered knobs.

I fondled Nani's head and neck, careful not to touch the distended belly. "Nani-nani," I said softly. "Are you going to have it soon, Nani?"

Lei, who was Holly's, struck me as looking unhappy. She was, if anything, larger than Nani, and she just stood there without grazing.

"Poor Lei," I said, stroking her. "Why don't you have your kid? Then your opu won't be so fat and you'll feel better."

I stayed with the goats until Kirey came out onto the brick terrace in front of the house to call me. Going down the hill toward her, I liked the way the setting sun lit her hair. I knew from brushing it that there was blond in it still, but the effect was white. "One of life's luxuries!" she would say when she took her hair down and I ran the ivory-backed hairbrush through it. "To feel really indulged, I'd like to have my hair brushed every day, and the sheets on my bed changed every other day." Kirey had linen sheets and soft, sheer wool blankets in blue and in peach color.

"Dinner as soon as you've bathed," she said as I ran across the terrace to her. "We're having one of your mother's good roasting chickens tonight."

I could smell it from the kitchen. Kirey had brought some of her lemon butter with her from Honolulu, to have with bread. Every year she made a big batch of it for the Fair at St. Andrew's Cathedral, and often gave jars to her friends.

After dinner I said, "Shall I read you a letter Grandpa wrote me?"

"I'd love to hear it."

The envelope with its round red two-cent stamp, addressed in black ink in his firm hand, was in my bedroom. I brought it out to the living room, and read: "Groveling in dust and ashes with much weeping, I confess that I forgot it was to be your birthday today. Your grandmother, ever loving and faithful and true, spoke of it this morning at breakfast.

"On the boat with this letter I am sending you a little pin, shaped like a star. And I enclose a picture of Abraham Lincoln. It is a kind of picture that it is good to have, to remind one of the fine man that he was. We wish there were a great many more like him.

"Your mother writes and tells us lots about you children 'and all like that'—but just lately we haven't heard much of your beloved father. Will you write and tell us how he is? As a rule he is so well, and accomplishes so much with little noise, that one seems to take for granted that he is as dependable as the sun and moon and stars. Please tender him my expressions of high esteem and regard, and my hopes for his welfare and long life and happiness.

"A few days ago we had a letter from your cousin Diane, a very nice letter indeed, although it might have been written by a crazy spider using all of its legs. What a great thing letter writing is so that we can communicate with each other and keep in touch, when separated!

"Do you read parts of the Bible sometimes? In the 6th verse of the 17th chapter of Proverbs, you will find: 'Children's children are the crown of old men.' (Solomon was some old man!) Well, we are all children, really, only some are younger. As for me, on my last birthday I did not feel one hoop older than I had the day before. Perhaps, though, today you feel a year older than you did yesterday! When next I see you, you shall have a shiny new quarter because I forgot.

"And now I must go and change my raiment for dinner. Afterwards, Grandma and I will be playing dominoes and spooning, as usual.

"Give our love to Kirey and tell her that I'll keep in practice to challenge her at cribbage.

"Your affectionate if absent-minded Ancestor"

It was delightful to wake with sunlight filtering through leaves of the tall eucalyptus trees on the hill, in Nani and Lei's pasture. I could see the two of them on the slope—no kids yet.

I dressed quickly and rushed through breakfast.

"Not too fast, now. Finish your porridge. This Dairy cream is so thick and good, compared to what the dairies in Honolulu call cream."

Nani and Lei were exactly the same as the afternoon before. I stopped in at the Ranch office to report to my father. He was there only until noon on Saturdays, and went down to the beach in time for lunch.

"No kids yet, Daddy."

His brown English boots, highly polished, showed under the big rolltop desk, and he smiled at me over it.

"They'll be coming along, don't you worry."

Across the stableyard, Masa was in the tack room. He was working on the straps of a saddle, which was on a rack where he hung those that needed repair. He sat on a high stool beside it and took tools from his overall pockets as he needed them.

I watched his deft fingers, and he looked up and smiled. "You like you saddle? Jack stay insi' pen."

"No." I'd go to see Jack, of course, but I didn't want to be far from the goat pasture. "No ride today, I guess."

The smell of leather mixed with the woolly, horsy smell of saddle blankets was good. The stable was the right setting for Masa, the place where he belonged.

Once when I had been given some initialed silver rosettes for Jack's bridle, he put them on upside down. When I remarked on it, he said, "So you can read when you stay on top Jack."

"Whassamatter, no ride today?" he asked now.

"No feel like," I said. "When do you think Nani and Lei will have their kids?"

"Pretty soon come, no worry."

Don't worry, no worry. But I *was* worried.

"Better you go watch, then you call me when baby goat come." His eyes teased me over the top of the saddle. "Maybe I no need help; you can fix 'em up OK."

Staying with the goats and then calling him was what I had in mind. He wasn't taking my concern seriously. I went to the back of the room, where the small saddles we had used in earlier years hung, and jumped down through the back door to the sick-horse pen below. There was a large bay in it, his knee bandaged, and I ran my hand over his warm neck and then climbed the fence to the outer pen where Jack was.

"Can't ride today, Jackie." I smoothed his mane and forelock, and lightly touched the diamond that starred his forehead. It was still a wonder to me that he was actually mine.

I crossed the road and went through the yard to the gulch horse pasture beyond. It probably *was* silly of me to think that I had to watch Nani and Lei every minute. Masa evidently thought so.

Holly was worried too, though. The afternoon before at the beach she had said, "You might be there when they have their kids. Be sure to telephone me right away." She had come out to the car with me and stood frowning abstractedly when Nagata drove us off, not even noticing when I waved.

Merry Legs and Butterfly were in the deep grass under the silky oak trees. Such gay names for two ancient mares! I jumped onto Butterfly's back, the rounder of the two, and let her amble along with me for a way. Then I left them and went down the steep side of the gulch to the bottom.

Here grew many of the trees I loved best: the mango, the jacaranda, the mountain apple. And the low, twisting fig tree. I climbed in the jacaranda and shook a spray of lavender petals down over me, then scrambled up into the fig tree and onto a branch that formed a perfect seat, with the trunk for a back-rest. I sat in this quiet, leafy place for a long time.

When at last I went back to the goat pasture, Masa was there. He wasn't smiling now. Lei was on her side, too weak to bleat. Her eyes were like those of a person; there was terror and pain in them.

Masa had to use his hands to help with the birth. Sweat rolled down his face and neck, which were a curious ashen color. A leg came first, and he said something in Japanese that sounded like a swear word. Then there seemed to be all legs—and blood; a great deal of blood.

"Go get water," he said to me in a voice that sounded strange. "Bucket water."

Daddy's car was gone from in front of the office. Kirey could have helped—but there wasn't time to call her. I raced for a bucket and filled it from the faucet at the goats' trough. Sun had warmed the pipes, it wouldn't be too cold. Water splashed over my legs as I ran back.

Gently, Masa washed off Lei and then the kids. They lay still. With beating heart, I watched for some movement to show that they were alive. Yes—so weak they didn't raise their heads, only "Baa-ed" faintly. But they lived.

I realized that Masa had turned from the kids and, looking around, saw Lei's eyes staring.

"Dead?" I wasn't sure whether I had spoken the word, but he nodded.

Dead! Lei! Oh no, it wasn't possible. I looked away from her and stared at Masa's hands, the back of one of them still streaked with red.

A shadow fell across his hands and part of Lei. Knowing in a flash of perception who it was, I turned slowly. Holly stood there. She must have got Daddy or Nagata to drive her up from the beach.

Her face, stark white framed by long brown curls, had an expression I had never seen. Stricken; the word came to my mind from somewhere. I could only gaze at her, could make no gesture to show that I understood how she felt. Her grief was too absolute.

After a while, I thought, *Nani*. She was nowhere to be seen. I ran up over the hilltop, and there she was, looking just as she had earlier that day. I thrust my nose into the furry warmth of her neck and thought, Oh Nani, not you.

Holly didn't seem to notice my return, or Masa. She was kneeling beside Lei. Finally, she moved round to where the kids lay, stirring now and trying to get up.

"I've got to stay and take care of them," she said. She looked at us now but with eyes that didn't appear to see. "They'll have to be fed with bottles."

In the morning, Kirey and I went to church, leaving Holly with the kids. Kirey always went to the Episcopal church—the "Church of England," she called it. For Easter that year she had given me a fat black book called *Hymns A. M. Tunes*. For a while I thought they were hymns to be sung in the morning, but knew by now that A.M. meant "Ancient and Modern." I always took it with me when I went to her church.

When we were back at the house, Holly said she had been trying to telephone them at the beach. But Central had told her, "I haven't been able to get a line to the beach yet this morning. I don't know what's wrong."

"How are the kids?" Kirey asked Holly.

"Better. They're a little stronger."

I tore out of my dress and into overalls.

"Lunch in a few minutes," Kirey said. "Cold chicken. But run see Nani first."

Nani was licking off a tiny creature who stood beside her. For a moment, I couldn't believe it. Then I thought, On wobbly legs, already! My tears fell on them both as I took them into my arms.

Kirey and Masa said they'd feed Lei's kids between them, and Holly said, "I'll come up to spend the afternoon tomorrow. I know Nagata will bring me."

When she and I got down to the beach late that day, Rob and our cousin Monty came running out to meet us. "Guess what you missed!" Rob shouted.

I shook my head dumbly, and looked past the boys to Holly.

"A tidal wave! We had a tidal wave!"

Rob's blond hair was standing on end and his eyes were round. Monty's freckled face shone with excitement.

Rob said, "All the water went out, past the reef, and we could see the bottom of the ocean, and seaweed and coral, and fish flapping!"

Monty chimed in, "The telephone wasn't working, and the lights were out!"

"And Mother and Monty's mother had gone to church in Wailuku and they couldn't go along the road by the harbor to get home, and they had to stay there."

"They didn't know what had happened to us."

The boys must know about Lei, I thought. But they hadn't been there . . .

"When the water came in," cried Monty, "you never saw anything so fast."

"It wasn't like a wave—just a whole lot of water coming at you."

"And it came up on the grass, and all around the house!"

Through their voices, I thought of Holly. I wanted to reach out and take her hand, but didn't know how to do it.

10

Rob

As I came back through the dormer window from the upstairs deck, I saw that Rob was in the big room where the three of us slept.

"What were you doing out there, Baba?" he asked. "I could see you looking up at the sky."

I hesitated, then decided to tell him. "I'm praying to be turned into a boy. It seems to me that God can hear me better from out there."

He laughed, and said mockingly, "You'd better tell Mother about it, so she can get you some boys' clothes."

"My overalls are just like yours," I retorted. "And my riding pants and boots." But it wasn't a bad idea, even though he had been teasing.

We called the upstairs of the Ranch House "the attic." The ceiling sloped at the sides with the slant of the roof, and the dormers made lovely alcoves, wide enough for a bed if you wanted it there. The main part of the attic was one great room, and Holly, Rob, and I placed our beds wherever we wanted them, moving them from time to time.

A bannister, lined with bookshelves, enclosed the flight of stairs at the center, and to one side of this was the red brick chimney from the living room fireplace below. The windows at the mountain end of the house looked up the hillsides onto horses and white-faced cattle in the Ranch pastures.

"The reason I want to be a boy is to be allowed to do all the things you can do," I said to Rob. "Like going on the Mountain Pasture cattle drive and sleeping at Ukulele."

My father had consoled me by saying, "There will be a drive of Waihou Pasture soon, and you and Jack may come on that. Rob's a year older, you know."

That would be fun, of course. But it wasn't like staying overnight at Ukulele, away up the mountain in the grove of eucalyptus and holly trees.

Rob went to work with the cowboys most days, too, and he had been to see the crater. He and our cousin Cho had ridden with Daddy to the top of Haleakala, to play in the snow, and Rob had had his first sight of the enormous dormant volcano there. Daddy had brought back snowballs in his saddle bag for Holly and me, still hard-packed, and tied to his saddle by its leather straps had been a silversword plant: strange, not like any plant we had seen, with its up-curving, spiky, silver leaves.

"Tell Mother," Rob said now again, with a grin. "Tell her about this cuckoo idea of yours."

All right, I would.

Before dinner that evening I found her and Kirey sitting together in the long, dusky living room. There were pools of light from lamps at the chairs where they sat, Mother knitting a sock, and Kirey tatting a long band of edging for underwear. Fire in the grate flickered near them, and there was a good smell of burning eucalyptus wood and leaves in the air.

Kirey was staying on at the Ranch with us for a while, after our having moved back from the beach. Best of all, she was going to move from Cottage Grove to a little house in the Brookside yard. Not the one across the brook, where

Mademoiselle had lived, but a cottage much closer to the house.

"Mother." I curled up on the sofa, wondering how to say it. "Kirey . . . "

It was easier to get Kirey's attention. She laid down her tatting, and I thought how pretty her high-piled hair was in the lamp's glow. The blond that was still in it was gold.

She smiled and said, "What is it?"

"I've—been wanting to be a boy and—" I floundered.

"You're a tomboy already," Kirey said.

"I know, but I mean really."

My mother looked up from flashing steel needles.

"What were you saying, dear? Oh, come hold yarn for me while we're talking." She thrust a needle through the sock and fished in her knitting bag for a skein of light blue wool— someone must be having a baby—and I pulled up a chair in front of her and held up my hands so she could put the wool across them. "Now, what was it?"

It began to seem very silly. How could one change from a girl into a boy, even by praying? *John Martin's Book* had said it would happen if a girl kissed her elbow, but I had found that to be impossible.

Kirey said, "Baba would like to be a boy. You almost might be," she added to me, "if it weren't for your hair."

My mother frowned slightly at me and my Dutch cut, and said as she wound the yarn swiftly, "Your hair's so awfully thin and fine. It might be a good plan to have your head shaved, the way Aunt Sybil does with her children."

Things weren't going right at all! "Mother! I didn't mean—I came to say—"

Oh, why had I started this? She was still looking at me, thoughtfully, and went on, "It's supposed to make hair grow out thicker and stronger. Sybil says it does. She shaves her children's heads herself, but I think—yes, I'd really rather have you go down to Hatae San."

Usually Mori, the cook, cut our hair on the back porch.

He sat us on a high stool in turn, put a large towel about our shoulders, and wielded the scissors skillfully. But sometimes we were taken to Mr. Hatae's barber shop.

Kirey was looking startled. "Do you really think it should be *shaved*?" she asked.

"No harm at all in trying it!" Mother said cheerfully. "It might improve her hair a great deal, make all the difference."

I turned to Kirey in despair. After a moment, she picked up her tatting and the shuttle she worked it with, and said quietly to my mother, "Would you like me to take her to Hatae San? I could ask his advice."

"Oh, yes! Would you? It would be a great help, I'm so busy just now." She put away the ball of blue yarn and turned back to her sock. "I'm sure it's a very good idea," she said absently.

Accordingly, the next morning Nagata drove Kirey and me to the barber shop in Wailuku, at the foot of the West Maui Mountains across the plain from Haleakala. The valleys of this western range were deep and shadowed, only their ridges sunstruck.

I had spent a perfectly miserable night. Because I had gathered the courage to say I wanted to be a boy, my head was going to be shaved!

On the trip down the mountainside, Kirey chatted with me all the way. For a few minutes at a time, I would forget what lay at the end of the drive.

Kirey asked, "'Why is this road called Pukalani? Do you know?"

"Yes." My father had told me. "It means 'Hole in the Sky.' Or you could say 'Hole in the Clouds.' It's because even on an overcast day, there's a streak of blue sky over it."

Kirey said, "I think 'Rift in the Clouds' would sound better."

"Maybe. Well, yes."

The road curved between fields of tall sugar cane, with its lovely feathery tassels.

"Have you ever chewed a piece of sugar cane?" I asked. "It's so good—sweet! But you can't swallow it, only chew it."

"Get the juice from it."

"Sometimes Daddy cuts us pieces with his pocketknife."

From here we could look across the fields and see the three Norfolk Island pines where my cousin Diane lived. I told Kirey that people often planted trees that would grow high, two or three or four of them, to mark where their houses were. You could see the ones at Diane's, like dark green spires, for miles around.

Occasionally the road crossed over an irrigation ditch, or a narrow one ran with water beside it. It was my Maui grandfather, who died before I was born, who had brought water from miles and miles along the mountain so that sugar would grow in what had been dry and barren soil. I thought of a story about him that had become a sort of legend, and told it to Kirey.

"When the ditches had been dug and the pipes laid a long, long way, with my grandfather and the men sleeping out there in the forest, they came to Maliko—that very deep gulch, you know? To get the pipe through, the men would have to let themselves down over a cliff on a rope and they were afraid to. You know that my grandfather lost an arm in a sugar mill accident, don't you?"

Kirey nodded and I went on.

"Well, to get the men to go down the rope, he did it with his one arm, and they were ashamed not to follow him. Every day after that he went first, until the pipe was across the gulch."

Surely Kirey knew this story, but she listened interestedly. When we reached the plain between the two mountains and came to a long stretch of road lined on both sides with monkey-pod trees, I was still thinking of him and said, "He planted these trees. Did you know that?"

The spreading branches met overhead, so that driving

under them was like going through a tunnel. There were many places on the island that made me think of this grandfather I had never known. Here, near sea level where it was hot, it seemed to me a wonderful thing to have had these long rows of trees planted, to look so beautiful and to shade the dusty road.

Hatae San greeted us at the door of his shop, with his usual bow and polite smile. When Kirey told him what we had come for, it looked as if something had erased the smile from his face.

"You like her head *shave*?" he asked in a tone of disbelief.

Kirey hesitated. "I told this girl's mother that I'd ask your advice . . . "

Holding my breath, I looked from her to Mr. Hatae.

He stood shaking his head slowly.

I clutched at Kirey. She held onto my hand, and said, "I expect her hair would come back in nice and thick? And—it wouldn't really take so very long to grow?"

"One year, hair same like now." Hatae San said it with an air of satisfaction. "Rong time, one year. Hair grow very slow." He shrugged and added, "No make thick, too."

Kirey looked at me. "Perhaps—a boy's haircut?" she suggested.

After the haircut, she asked Nagata to drive us to the Paia Store. At this plantation store that stocked everything from gunny sacks of rice to saddles, she bought me two boys' suits, the kind Rob had worn until recently when he got dressed up. They were shorts and middy blouses, one blue, the other with green stripes. I was speechless. She had me put on one of the suits in a little dressing room.

On coming out, I gave her a quick hug and whispered, "Thank you, Kirey."

"Between your overalls and these suits, who's to know you're a girl?"

And when Daddy saw me looking like a boy, he was sure to let me go on longer cattle drives, and ride Jack to the top of the mountain!

Mother said: "Oh, Kirey!"

"She would have looked so—so—and the barber said—"

Mother put her arms around Kirey and hugged her hard. "It would have been pretty awful," she agreed. Laughter began to bubble up in her so that she could scarcely speak. "I might have known!" she gasped.

Kirey smiled complacently, and all at once I knew that she had planned it this way from the beginning.

"Why don't we call you 'Bob' now?" she said to me.

11
Stolen Goods

Jamie was spending the day with us, the time when Brownsey drove up to the brick steps of the Ranch House terrace in a roadster.

Jamie was younger than any of us three. He had an anxious looking face with a little pointed nose, and hair so pale that it was lighter than Rob's. Holly and I thought he was adorable.

"I wish he was ours," she would say, wistfully twisting one of her curls round her finger.

We all ran out to see Brownsey alight from her roadster. It was beautiful; dark blue with a dashing red stripe all around, at the level of the door handle.

And how smart Brownsey looked! "You're chic," Holly said, a word she had just learned. Brownsey was wearing one of the new short dresses, with a belt around her hips instead of at the waist, and her driving hat had a red band on it to match the stripe on the car.

"You driving!" cried my mother.

Mother herself had a driver's license and on occasion we

saw her, looking very small, at the wheel. But as a rule she was driven by Daddy or Nagata. And as for Brownsey—what a surprise!

Brownsey laughed in the lilting way that made you want to laugh, too. "I've been taking lessons for weeks and didn't even tell you. I had to learn to get around on my own."

Rob said, "Boy oh boy, it's a swell car. It's got a rumble seat!"

"Sure it has," Brownsey said. "And a horn." She pressed the rubber bulb to 'beep' the trumpet-shaped brass horn that hung on the driver's door. "I'll take you for a ride sometime soon."

Jamie looked hopeful, as if he were wondering whether she meant him as well. I wondered, too. Oh, poor Jamie, if she meant only the three of us!

My mother frowned slightly. Wouldn't she let us go for a drive with Brownsey?

Jamie trailed after Rob, who was inspecting the roadster all the way around.

"It's a bonny wee car, isn't it, Rob?" he said solemnly, walking after him in his slow-gaited way.

Jamie's parents were Scottish and he said cute things like that. They lived a half-mile or so down the road from the Ranch House.

All of us admired the car from every angle and got Brownsey to sit in it again to show us how it worked.

"Gee whiz!" Rob said, peering in. "I bet I could drive it myself."

"Bet you could, mate!" echoed Jamie.

"You'd need to sit on a cushion to see over the wheel," Holly said, "and then you wouldn't be able to reach the pedals."

"Are you sure the brake's on?" asked Mother nervously.

After Brownsey's arrival in this spectacular manner, Rob, Jamie, and I played in the gulch pasture. We climbed trees— mango, alligator pear, Pride of India—and ran along huge fallen eucalyptus trunks. We jumped onto the backs of the aged Butterfly and Merry Legs, and let them laze along with us. Then we smoked, stuffing leaves into the hollow stems of bamboo stalks. It was fun having Jamie there. If only he did live with us!

Holly was catching caterpillars in the yard. She kept them in jars in her bedroom upstairs and watched them turn into chrysalises. She made air-holes carefully in the lids, and gathered milkweed and other leaves that they ate, wetting some in case the caterpillars were thirsty. Nearly all of the jars were labeled now; she pored over books to find the exact names and could tell you what sort of butterfly or moth each would turn into. Imagine anything like the fat green one, or the funny black and white striped, turning into something as pretty as a butterfly! "This one will be a monarch," she would say. "*Danaus plexippus*. Monarchs are very interesting. Every year on a certain date, they fly from Canada to Pacific Grove in California, and when it's warm enough in Canada, they fly back. Each year the flock is different—the *children* of the year before's butterflies."

When we went in to wash for lunch, Jamie looked sad as he soaped his hands, slowly and thoroughly.

"Are you homesick, Jamie?" asked Holly, putting her arm around his shoulders.

"Can't I go home now?" He looked up at her with big, earnest eyes.

She knelt beside him to be closer to his height. "Your mother is out today, and your father is at work. But you can have fun with Rob."

Rob was saying, "Brownsey, when are you going to take us in your roadster?"

Jamie whispered, "Do you think she'll take me, too?"

"I don't know." Holly looked worried. "But I'll show you my caterpillars."

Jamie looked appeased, and went into the dining room with us.

After lunch, Rob and Jamie went outside again. The thing to do at the moment was to curl yourself up in an automobile tire and have someone roll you. We stood at the lanai screen door watching Jamie's struggles to propel Rob toward the bank at the edge of the lawn, and Brownsey said, "Jamie is a comical little fellow." She pronounced it "cawmical," which made it sound deliciously funny. Then, with a little peal of laughter, "His knees come into the room a week before he does."

I bent double, convulsed at this description of Jamie's unique manner of walking.

"He's such a funny, cute little person," Holly said. "Oh, I *wish* he was ours."

She wandered out, jar in hand, toward nasturtiums clambering on a wall, with a flutter of white winging above them. Her dog Rufus was nearby, as usual. Rufus was the son of Daddy's English setter, Don, and a mother of unknown breed—a lovable dog.

I followed her and suggested, "Maybe Jamie's mother will let him stay with us for a while."

"She'd never! But you know what, Bob? We might hide him . . ."

"She might forget about him!"

Holly shook her head. "No chance of that! But we could keep him till she found out where he was."

Later that afternoon, Rob and Jamie came in to have a look round "Mother's closet." This was a huge closet off her and our father's bedroom. The back wall of it, beyond her dresses hanging on rods, was a cabinet of drawers and shelves with doors. Here you might find anything from discarded plumed hats, ostrich feather fans, yarn and knitting needles to paper dolls, puzzles, boxes of plasticine, and books ready for any of us who were sick. Sometimes Mother let us rummage through this intriguing array, and we wished we'd get sick.

Holly stood at the closet door. She grabbed my arm and, shushing me, called, "Rob! Come here a minute. No, not you

Jamie." She shoved him back and he retreated obediently.

Holly closed the door and put her weight against it. "Find a key!" she said frantically.

I don't know what Rob thought, but I knew what she was doing. We ran round the big square room collecting keys: from the door to the living room, the wide double doorway to the lanai, the bathroom. One of them fitted the lock, and Holly turned it with a sigh of relief.

There were muffled sounds from within and Jamie's little voice crying: "I want to come out!" Holly called through the crack, "Don't be scared, Jamie. You can keep the light on, and by and by we'll bring you some dinner. See what you can find to play with."

He was sobbing, and knocking on the door. "It's all right, Jamie!" I called. "We'll let you out after a while. Don't cry."

Should Holly really have told him to play with things? What fun it would be, though, to have him stay with us! Maybe his mother wouldn't know he was gone, I thought hopefully. He was such a quiet little boy, she must hardly know he was there.

He was still making small whimpering noises. "Play with something, Jamie," I said recklessly.

Our mother came in, and we slipped guiltily away. From upstairs, Melbie's voice floated down in anguished tones. "Holly! Come quickly—hurry!"

Melbie was always, in our experience, in entire command of herself—and of us. Her sounding distraught made the summons very urgent indeed.

She was standing in the middle of Holly's bedroom, pointing a shaking finger at a fat caterpillar that inched its way across the floor.

"Oh!" Holly picked him up tenderly and returned him to his jar. "Oh, oh! I was giving them some extra air with the lids off and I forgot them." She tore at her hair in a dramatic gesture she had been practicing lately.

There were twenty-six empty jars. Holly looked feverishly

around the room, and Rob and I helped her. We found twelve without too much trouble—in her shoes, on and under the bed, crawling up the legs of tables. When Melbie spotted a stray, she waited for one of us to pick it up.

It surprised us very much that Melbie should be afraid of anything—and of all things, a little caterpillar! She did show interest in Holly's collection and had found a book on the subject for us to read. And she shared our delight when they became chrysalises and were transformed into butterflies and moths. We had never dreamed she would be squeamish about touching one.

The bathtime gong sounded its four rising and descending notes, and Melbie said: "That leaves fourteen of them still loose. Hurry with your baths, children, so you'll have time to go on looking for them before supper."

Our parents and Brownsey were going out so we had a quick early supper with Melbie, in the pantry.

Rob whispered to Holly, "Don't you think Jamie must be getting hungry?"

She whispered back, "Later."

After supper, though, we scampered back up the stairs to continue our search, without thinking of him again. Roving caterpillars occupied us for some time. "Here's one!" Rob would shout, lifting it from Holly's dressing table mirror or the edge of a picture frame.

Once he stood gazing out of the window, and I went to see what he was looking at. Brownsey's roadster, in all its new splendor, was parked on the grass beside the driveway circle.

"You don't s'pose she'll forget, do you?" he said. "To take us out in it."

"We won't let her forget!"

We could hear the telephone bell giving two rings downstairs and our mother answering and having a worried sounding conversation. She came running up the stairs in her new evening dress. It was of crepe de Chine, with splashy pink and orange flowers and green leaves making a wonderful pattern. The neck and hemline (not so very much below her knees) were silver-spangled beige, and there were rhinestone-bordered straps over the shoulders. A large clasp of green and silver rhinestones gathered in the hipline. It was gorgeous; she looked elegant! Her silver shoes were new, too—in size three.

"Children!" she cried. "Jamie's mother is beside herself—he isn't home yet! Didn't he start down the road when you had your baths?"

Jamie! The three of us stared at each other. We had forgotten all about him. Melbie looked as blameworthy as we, because she hadn't sent him home.

No one spoke for a minute. Then Holly said in a quavering voice, "He's in your closet."

"In my *closet*. But I was just there, getting my dress and things. The door was locked . . ." She looked at us in a puzzled way, then with a dawning thought, and at last severely. More severely than I remembered her ever looking.

We went pell mell down the stairs and through the house, and Holly opened the closet door. All was silence within. Mother had turned off the light and there was only a faint streak from the bedroom, on the floor and outlining the edges of her dresses. He *couldn't* have vanished. Could he? Holly switched the light on and we pushed past the dresses to the back of the closet.

Jamie's white head was on a cushion he must have found in the cabinet, and tears streaked his cheeks. His little pointed face looked anxious even in slumber. Stirring, he said sleepily, "Mummy?"

Mother leaned over and picked him up in her arms. To Holly she said, sternly, "Please telephone his mother right way . . . There, there, Jamie. It's all right, little boy." She stood patting his back and gently rocking him, and the small pale head snuggled against her neck.

Holly began to cry. "It was me, Mother, all my idea, because I thought—I thought—and then the caterpillars . . ."

Brownsey had come into the room, looking nearly as nice

as Mother. She had on an evening wrap in shimmering brocade, lined with velvet, and with a white fur collar. The white was a wonderful contrast for her gleaming, waved black hair.

She said to Holly, "Tell Jamie's mother that I'll drive him home right away."

We three stood on the brick steps to watch them go.

Brownsey sat very straight and looked determinedly over the wheel. She wore her shining, fur-collared cape, and not a hair of her marcel was out of place. Mother clutched Jamie to her gaily printed but now tear-spattered bosom.

The little boy's cheeks were dry now, and there was an expression we had never before seen on the small serious face we knew. He was grinning from ear to ear.

Jamie was having first ride in the roadster.

12
Kirey's Ship

When Kirey wasn't in her cottage or garden, I knew where she was: in the greenhouse. On the day when I got the idea of the question box, that was where she was. I ran through the door and said, "Guess what I'm going to do!"

She was watering the pots of ferns on the shelves at one side of the little structure. She turned and smiled at me, keeping her watering can tilted so that its fine spray washed the fronds clean and filled the brick-red pots. Her gardening smock was green, and her hair mostly covered by her lau hala gardening hat.

"What are you going to do?" She was always interested and never made me feel silly.

"I'm going to have a question box and put it in the dining room, and everyone can write questions and put them in and I'll answer."

"You'd better have an answer box too, then."

"And you can put in a question about when you'll go to England!" I said this because Kirey always said, "When my ship comes in, I'll go home for a visit."

119

"I have a secret to tell you," she said. "When we go indoors. You must be a good girl and not tell."

A secret! I was dying to know what it was, but knew very well there was no use in asking yet. I walked round the greenhouse, looking at the ferns, anthuriums, and orchids. It was cool and dim and fragrant in there. The fragrance was a sort of cool dampness, a shady, leafy scent. The slatted sides of the lath-house, the plants, and Kirey's smock made of this place a small green island, even in the surrounding greenness of the yard.

"Almost done now, and we'll go in for tea. He's thirsty, over in the corner here." She gave the last that the watering can held to a maidenhair fern. Kirey always called her plants "he" or "him," as if they were real personalities. Well, they were, when you saw them with her.

On the way in, she plucked two or three sprigs from the stephanotis vine that climbed its trellis to her window. They were like a handful of sweet-smelling porcelain.

At the bottom of the steps, she turned the faucet handle to let the hose run slowly about the roots of a kahili ginger. "He likes his head in the sun, and his feet wet. Now come! We'll put the kettle on and when I've tidied my hair, it will be boiling."

It was wonderful having Kirey right here at Brookside. She had moved into a cottage that wasn't far from the house, with its own entrance on Bates Street.

Her sitting room was nice and big, lots more space than she had had at Cottage Grove. All the things from Ah Inn's store looked right at home. Her bed, in one corner, was like a pune'e with its blue cover and pillows embroidered in Chinesey designs, or of blue or gold Chinese silk. I stood in front of a delicate table inlaid with mother-of-pearl, on which was her collection of tiny figurines. There were minute rickshas drawn by coolies, an ivory Buddha and a Kwan Yin, china vases an inch high, birds, jade elephants, other animals. The familiar tea tray was there on its table beside Kirey's rocking chair, vases of many shapes and sizes stood about the

room, and an intricately carved teakwood screen hid the door
to the kitchen.

"Here we are!" She came in with the teapot steaming, and
a pitcher of hot water, bringing with her into the room a whiff
of English Lavender. "Get the cream, child."

Her hair was brushed neatly in coils at the top of her head,
held by the usual bone hairpins, and she had taken off the
smock. Her dress was flowered in a prim design of cornflowers
on white.

"Which cup today?"

I made this important choice, picking out from the tea
tray a gold and white cup of fragile china with fluted edges,
and she poured my Cambric tea and then her own. Her cup
today was the one encircled by a tracery of violets.

"The English use milk in tea mostly, you know," she said.
"But this Dairy cream that your father brings me is so
delicious! Have a biscuit, now." Nothing was so good with tea
as Kirey's Huntley Palmer biscuits, which came in tins from
England.

Her eyes smiled at me over the rim of her cup, and I knew
the secret was coming.

I couldn't wait a minute longer. "Has your ship come in?"
I asked. "Has it, Kirey?" I could see Kirey's ship perfectly, piled
with some mysterious cargo, sailing into Honolulu Harbor. It
had something to do with a rubber plantation far away. Tan
Janding, those were the words. Perhaps the cargo was rubber,
then. Once I had heard my father say to my mother, "I don't
like Kirey's investing everything she has in rubber. I've asked
her to put half her capital in sugar, or something else. It isn't
good to have all in one company." "But you know Kirey!"
Mother had replied. " ' Miss Independence,' she says they
called her when she was nursing. Well, I love her that way."

Kirey said now, "My ship has almost come in. Think of it!
England . . ."

Her face became rapt; she was halfway around the world.
After a while, she said dreamily, "The daffodils! I'll go in the

spring. You've never seen anything like them on the moors of Yorkshire, a brilliant carpet flung down on the hillsides. 'A crowd, a host, of golden daffodils.' "

It seemed to me that it must be the most wonderful sight in the world. And Kirey would be seeing it soon!

"Will you go to Auld Reekie, too?"

"Ah, yes. And I'll see the Wee Sprite."

I knew her only by her picture, a small woman with a humorous face. What fun for those two to meet again! It was thirty years since Kirey had left Britain, longer than I could imagine. Ever since I could remember, she had spoken of "going home."

In leaving, I said, "Why don't you ask the question box when your ship will be coming in?"

"I shall. Now don't forget, what we've been talking about is a secret still."

I nodded importantly. It was flattering to be entrusted with a secret. On the way home I thought, Lucky Kirey, to have a ship all her own. And to be going to England on it!

At dinner that evening, I told my family about the question box.

"And *you're* going to think up the answers?" asked Rob.

I said yes. "You can ask anything you want."

"I'll ask what I'm going to get in the arithmetic test we had today."

"Well . . . "

"I can't imagine your being able to answer anything *I'd* want to know," said Holly.

"What about if Harvey will talk to you at recess Monday?" That would be a pretty sure one.

"Now, let me see," Mother said. "I'll have to put on my thinking cap."

My father, at his end of the table, was wriggling his eyebrows thoughtfully. I looked toward him, waiting.

"How about if Lanai School will burn down and we can't

go to school?" asked Rob.

"Quiet!" commanded Holly. "Can't you see that Daddy has a question?"

"Thank you, my dear. I was thinking of asking whether we'd have rain soon at the Ranch."

"All right. But now don't anybody else tell me what you're going to ask. Just put your questions in."

"How can we, if the box isn't even there?" demanded Rob.

He and Holly weren't taking this seriously enough. Well, I'd put up the box, and then maybe they would. Or two boxes, one for answers. The dining room seemed the best place, where we all met at least twice a day.

I was kept fairly busy answering questions, as it turned out. Otoru asked if she would get a letter from Maui soon, and I wrote, Yes! 'Toru was so pretty with her hair in a big roll and a tortoise shell comb stuck in it; Kiyoshi would be very silly, if he let her forget him. Misao asked when Ka-chan would have a brother or sister, and which it would be, and I answered, Soon! A brother, because we had a girl baby, who was so much fun to play with, and I thought it would be nice to have a boy baby too. My father asked about the rain but went back to the Ranch before I'd answered. Mother said she had heard there were fairies down near the brook and wondered if it was true. I said yes, because once I'd almost seen one of them. Holly and Rob put in some kind of pointless queries, but at least they were something in the box. Melbie asked when Keiki's new tooth would come in. I told Nagata he should ask one, and he said: "I try think." Misao brought one in for him later. It read: "How fast can the new Pierce-Arrow go?" I wrote back: "Thirty miles an hour." I didn't ask Mori for a question. I wasn't exactly scared of him, but didn't think he'd ask one.

Kirey wrote hers in her small, neat hand, and my reply was, *Very soon now*! She laughed and said yes, she thought it could be managed now. She told the rest of the family and we were all excited for her, and looking at maps, and at a book she had called *In Search of England*. There weren't many pictures in it, though. My school geography was better.

When the day was set, you could feel a stir of anticipation at Brookside. I ran across to the cottage several times a day, and asked again and again, "Your ship—is it almost here?" Then the ship had a name: the *Aorangi*. "A Maori name," Kirey said. She would go to New Zealand on it, and from there on to England.

My father said to her one day, "I know of a sugar stock that's bound to go up, and it's paying good dividends now. Don't you think it would be wise to consider it? You could still keep half of your Tan Janding."

But she only laughed and said, "We'll see—when I come back."

Her valise was out, and her steamer trunk—both had been sunned on the lawn and were ready to be packed. Kirey took me with her to the dressmaker's, where she was having a dark blue traveling dress and other things made, and downtown when she bought a hat and some gloves. "A lady is known by her shoes and her gloves," she told me. I wondered if I'd ever wear gloves. They looked nice on her slender hands. She wore white ones to church, but these were darker.

England! The thought of Kirey's trip was so enthralling to me that it wasn't until a short time beforehand that I began to realize how much I'd miss her. She was to be gone six months, and come back before the winter.

As we came home from school one Friday afternoon, we could hear our mother and father talking in the den. Their voices were quiet, but there was an undercurrent of tension that arrested me as I was about to follow the others upstairs to change out of school clothes. As I hesitated, I heard the words, in a despairing voice, my mother's: "Tan Janding. Why *now*?" I was struck to stone. Not understanding, from those words and their tones I knew that something was wrong. Dreadfully wrong.

When I could move again, I took my hand from the bannister rail, walked through the end of the long, dusky living room, crossed the back porch and went down the long flight of steps—and then began to run.

The valise and the trunk were gone. Kirey wasn't there. But Misao was, with Ka-chan. Kirey's traveling dress was over her arm, and others of the new things were folded on the pune'e.

"What are you doing?" I flung myself at her, and she laid down the dress and put her arms around me to hold me quiet. Her sober married-lady kimono was crisp and clean smelling against my face.

"There now. Kirey's all right."

"But what—?"

"I'm putting a few things away for her, so she won't have to bother."

I drew away from her and said, "Where?" But I knew. In the greenhouse.

She was there, in her green smock, with her watering can. She smiled at me, just as usual.

"What's the matter?" I blurted out. "Kirey, what's wrong?"

"It's all right, dear." She didn't look quite as usual. Her face seemed—thinner, somehow. "It's only that I'm not going to England just yet. Later, perhaps. When you're a big girl, we might even go together."

"But—but your ship. You said it was coming, and you would go, and the daffodils," I babbled.

"Look at this poor fellow." She snapped a stem from an anthurium plant. "He needs a drink badly . . . No, you see, I thought it could be managed now. But then something happened . . ."

"Tan Janding?" I whispered.

"Yes. The stock is away down at present, and there will be no dividends for a time. Perhaps not ever. So you see—"

"But your ship, and your trunk, and your new clothes," I pleaded. The ship was bound up somehow with Tan Janding, I knew that. But was there no other way she could go?

"I'll bet Daddy could do something about it, if he thought hard enough. I'll just bet he could!" I started for the door.

"No!" Kirey had never before spoken to me in that tone of voice.

I turned back. "I was only going to see Daddy, just ask him—"

"I've told your father and mother that there is nothing anyone can do," she said more quietly. "They understand that I must wait, and go another time if I can."

Another time if she could! When she had dreamed of this for thirty years . . . Somehow, I must make it right, make it that she'd know she would be going soon.

"I know," I said slowly. "We'll ask the question box when you can go." If it were down in black and white: Soon.

She spilled some water on me as she set the watering can down. "Let's go in and have some tea, shall we?"

While she was making the tea, I walked aimlessly round the room. I picked up her *Longfellow Birthday Book* from her desk and looked through it absently. Usually she had people write opposite the dates and quotations for their own birthdays, but some of the entries were in her curly writing. I turned to Kirey's birth date and read the quotation: *Brave as man is, soft as woman*. She hadn't written her name in the space opposite. Some day I'd do it for her.

When she came into the sitting room with the teapot, I had her pad and pencil from the telephone table on my lap and looked up at her questioningly. "Why don't we ask, 'Will Kirey go to England next year?'"

Her expression as she stood looking down at me gave me my first glimmer of understanding of a word that I didn't know: acceptance.

"Come, we'll have tea," she said gently. "Which cup would you like today?"

On my way back through our house after leaving her, I took down the question box.

13
Numerology

Otoru scuttled out of the Professor's cottage just as I reached Round-the-World's. Her face in contrast to her flower-spangled kimono made me stand up and gape, leaving my jacks and ball scattered all over the cement walk. Her eyes were wide with fright, and dark against skin that had an oddly pale look under its golden-brown coloring. I had never seen her look that way.

She motioned toward the cottage and I said, "What's the matter?"

She answered something about a pillow that didn't seem to make sense. The Professor's pillow? When Otoru came that morning to do her weekly cleaning for him, I had come with her across the brook.

The Professor lived now in the cottage where Mademoiselle had been. He was a jolly sort of man, with reddish-brown hair and a moustache, and long, skinny legs. Jolly, yes—but in a funny way. He made a lot of noise and laughed a good deal in a high voice (except when he was in the wilderness looking for birds), and he sounded jolly enough, but there was a difference that I couldn't quite pin down.

The Professor had lived in the cottage for some time, but we children didn't feel that we knew him any better than when he had come. He had been a teacher and was now retired, we knew that. That was why we called him "the Professor," a name that had caught on so that even Mother called him that now. He seemed foreign to us, unlike the Islanders we knew. German? Perhaps.

I said now to 'Toru: "What's wrong?"

There was something in there that I must see, yet looking at her, I didn't want to go in. She said in a low voice, as if she might be overheard, "Under the pillow. Come in and look."

The traffic sounds of Nuuanu Avenue were like a background to the thumping of my heart. Otoru was being brave; I'd have to go in with her. We went together through the tiny living room to the bedroom. On the bed, where she had pulled aside the pillow, lay a revolver and an unusual looking stone.

"He's a queer man," Otoru said. "Look."

She showed me a spear that leaned against the wall of the closet. It could be an old Hawaiian one, I thought, of wood, long and very sharp. I had seen ones like it at the Bishop Museum.

"I never thought much about this," she said. "People collect things, the way your grandpa does. But then they don't keep them in closets. And come see. There's something in the bathroom that's, well—that's strange."

She opened the door of the cabinet over the washstand. The shelves were crammed with empty bottles, small ones like aspirin or pill bottles, of all shapes and colors. Lavender, blue, red, besides clear glass. There was room only for his toothbrush and shaving things besides.

"One day I got them all out to throw away and he saw me and was furious. He told me never to touch them again and wouldn't even let me put them back myself. I think there's a special way he arranges them."

The bottles were strange, but not frightening. Unless—unless they were for poison? How could they be! "What are you going to do with the stone and gun?" I asked.

The stone puzzled me. It wasn't big, less than half a foot long, and there was a narrow place in the middle. I had seen one like it somewhere. The Bishop Museum, too? Yes! It was like a stone club. The narrow place, of course, was a hand-hold. What would he have it for? A man might want to have a gun at hand—but a club? My throat felt dry.

Otoru picked up the two from the bed and held them out in front of her. Her arms were bare above the elbow with her kimono sleeves pinned back while she worked, and I could see that she was trembling. After a moment's hesitation, she put them on the bureau.

"I'll help you change the sheets," I offered, and stayed with her while she swept and tidied the house.

The Professor came in when we were nearly finished. He had his Kodak in one hand and his hair was mussy, and I knew he had been skulking in the wilderness.

The day I had seen him there, Rob and I had been playing Robin Hood with some of the kids who lived near us. We were allowed now to play in the wilderness, where we couldn't go when we were younger. It was across the little 'auwai, the narrow stream in our yard that flowed into the brook. The perfect place for Robin Hood—a tangle of trees, bushes, and vines, with a lovely foresty smell. A wild smell, cool and green and sunless, and damp because of the brook's nearness.

After the others had gone that day, I stayed on to be Robin Hood myself—quite often we had to let Rob be him because of his name. While taking aim with my bow made of a branch and some string, and a stick for an arrow, I saw the Professor. He had the Kodak and was watching a mynah bird in a mango tree. I almost said hello but something in the way he looked stopped me. He didn't seem to want to be seen. He crouched there for a long time, then took a picture of the bird and went away, as quietly on his long legs as if he had been an Indian.

What did he want a picture of a mynah bird for, I wondered? They were everywhere, not just in the wilderness.

This morning the Professor had the sort of look he had had the day I saw him with the bird—as if he had been hiding, it flashed on me. He put on his jolly look when he saw 'Toru and me.

"Well, well! Otori has a little helper this morning." He always got her name wrong, and never remembered mine at all. He smiled widely at us and ran a hand through his hair, tousling it more. "You are learning to be a housekeeper, yes?" All at once, I knew what it was that kept him from being really jolly. His eyes didn't smile—only his mouth, under the big moustache. His eyes had a queer look today, a secret sort of look.

"We were just going," I said, sidling toward the door before he could see that we had found the things under his pillow. "Come along, 'Toru."

At lunch, Rob could talk of nothing but the Olympic title in swimming that had been won by Duke Kahanamoku. All of us were excited. One of our own Islanders, a world's champion!

"It's the second time he's won it, you know," my mother said. "It's not surprising, really. The Hawaiians are natural swimmers. Think of the centuries when they lived half of their lives in the sea."

"Half their *lives*?" I was incredulous.

"Fishing, swimming," she said vaguely.

"What did you think?" jeered Rob. "Either the first half or the last half of their lives?"

"And how would they know when they were halfway?" asked Holly.

"Now children, don't be silly." My mother spoke abstractedly, though. She was in one of her Don't-bother-me-now moods. "I must go along to the Professor's right after lunch. I don't want to keep him waiting."

The Professor! I remembered then that it was the day for

her lesson in numerology.

Mother always had some such interest. We all thought of her as "psychic," and actually she was. She could find water with a forked stick, a ouija board went mad when she touched it—and the really interesting thing was her automatic writing. She began by receiving messages from the dead, and then on a trip to New Zealand she wrote something in an ancient tongue, a combination of Persian and Hebrew or some such peculiar thing. It was translated by the British Museum as the log of a ship that had passed that way a long time before. Spooky, we thought! One year, it had been astral bodies. There was a woman who stayed with us on Maui, who told us that if we lay at night perfectly still and made our minds "receptive," we would feel our other selves floating up to the ceiling, or out the window and away. Once I did get up to the ceiling. Then there was the faith healer. And now, the Professor!

I stared at the castles on the wallpaper of the dining room. "Munna," I said.

She looked at me surprised at my using the babyish name, and it surprised me, too.

Rob was saying, "I wish my name was Duke. That's a good name. Duke. Duke."

"Well, why don't you change it?" asked Holly.

"*Change* it? Change my name?"

"Why not? People do."

I couldn't help laughing, thinking of Rob with his blond head and a Hawaiian name.

"What's so funny?"

I told him, and he looked dejected.

"It isn't a Hawaiian name," said Holly witheringly. "He was named after his father, who was called for the Duke of something-or-other of England, who arrived in Honolulu the day Duke's father was born. Anyway, what dif would it make? I think Duke would be a good name for you."

"You *do*?"

"Now, children," Mother said. She smiled, bringing her attention to them. "Robby can't just change his name."

"Not really. But we could call him that. I like it. Duke."

Mother frowned a little. "The wrong name can have a bad effect on one. It can make a person vibrate out of tune."

"Huh?" said Rob.

She hesitated. "I'm learning all about this from the Professor. I'll explain it to you when there's more time." She was in a hurry. Oh Mother, I thought. How can *I* explain to *you*? She folded her napkin carefully and put it into its silver ring, and placed it beside her plate. "Are we all through?" she asked briskly. "I really must go. If you like, Rob, I can ask the Professor about 'Duke' for you."

I followed her out of the house and, as she was going down the broad lanai steps, asked, "Mother, why do you go to the Professor's?"

She paused on the landing and said, looking back, "I find these lessons most interesting. I'm doing numberscopes for all of you children, you know, with his help. You wouldn't understand yet, but some day you must learn all about it." She had some papers in her hand.

"Mother . . ."

But she was hurrying on, across the driveway, down the steps of slabs of granite that had been carried as ballast in my great-grandfather's sailing ship, to the long slope and the brook.

I went with her, and on the bridge said, "I wish you wouldn't go today. Why don't you wait till Daddy comes from Maui next time, and let him decide whether you should?"

She turned and asked, "What's worrying you, dear?" I thought how like a splash of sunlight she was in her yellow dress, standing over the dark water in the shadow of the trees. I wanted her to stay there and listen. How could I convince her?

"The Professor goes to the wilderness," I said quickly. "All by himself and looking—well, funny. He takes pictures of birds but he really seems to be wanting to hide there. The pictures would never come out, anyway, it's so dark." Why had I not thought of this before? It was almost as if he took the

Kodak along as an excuse to go into the wilderness. She was turning away, she had barely heard. "Mother! You've *got* to listen." She half turned back, and I blurted out, "He keeps a stone club under his pillow!" Even as I said it, I wondered if he could have found the stone in the wilderness. It might not really be an ancient club, but one that could be used in the same way.

Mother laughed in a grown-up way and said, "People spread stories about the poor Professor but you mustn't believe them. He's a very intelligent and well-educated man. There he is now!" She waved as he came to meet her.

Oh Mother! I had known she wouldn't take it seriously, about the club. All I could do was to follow and be there if anything happened.

He called to me, "Hello, little girl!" and smiled cheerfully. "You have a young housekeeper in the family, did you know this?" he said to my mother.

Why had I never realized about his eyes before? Watching as he held the door for my mother, it occurred to me that something under his air of affability had always bothered me. Mother's being so enthusiastic about her numerology lessons had kept me from quite seeing that I had never really liked or trusted him. It seemed funny, too, that he got people's names wrong, like Otoru's, or couldn't remember them, like mine. His work was with names, wasn't it?

When Mother and he were in the house, I went by a roundabout way to sit on the grass under the windows.

Mother was saying, "I'm having a fascinating time working out this numberscope for Keiki," and the Professor's high-pitched voice replied, "I knew you would. Such a vital little personality. What potential that child has!" I could hear them quite clearly.

"Let me see what you have done," he continued, and papers rustled as they looked over my little sister's chart. "Very good, very good. 'Vibrates chiefly in the Trinity of the One, although she also touches the Trinities of the Many and of the All.'"

"Now this is something I've been wanting to ask you," Mother said. "Since her inner self is three and her outer self is seven, it seems to me in comparing them that her inner self will, as she grows older, develop its latent resources."

What on earth were they talking about? It seemed to me that a baby of scarcely two was a bit young for them to be discussing her in such odd-sounding terms.

I could hear him get up and walk toward the bedroom door, saying, "Yes, I think you are right. You are a good student. Now, I have something in here that I'd like to show you."

The bedroom . . . the gun and the club! I ran around to the door and burst into the room.

Mother was sitting at the Professor's desk and he was coming out of the bedroom, holding in his hand a book with NUMEROLOGY printed on it in big letters. They both turned to me, and I thought he was annoyed at my presence, though he smiled as usual.

"Mother," I implored.

"Come here, dear." She held out an arm and I ran to her, welcoming her nearness. Surely nothing could happen—to her with me there, or to me with her there?

"This funny child has heard something about you that's quite ridiculous," she said, laughing toward the Professor.

I wanted to cry, Mother, it's *true*, but couldn't speak or take my eyes from him. There was a curious expression on his face—that secret look, intensified—and he said softly, "It was about bottles, yes?"

"Bottles!" repeated my mother, startled.

Now, I thought. Now she's going to find out. There was a tightness about him; had she noticed it? I stood as close to her as I could.

"Lovely bottles, such a charming collection. Little bottles, so nice, so pretty." The thought of poison returned to my mind, and I shivered. "They must be in a certain order," he went on, "or something dreadful may happen—that's what nobody understands. I have to watch very carefully."

"And the stone club?" Mother asked.

I said, "Let's go," tugging at her.

"Ah, the club." Mother rose now and he came very close. "The club is for the intruders, the ones who come at night. They're very hard to kill. I've killed only two," he said.

Mother stood very still beside me and gripped my hand. "Thank you for this lesson, Professor," she said. "It's been helpful, but I think we must be going."

At home, she talked with Otoru and sent a wireless to my father at the Ranch. Then she went across the street to Grandpa's house and was there a long time.

Before Daddy could reach Honolulu by boat, the cottage was empty. Grandpa did some telephoning, and later Holly, Rob, and I watched from across the brook while some men came and took the Professor away with them. Poor Professor— I was sorry for him now. He looked toward the wilderness, as if wishing he could be in it. I almost wished he could be, myself, seeing the men taking him down the walk.

"He's gone to the hospital," Mother told us. "From there he'll go to a place where he can be well taken care of."

"You mean the Insane Asylum?"

"Well—yes."

I knew all about the Insane Asylum. Grandpa had a friend there. Sometimes he took me along when he called on him, as Diane had told me he took her. I had to wait with Taka, the chauffeur, outside the high walls, while Grandpa went in. He took them all cookies and magazines and things.

We were full of what had happened to the Professor at dinner time. I was telling them a story of Diane's about the day Grandpa came out of the Insane Asylum chuckling because a man had held out his hand and said, "I'm George Washington," and Grandpa, shaking hands, replied, "I'm so glad to meet you—I'm Abraham Lincoln," when Rob interrupted.

"Mother!" he exclaimed. "I'll bet you forgot to ask the Professor about the the name 'Duke'!"

14 The Horse Party

Jack was getting his morning brushing and currycombing outside the stable when our cousins, the four Knapps, came walking up the road from their house.

"It must be about school time," I said to Jack. "We'll have to finish you up in a hurry."

Cathy came over to us, while the three boys went on through our front gate and toward the schoolhouse, on the hill above the Ranch House.

Her eyes sparkled, and she said, "Guess what! Today is Mary Paku's birthday and I'm going to have a party for her this afternoon. Can Jack come?"

"Jackie, a party!" I sniffed his neck and put my hand up under his left-sided mane to stroke him.

"What other horses shall we invite?" asked Cathy. "Lorry wants to bring Daisy White."

"Let's have Merry Legs and Butterfly. All they do is graze in the gulch all day. I'll bet they'd love a party."

"Too bad Jenny died."

"Yes, and just the day after we gave her to Jamie! I don't

think they should ever shoot horses, only because they're old."

"Me either!" said Cathy. "Poor Jamie."

"And poor Jenny."

I had written a *Pony Note Book* about all of these horses, and Bessie, Wiwi, 'Ilima, and Holly's ex-polo pony, Lady Gray. On the first page was the warning: "Return too Bob Lamberton, esq."

Jack's brushing finished with his tail, and I put him into his pen before we started off for the schoolhouse. Looking back, it seemed to me that Jack wasn't very interested in the party, or in anything else. But when the time came, he'd realize what fun it was going to be!

Most of my time outside of school was spent with Jack. Mostly I rode him bareback, often with a punuku, a rope around the nose instead of a bridle. In the yard and gulch pasture, sometimes without even a rope.

Jack and I could go farther afield than Wiwi and I had been allowed to do. We went through the cattle and horse pastures above the house, and at times up the Olinda road. It was a good road to ride on, because of its being dirt, not macadam. In some places the eucalyptus trees lining it grew so thickly that sunlight only dappled the roadway, or it was entirely in shadow.

When he was grazing, Jack let me climb up his neck to his back, and sometimes I rode him sitting backwards. It was safe to climb up his tail, too, or to crawl under him. He was an easy horse to learn to get on bareback. The technique was to clutch the side of the knee with the toes of your left foot, hold onto him at the withers, and propel yourself to his back.

Duke had told me that you had to fall off a horse three times before you were a good rider, and I made it easy by sitting sideways, bareback, and galloping downhill. I practiced riding Jack standing up and thought how exciting it must have been to be a Roman Rider.

Kirey had given me a wonderful book called *Riding and Driving for Women*. Most of the riding part was about the

sidesaddle, with brief mention of riding astride. There were
chapters on jumping and hunting, correct dress, and of course
on tack. Kirey had told me something of sidesaddle riding; she
had been a fine horsewoman when she was younger, before her
back began to trouble her. I had a picture of her looking very
smart in a derby hat, mounted on a powerful looking hunter.

From the dictionary sketch, I had learned earlier the
"Points of the Horse," and reviewed them in this fascinating
book; and devoured the less familiar sections on driving a trap,
and four-in-hand and tandem driving. Some of my aunts had
driven their own traps, Aunt Ella among them. But now ladies
went about at the wheels of their autos, even Mother, who had
been inspired by the fun Brownsey was having with her
roadster.

As Cathy and I went up the hill through the goat pasture,
we discussed the party.

"How old is Mary Paku?" I asked.

"Twenty-two, I think. Or maybe twenty-three."

"Merry Legs will be the oldest guest, then. She ought to
have a place of honor—she's thirty."

"But it's Mary Paku's birthday," Cathy objected.

"Well, yes. But she can be next to Mary Paku, can't she?"

Nani was standing near the path, and her kid Kolohe
frisked to and away from us. I stopped long enough to stroke
Nani's pale soft coat and to tell her about the party. "But you
can't come, because it isn't a goat party." Kolohe stood on a
grassy mound beyond, ready to dance off and wanting us to
chase him. His name suited him, I thought—Hawaiian for
"Mischief."

"Can't play now!" I called to him. "We'd be late for
school."

As we came into the room, Duke looked up from his desk
and said, "A horse party! Gosh, what kid stuff," and Lorry,
who must have told him about it, looked abashed. He was two
years younger.

Cathy too looked crestfallen, and I said to Duke, "You don't have to bring 'Ilima if you don't want to! Has Mary Paku even invited him?"

Melbie said, "Everyone at his desk, please, children," and we pulled out our chairs as quietly as we could and sat down. There were nine of us: two girls who lived farther along the mountain, four Knapps, and Holly, Duke, and me.

The schoolhouse was cozy, with a raftered ceiling and a fireplace for cold mornings. At the back, looking up the slopes of Haleakala, was a sunny, enclosed lanai with an enormous blackboard on the inner wall. There was a bathroom on whose wall hung a toothbrush for each of us, with the owner's name pasted above, to be used after the "morning snack." Each of us had his own towel, too, and a goodly supply of soap must have been gone through each year.

Melbie had trained under Madame Montessori, and during the few school years that we didn't spend in Honolulu, she ran our little school on Maui with firm discipline and in a way that kept us interested. At our youngest, we learned to lace, button, and tie on frames; and became familiar with numbers, simple arithmetic, letters, and sounds through the use of large printed cards. We fit square pegs into square holes, and round into round. It was fun. This year we had our own unofficial Scout troop—using the Girl Scout Handbook, to the chagrin of the four boys.

In the afternoon, we made horse leis from whatever flowers and vines we could find around the yard, and assembled the guests for the party. This was to take place at the bottom of the gulch. Cathy rode her old mare down, but I led Jack because he didn't look as if he wanted to be ridden. All the way, we told them about the party. "It will be fun, Jackie!" But he didn't look enthusiastic.

Lorry came along behind on Daisy White, and Bubbles (who did have a real name now) rode Merry Legs. He had to kick her sides as hard as he could with bare heels. The smallest boy, whose hair was as white as Duke's had been once, led Butterfly down one of the gulchside paths—with a good deal of difficulty. What reluctant guests they were being!

"Don't be so silly, Butterfly," Cathy said. "You're going to a party. You and Merry Legs just don't know what you'd be missing."

I frowned over my shoulder at Jack, wondering why he was moving so slowly today. Could he be catching the mood of the elderly mares? I leaned back and whispered into his ear, "What's the matter, Jackie?" He plodded along, head hanging low.

Masa had given us some of his lovely-smelling feed from the saddle room bin, and each of us provided one or two carrots and some sugar lumps. "They've got to have dessert," Cathy said. "After all!"

Lorry produced a pineapple from a paper bag, saying, "Daisy White loves this. Maybe the others will, too."

We arranged the horses in a semi-circle, and it was a splendid party in spite of the unwillingness to come on the part of the guests. For all but one, that is. Once there, the others proved to be hungry, as befitted a birthday. Mary Paku was quite greedy and tried to get Merry Legs' share as well as her own—not knowing that Merry Legs' age should be revered. The neck leis and the flowers stuck into their forelocks lent a festive air.

Jack wouldn't eat at all, no matter how I coaxed. Not even a sugar lump, held on my palm against his soft lips. He looked tired, and his eyes were dull and lifeless. Before the party was over, I led him back through the pasture and yard to the stable and Masa.

Masa sucked in his breath and said, "Yeah, sick I think. This morning, Jack no look too good. Better stay sick-horse pen tonight."

We put him in the stall back of the stable, where the sick-horse pen was, and I stayed with him until bath time. Masa brought a bucket of water and put it in a corner but even when

I held it up for him, he showed no interest.

Masa said: "Better he no eat. Horse no can throw ou'."

"They can't? Why not?"

"Neck too rong, that's why."

It was news to me. *Poor* Jack, if he felt sick but wasn't able to throw up. I sat on the sawdust near him so he would know I was there, and got up now and then to stroke his neck, back, or his face, forehead to nose. He didn't have his usual afternoon brushing, only his mane. I ran the brush through it gently, outside and underneath, hoping it might make him more comfortable.

Doctor Fitz came and gave him some medicine.

"Is he very sick?" I asked.

"Pretty sick, poor old fellow."

In the morning, he seemed the same. Doctor Fitz came again and gave him another dose of medicine.

I worried all through school, and again spent the afternoon with him. He just stood there, head drooping. Once he lay down with quite a commotion, as if he were stiff or hurt somewhere. I ran for Masa, knowing that it was a bad sign for a sick horse to lie down. Together we managed to get Jack to heave himself up again.

Late in the afternoon, knowing it was time for me to leave him, I put one arm around his neck and the other hand up under his mane, lifting it to cool him. It was getting dark; I was late already. "Good night," I whispered, and started across the outer pen toward the road. But something made me turn back as I was climbing the gate, and I ran and kissed the diamond on his forehead.

My mother looked up from her knitting as the screen door from the lanai closed behind me.

"How is Jack?" she asked.

She wanted to know but I just shook my head, unable to speak.

In the attic, I lay on my bed, lacking the energy to take my bath right away. My bed was back of the chimney now, near the bookshelves of the bannister. My eyes were on the cover of *Robin Hood*, with a picture of Robin and his merry men on a forest path, dressed in Lincoln green, bows and quivers of arrows at their shoulders, hunting horns and knives at their belts. I was reading the book for the seventh or eighth time, but gazed at it without really seeing it.

The next morning, my father called me to him and put his arm around me. It was not a surprise when he told me that Jack had died. Not a surprise—only a hollow feeling inside, a great aching emptiness.

I never asked what had been done with him. You couldn't bury a horse, he was simply too big. Ranch life had taught me that when a horse or a head of cattle died in a pasture, the body was burned right there. But if at the stable—what then? My comfort was that he hadn't been shot, like Jenny.

As I went up the hill toward the schoolhouse that morning, a skylark swooped over my head and up, up toward the sky, singing its song of life. There goes Jack, I thought, to Horse Heaven. I stopped on the path, looking upward and listening to the song even after the bird had vanished into the blueness.

15
Silversword

As I practiced roping Frisky on the lawn early one morning, my father came round the end of the stone wall that bordered it. He was coming in from the Ranch office for breakfast.

He watched me for a minute, then said, "You need a bigger loop. See?" He took the lasso in his well-shaped brown hands and uncoiled it a little, shaking out the loop. "And your throwing hand, holding the two lines together, should be farther from the ring. Try again. A girl can rope just as well as a boy."

Frisky wasn't much of a target, a Boston bull terrier not being the right size for roping, and I was throwing the loop right over her as she scampered around on the grass, not even attempting to catch her by the neck. It was more fun than roping a post, though. We weren't allowed to rope calves in the pastures, or the Dairy cows, or even the old mares in the gulch behind the house.

Daddy took off his light gray felt hat and ran a hand over his forehead, which was white compared to the rest of his lean tanned face. "Why don't you go for a ride?" he asked.

143

After Jack died, he had suggested my trying several of the other horses. One of them in particular, a bay named Kula Boy who was a pacer, was fun to ride. But everywhere I rode reminded me of Jack.

"You know," Daddy said, "when you've fallen off a horse, you must get right on and ride again. It's something the same when you've lost a favorite. You should ride another. It won't be Jack, and you'll never forget him—but you'll feel better about life in general, if you make yourself do it."

I looked up at him, the rope in my hands.

"Would you like me to go out to the stable with you?"

"No," I said. "No, you don't have to. I'll go and see if Kula Boy is there."

Daddy was right. I realized now that I had known this was what I should do.

Kula Boy was in one of the pens, and I got a neck rope from the saddle room and led him to its doorway. If it had been Jack, I'd have ridden him across the road with the rope around his nose as a punuku. Kula Boy was tall to get on bareback.

Masa looked up from the bridle he was working on and said, "You like ride?"

He smiled, and I said, "Yes."

"Jack saddle too small, I think."

"I'll ride him bareback." I could use Mother's tree stump mounting block to get on him, at first.

"Better saddle. Kura Boy need martingale." He went down the length of one of the hanging racks and swung off my mother's saddle. Mother's saddle! "You mama, she no mind. This one fit Kura Boy good. You mama like this kind pekipeki horse."

Mother's initials were on the cantle, "K.S.L.", probably tooled by Masa himself, and the design around them. It was a newer looking saddle than the one I was used to, when I rode with a saddle, and it was highly polished. A ladies' saddle, not like any I'd ridden before. It was heavier than Jack's but I managed to get it onto Kula Boy's back.

Kula Boy seemed very high. That, and using a saddle, and the bridle's being a different one made it unlike riding Jack. I walked him round the curve of the pens, between blacksmith shop and cowboy stable, and headed into the straight stretch of dirt road toward the two gates leading into pastures. He needed only to be touched lightly with my heels to break into his pekipeki, the pacing gait. He held his head as high as the martingale, held in place by the saddle girth, permitted.

Cool, early morning breeze blew gently against my face and lifted my hair. The pacing motion was novel, and fun. I leaned over and stroked Kula Boy's neck.

From behind came a flurry of hoofs on the hard-packed dirt, and a voice saying, "Giddap, you!"

I drew rein and waited for Lorry to catch up with me.

"Darn you, Daisy White," he said. "What makes you so lazy?"

There wasn't anything to say in reply. She *was* lazy, which was at least partly why Lorry didn't get the best out of her. He'd let her stop and take a mouthful of grass at the roadside, then flail his legs, stirrups flapping, as he kicked her sides. He switched her with the ends of his reins and grumbled at her, while she walked or trotted slowly along as she pleased, streamers of grass drooping from either side of her mouth.

"Where you going, Saburi?"

Lorry had his own name for me, and I had mine for him. "I don't know. Shall we go up past the Green Tanks, or do you want to go over into Poepoe? You say, Lorranto. I don't mind where we go."

"Let's go by the Green Tanks," he decided. "That way's not quite so steep for Daisy White."

He took the wire loop off its post and opened the big gate, and Daisy White turned against it so that they looked particularly awkward. As Lorry struggled with her and with the gate, I saw my uncle—Lorry's father—riding down the hill just above us, from the slaughterhouse.

He watched his son with an expression that was partly

amusement, but even more annoyance. He would have to come along right now!

"Good God, Lorry!" he called. "Can't you even open a gate without getting your horse all tangled up?"

Lorry's face got red, and I said, "Daisy White's pretty stubborn."

My uncle grunted. "She shouldn't be *that* pa'akiki. Why can't you manage your horse better?"

"Because she's a darned old lazy mare!" Lorry burst out, and turned away. I could see that he was close to tears.

"I'll shut the gate," I said, wanting my uncle to go on through.

We went silently up the wagon track that led toward the gate at the tanks. I did think Lorry should have a younger and better trained horse to ride.

After the second gate, we stopped for a blow. Early sun rays were slanting down the mountainside, lighting ridges and grassy hilltops, and glinting from the tops of eucalyptus stands. Gulches and hillsides away from the sun were still deeply shadowed, and so too were slopes below the groves. The trees stood dark and quiet, as though they held a secret. On a ridge beyond, groups of Herefords grazed or stood basking in the first warmth, their hides shining red.

In the wood just above us, a shaft of sunlight streaked an occasional tree trunk and lighted patches of grass. The scents of warm horseflesh and of tall pasture grass mingled with that of saddle leather and of eucalyptus.

We went on up through the trees, and as we came out onto the clear hillside, we saw the colt. He stood on the brow of the hill, alert at our coming; head up and ears pointed, long slender legs poised for flight. With the early sun on his coat, he was the silver of mist with light shining through.

"Silversword," Lorry whispered. That rare, most regal of plants, that grew on slopes of the volcanic cones in the crater of this mountain, Haleakala. Silversword, touched to radiance by the sun. We stood our horses and watched him. I had never seen so beautiful an animal, and knew it was so with Lorry.

At last he said, wonderingly, "If I had a horse like that, I could ride, Saburi."

I glanced at him quickly and said, "But he's only a colt, Lorranto. He's too young to ride."

"He will be a horse," Lorry said.

On the ride downhill, Lorry asked, "What does the Ranch do with all its colts? Do they grow up to be cattle horses for the cowboys?"

"The ones we saw just now are the Thoroughbred colts." There had been others, but we had hardly noticed any but the gray.

"You mean they'll be polo ponies, or something?"

"Some of them. Or race horses. Sometimes my father will keep one as a riding horse, for himself or my mother. Or— they're sold, some of them, too."

He didn't speak again, and when we reached the stable he tied Daisy White to the rail in the shed, and walked across to the Ranch office. I followed, wondering what he was up to.

He went through the door into my father's office, and I sat on the steps and listened.

After a minute my father's voice said, "Oh, hello, Lorry," as if he had looked up from his desk and seen the boy there.

"Uncle Dan. Uncle Dan—you know the colts up there. The ones in the second pasture above the Green Tanks?"

"The Thoroughbred colts, you mean."

"Yes. If I had some money, could I buy one of them?"

There was a silence. I could imagine Daddy looking over his rolltop desk at Lorry.

"I want—I've got to have a decent horse to ride, and if I could have one like *that*, and train him . . ."

"Thoroughbreds are very different from any of the horses you've been used to, Lorry," Daddy said gently. "And these colts won't be old enough to be ridden for a couple of years."

"I don't care! I'd wait all my life!"

My father paused again, as if he wanted to try to explain without hurting Lorry's feelings. "These colts grow into very high-spirited horses."

"I know! You ought to see them! Especially—the gray."

Another short silence. "We use them for polo, you know, and some for the races at the Fair."

"And sometimes you sell them!" cried Lorry excitedly. "Saburi said so."

"For polo ponies mostly, when we have more than we need."

"How much—how much do they cost?"

"Different prices. Several hundred dollars, at least."

I could sense the stunned quiet that surrounded Lorry. But he had to know, and my father was telling him as kindly as he could that those colts were not for him.

Then Lorry surprised me. "Could I have a job on the Ranch this summer? Not being a cowboy, I wouldn't be good enough for that. But—any kind of job."

Daddy didn't answer for about a minute. "Masa might use another boy in the stable, besides Tony," he said at last. "You'd be working with horses only part of the time. Polishing saddles and bridles, filling the feed bin . . . sweeping out manure."

"Could I have the job?" Lorry asked in a hushed voice.

My father pushed back his chair, and he and Lorry appeared in the doorway. "Yes. It would be good experience for you. And some day . . ." he smiled down into the round, earnest, smudged face. "Your day will come, Lorry. It's a good thing—holding onto a dream."

Riding again every day, and spending the rest of my time at the stable, I knew how much I had missed it. And in some strange way, it brought Jack back closer to me. The first time I ran my hand over his saddle, and took his bridle from its peg, it was almost as though Jack were there.

The upside-down initialed rosettes looked up at me. I'll put them away, I thought, so no one can ever use them on any other horse. Then a picture of my father, on the lawn as I roped Frisky, crossed my mind.

"You'll feel better about life in general, if you make yourself do it," he was saying. And they were my initials . . .

I went round the end of the racks of saddles to where Masa sat in a corner, working what would be the browband of a bridle. With Jack's in my hands, and touching the coolness of a rosette's silver, I said, "Do you think—could you put these on Kula Boy's bridle?"

"Sure, can," he said. "Look nice, I think."

"And—upside-down. I mean, same like this."

"Yeah, yeah. Then you can read, when you stay on top horse."

Lorry came in with the big stable broom, after sweeping out the shed at the end of the building, where the hitching rail and wooden mangers were. His overalls, face and arms, and heavy boots were filthy, and he looked completely happy. Most of his job consisted of helping Masa in the stable—learning to work with leather, treating saddle sores with "horse iodine," sometimes "saddling up for the Boss," and every day sweeping out the tack room and shed—and he loved every minute. Now and then he and Tony were sent out to round up horses, or take feed or salt to the pastures, and then he was in seventh Heaven.

"What are you doing this aft, Saburi?" he asked. "Pau hana time."

"Ride, like always." That was funny. Lorry never rode with me now in the afternoons. I hadn't thought about it before. Quite often I saw him on Daisy White, or saddling her after work, but we would go our separate ways. I liked best to ride alone, especially now when Jack was so miraculously being restored to me—and it was a much better ride, too, without Lorry forever trying to catch Daisy White up to Kula Boy.

"Want to come?" I asked.

He looked mysterious—or as mysterious as such a round face could—and said, "You come with me."

Masa put him to work then, filling up the feed bin near the

door with grain from gunny sacks.

Tony came in, teeth flashing white against olive skin, and said, "You working hard, Lorry?" He winked at me. Tony was a good looking Portuguese boy, a few years older than Lorry or I. He was rubbing a skinned knuckle with some of the strong mixture from the "horse iodine" bottle, which made me shudder.

Masa said, "You come this side, Tony. I like you wash saddle blanket now."

Sounds of the stable and its surroundings came through the wide doorway and the narrow one opposite: a horse moving slowly in the pen for sick horses, or drinking at the trough; the clang of iron from the blacksmith shop; a wagon being unloaded of its bags of feed at the warehouse next door. From farther off came the intermittent lowing of dairy cows and the sharper bleats of calves. Here in the tack room, the varied scents of leather, wool, and a pervading horsey smell were exciting. It was a good place to work.

At three o'clock, pau hana time, I was saddling Kula Boy, and in a few minutes Lorry brought Daisy White from the pen where she had been while he was at work.

"Where shall we go?" I asked as we turned into the straight stretch of road. The rosettes were on my bridle, and it gave my heart a lift to see them. Your rosettes, Jackie, I said to him silently. I'm using them still, see? My initials were upside-down as Masa had promised, so I could read them while mounted.

Lorry's mind was too much on something else to notice my bridle. "To the colts' pasture," he said.

When we had gone up through the final pasture gate and closed it, Lorry got off and tied Daisy White to a fence post. Some of the colts were on the hillside above. Lorry took a few steps toward them and waited, his hand in his pocket.

Silversword made the first move, trotting toward him at first, slowing warily as he neared Lorry. A half dozen other colts came behind, but stopped short of Silversword. Lorry took a sugar lump from his pocket and held it on the flat of his hand, and Silversword came with graceful neck outstretched to brush Lorry's palm with his velvety lips as he took the sugar. The boy stroked the slender face from forehead to nostrils, while the colt stood regarding him with gentle, inquiring eyes. Then Lorry curved an arm under his neck and they stood there together, quiet.

I dismounted and the movement frightened all of the other colts, and they turned and trotted uphill to a safe distance.

"Silversword was the shyest of them all," Lorry said, his eyes shining. "At first I just sat on Daisy White and let her graze, to get them used to our being here. Then one day I got off, and they all ran up over the hill."

I could picture Silversword, standing watchful, hesitant, slim legs ready; then with a leap and a toss of his elegant head, frisking away and galloping across the pasture with mane and tail flying, as if in sheer love of stretching his limber muscles, of the sun-warmed breeze he created, of leaping hillocks of grass. How beautiful that colt was! Fluid grace in every line, lithe power in each motion.

"Finally one of the others, that little bay filly with the blazed forehead, came and took some sugar from me. Then some of the others did—and last of all, Silversword. By now he's the tamest one."

"Have you been doing this right along?"

Lorry nodded. "Every day. Since the time you and I first saw him."

He took his arm from Silversword's neck, but the colt stood there still, and began to nuzzle at Lorry's pocket.

"I know now that you're not supposed to give them sugar lumps," he said. "It might start them nipping. I've been reading about training colts. But Silversword doesn't nip. And he was so shy of me, with so much life in him, it seemed the only way to get him to come. Now I can put a rope around his neck."

He took the coiled tie-rope that was strapped to his saddle, and gently, gently circled Silversword's neck with it.

I looked curiously at Lorry. He had changed; there was a confidence in him that had been lacking. He spoke softly to the colt, which showed no fear of him. I was careful not to move again.

We stood there together, looking up over the mountainside, hill rising into hill to the curve of summit line. The sun on our backs was a benediction, we heard wind in the trees like a faraway sea. I glanced at Lorry. He was touching Silversword again, stroking the warm neck, and his face was transfixed. Lorry was "holding onto his dream."

Riding downhill, he said, "I'm saving every cent I make on the job. My mother pays me for work around the house and yard, too."

I didn't answer. What was there to say? Never in the world could Lorry save up as much as he would need.

The next morning my father came out to the stable and said, "A man named Mr. Harris is coming to look at the colts today. He needs one to be coming along for polo, and we have an oversupply this year. Tony and Lorry, I'd like you to drive them down to the pen, so he can pick one."

Lorry stood with a rope dangling from his hand, stupefied. "You mean the—you mean the *Thoroughbred colts*?" he stammered.

My father said yes.

"But I thought—I thought they were going to be broken first, before—before you—"

"Mr. Harris prefers breaking his own, so we're letting him have one now."

Lorry, in a daze, gaped after his uncle as he walked back toward the Ranch office.

"C'mon, shake a leg," Tony said. "You heard the Boss."

I rode up with them, to help. Colts were hard to drive, one after another leaving the group and having to be coaxed back. I couldn't have kept from going, anyway, I felt so keenly for Lorry.

Never had day been more glorious. A light breeze caressed our cheeks, and bent a little the tall grass of the pastures. On a slope beyond, a patch of redtop, burnished by the sun, shimmered so slightly that it might have been only the sun's radiation. Stands of trees above their deep slanting shadows were dark against the pale summer grass, gulches cut clearly defined rifts in the mountain's side. It seemed to me sometimes that the mountain lay under the sun's warmth quiescent but living, as if the volcanic crater at its heart merely slept.

Far above, a skylark sang, its trilling a mockery in our ears.

In the large pen across the road from the stable, my father and Mr. Harris walked among the colts, marking their gaits, studying their conformation. The colts trotted about, bewildered and unresigned to this confinement. Reddish dust clouded up under slim hoofs.

They had not been easy to corral, and Silversword had been especially wayward. Now he shied from the men's advance, with a whinny of distrust. Perhaps Mr. Harris would think him too wild! Oh, how I hoped so! Lorry and I were perched on the top board of the fence, watching.

Mr. Harris pointed toward Silversword. "I like that one best," he said. "The gray."

There was something coarse in the man's profile, turned toward us, something that made the idea of his owning Silversword particularly abhorrent. I pictured the grown colt on the polo field, jerked by a heavy hand, spurred by exhaustion.

"But I can't get near him," Mr. Harris said. "He has life, that colt!"

My father was summoned to the Ranch office for a telephone call, and Mr. Harris said to Tony, "Get a rope on the gray, will you?"

They had him cornered, they were converging on him, a long neck-rope looped in Tony's hands. But he broke away! By God, he went right through them! Now he was in the far corner, separated from the other colts. He leapt toward freedom, and before Lorry and I realized what Tony was going to do, he had thrown the rope like a lasso.

Lorry shouted a protest but it was too late. The rope encircled Silversword's neck. How he plunged, kicked, bucked, reared! whinnying now in fear. This was something quite different from having a rope placed lovingly about his neck by Lorry. With a desperate lunge he tore the rope from Tony's grasp and galloped off, shaking his head, twisting in frantic efforts to free himself. The rope flapped against his side, frightening him further.

Lorry flung himself from the fence. Mr. Harris was rubbing his arm. Had the colt kicked him, then? Good! We heard the man saying, "I'll let that one go. He has too *much* life!"

He didn't want Silversword. But Lorry couldn't wait, he couldn't let Tony be the one to catch him roughly and terrify him anew in setting him free. Lorry must have known that Mr. Harris could change his mind when he saw the colt gentled, must have seen that by his own action he could lose Silversword. But he went toward him.

My father, returning, called, "Get back, Lorry!" as the colt plunged by. Lorry didn't seem to be aware of his voice. Wildly Silversword ran from one fence to another, scattering the other colts, who milled about confusedly.

Lorry stood in the center of the pen, waiting until Silversword should pause. When my father went to order him away, he shouted, "Watch out, you fool!" He started toward the colt, slowly. When Silversword saw him, he stopped, and held out his hand as he was used to doing in the pasture. The other colts were now at the far side of the corral.

Silversword stood trembling, eyes rolling in fear and defiance, legs balanced to strike out and away. Watching Lorry, he uttered a low whinny like a prolonged snort. The boy advanced a cautious step, halted. The colt stood eyeing him. Lorry went forward. Two or three lengths from the colt he stopped again, the sugar held out on his palm. Slowly, slowly, Silversword came, long slender neck arching toward him. At this pace, the rope no longer slapped his side.

The soft muzzle touched Lorry's palm as he took the lump of sugar. Lorry stroked his neck, with one hand slipped the knot loose, releasing him. The colt's nose went to Lorry's pocket, nuzzled his side.

Mr. Harris was saying, "Well, what do you know?" His voice had a smiling sound. "That kid really has a way with horses. It's a rare thing to see an animal so easily subdued. I'll take him, Dan. First choice."

Lorry's forehead was against Silversword's neck. He knew it was a risk, I thought. But he had to set him free. My heart ached for him. Lorranto! And you did it yourself.

From a distant place, my father's voice came. "He's not subdued, Mel." Something in his tone made Lorry look around. My father was staring at the boy in an unbelieving way, as if he had never seen him before. Lorry stared back, mesmerized.

Daddy was speaking again. What was he saying? "You've already turned this one down, Mel." His voice was crisp. "He wouldn't suit you, anyway."

Mr. Harris said: "I've changed my mind, Dan. I *do* want him."

My father said nothing for a minute. Then, quietly, "I've changed mine too, Mel. The gray is not for sale."

Lorry's arm tightened about Silversword's neck. He couldn't speak, and when he turned his head away, I knew it was because there were tears in his eyes.

At last he said, in a muffled voice, "I'm sorry I called you a fool, Uncle Dan."

My father stood looking at the boy and the colt, smiling a little. Then he said, "You didn't know what you were saying, Lorry. And it turned out that I *was* being rather foolish, didn't I?"

16
The Valentine

Almost every boy at Lanai School had a case on Meg, from Chuck (I feared) down to the third-graders. You couldn't blame them. She was the prettiest girl in school, and there was a quality of elusiveness about her that was somehow very attractive; even another girl could see how intriguing it must be to a boy.

That was the year that there were five of us in fifth grade. Our desks and Mr. Kiehl's were on the lanai at the far end of the building, around the corner from the rest, a position that set us apart from the school as a whole. Besides, we were the "big kids" that year, and morale was high among us.

Duke was at Punahou now, where there were three sections of fifth grade, each with twenty or so pupils! At home, I was aware of the terrifying aspect of such an enormous school, but at Lanai it was unimportant. The time when I would have to go there seemed far away.

On Valentine's Day, after Assembly and morning prayers, then flag-raising on the lawn and the Pledge of Allegiance, we wasted no time in getting to our desks. Everyone had come early that day and had made hurried, hopefully surreptitious rounds of the classrooms before Assembly.

Meg opened one of her envelopes, looked hard at the red heart, and blushed. Her skin was very fair and her hair a pale blond. She had a remote sort of look and one might never have known she ever felt any self-consciousness, had it not been for that occasional betraying blush.

"Who's it from, Meggie?" whispered Kit.

Meg fumbled putting the heart back into its envelope—we could see that there was something written on it, a verse—and just shook her head and went on to the next. She had more valentines than anybody.

Mr. Kiehl looked over his glasses at us and, after the usual moments of silent scrutiny, asked, "Can anyone here tell me who Saint Valentine was?"

We all looked up, interested. Then four of us turned toward Edgar who, after some hesitation, said in his shy voice, "He lived in the third century, a Christian martyr."

"I never even thought about it!" said Kit. There were three of us girls in the class, and Edgar and Chuck.

Edgar cleared his throat, and after a moment went on, "But giving valentines really has nothing to do with him. It was thought that birds—er—began to mate on that day. Long ago, names were put in a box, and each young man took out the name of a—er—maiden, and she was his valentine for the next year."

"Quite right," said Mr. Kiehl.

"How do you know all that, Edgar?" demanded Kit.

"I looked it up."

"A good example for the rest of you," Mr. Kiehl said severely. He stood up the three valentines that he had found on his desk, so that they faced us. One of them had very delicate white frills surrounding a red heart—handmade by Meg, we all knew, but so carefully done that it might have been bought in a store, like Kit's and mine.

"Now," he said, "we'll proceed from the fascinating and pretty custom of giving valentines to—fractions."

Kit and I groaned, and Chuck scowled at his arithmetic book.

Chuck was my hero. He was a good-looking Portuguese boy, and captain of the soccer team. Not the best student among us, perhaps, but certainly the most popular boy at school.

I couldn't be sure about his attachment for Meg, and not at all sure about her regard for him. But it was a suspicion that at times made me feel actually sick.

Chuck was, to me, as romantic as—well, as Ramon Novarro. Both of them had that dark glamour that made you feel tingly inside. Once, in a confidential mood, I had told Meg how I felt about Chuck; this was, of course, before I had begun to be afraid that that was how he thought of *her!*

Besides being handsome and charming, Chuck was so much fun. He always had a joke to tell, or a trick to play, and the rest of the class responded to his flashing dark eyes and his, "Let's put a lizard in old Kiehlie's desk drawer."

It was always Chuck who caught the lizards or the giant, many-legged spiders who waited high on the wall for a passing fly or occasional mosquito. Or who turned his book upside down until Mr. Kiehl noticed it, or stood on the railing when we were alone and gave very bad imitations of Miss Maxfield, the principal, or Mr. Kiehl. It didn't matter to us that he wasn't much of a student. And at recess time, Chuck came into his own.

The really important thing at Lanai was soccer. Sides were chosen up each day, and Chuck quite often chose Meg third or fourth. She wasn't a very good player so he could hardly pick her first, and when he said her name it was in an offhand kind of way. As for Meg, she never looked as if she cared whether she were chosen or not. She usually didn't even glance at Chuck but strolled slowly toward his group.

We played on the school lawn, which had one huge Chinese banyan tree on it. No playing field, nothing organized about our games except for Mr. Kiehl on the sidelines with his whistle. As the only man teacher, the job of referee fell naturally to him.

If unorganized, our games were certainly enthusiastic. On Valentine's Day, to my surprise, when I kicked the ball it went high, far, and in the right direction.

"Good kick, Bobora!" cried Chuck. I felt greatly set up, and for the time being forgot my conviction that Chuck had sent Meg the valentine that had made her blush.

But that kick, it seemed, was to be my only claim to fame in soccer. Kit was very good and was on the first team. This had to be composed mostly of fourth graders because of the smallness of our class, and the unathleticness of Meg, Edgar, and me. We had one game a year with another school, Hanahauoli, which we called "Hanapupule"—pupule meaning "crazy." There was a school song for such occasions and one school yell. "The Green and Gold are brave and bold," we would chant.

Our recess games ended with Miss Maxfield ringing a bell that she held in her hand and calling, "All right, children! Come along in, now." Miss Maxfield was a rather frightening person to us, I think because she had a large front and a deep, resonant voice. We admired and really were fond of her, and she was a friend of my mother's and came to our house. But even there I was in awe of her.

When we got back to class that day, Kit and I hovered near Meg's desk. Kit didn't have my romantic interest in Chuck but I could see that she was curious about the valentine, too. We three were "best friends," yet there was some intangible thing about Meg, a sort of unseen veil—no, not even a veil, perhaps an aura described it better. I thought back to the days when I had imagined (seen? I still didn't really know) auras in different colors about people's heads, and tried to think what Meg's would be like. Pearl gray? Fragile rose, like a blush? No-color? Meg always looked as if she were thinking of something else, something she'd never tell you. Yet she was not absentminded in the way both Kit and I were. "Her mind on higher things . . . " occurred to me. Were they higher? I simply didn't know. Anyway, there was something that kept Kit and me from being quite as free and easy with her as we were with each other.

Kit had asked her once already about the heart with writing on it, and she didn't want to again. Instead she reached back to her own desk and picked up her six or seven valentines and riffled through them.

"I'll bet this one's from you, Meggie-meg." She held out a white heart with little red ones pasted on it, surrounding a Cupid with his bow, and with the rim of a larger red heart just showing round the white. Meg was so clever with her slim fingers, we were sure she had made all of hers.

She said, "They're not very good, but it's fun to do them."

Chuck and Edgar were coming back round the corner. Feeling rather high-flown after Chuck's comment on my accidental good kick, I whisked into Mr. Kiehl's chair and put on the glasses he had left on his desk, and looked over them and tapped a pencil on the blotter just as he returned.

Mr. Kiehl said, "Do you know what your name means? It means 'barbarian' and that's what you are. As part of your homework, will you all please look that word up . . . or does anyone happen to know it already?" He peered over the glasses he had retrieved from me.

After a pause, Edgar said hesitantly, "An uncivilized kind of person, in ancient times. Cruel and—er—brutal."

"Exactly," said Mr. Kiehl.

Nagata was late in picking us up that afternoon, an unheard-of thing. He was always five minutes ahead of time. I went out to the street and sat on the grass sidewalk, watching for him. Meg was still in the school building.

She went to and from school with us because she lived nearby, a little farther up the Valley than we. She and I were left first, on the way to Punahou where Holly and Duke were taken, and we were picked up first because Lanai let out earlier in the afternoon.

After a while the big Pierce-Arrow turned the corner and Nagata stopped it at the school entrance. He got out, smiling, and said cheerfully, "Frat tiah!"

Nagata smiled often and his solid, neat appearance in uniform and cap was reassuring. He took such pride in our cars that they glistened, and any dust or mud was immediately wiped off. He was careful to put up the canvas side pieces with their little windows of isinglass as soon as it started raining, and the insides of the cars were always spotless.

The metal spare tire holder on the fender was empty. "Too bad!" I said, getting up. "You change 'um?" This was merely the politeness of conversation-making. Naturally, he had changed the tire himself, and as naturally looked trim as ever afterward.

"Yeah. Runariro Street. Big nail!"

"I'll go get Meg."

Instead of going up the steps and down the length of the lanai, I ran across the grass and reached our end of the building to see Chuck leaning toward Meg, his hands on her desk as she tidied its drawer. His face was very serious, quite unlike Chuck as we knew him; hers was nearly hidden by the fall of her shining blond hair.

I stopped in mid-run, with my mouth open, ready to call out to her.

Meg looked up into his face with an expression I had never seen on hers. Not remote; not at all. Chuck was about to speak when she became aware of me. The color rose in her lovely smooth skin, but she smiled at me as she got up quickly and said, "Coming!"

Chuck turned with a gesture of annoyance, which he tried to cover up with a vivid smile in my direction. "Be seeing you tomorrow," he said to us both with a sort of salute. "Worse luck!"

He sauntered along the lanai after Meg, and I joined them at Miss Maxfield's office to say goodby to her. Every day she stood at the entrance on the street as the pupils left, but as we were late this afternoon she had returned to her desk.

Meg and I got into the back seat. Duke always rode in front with Nagata, in the separate seat with a space through which one could pass between the two, and Holly sat in back with Meg and me.

I felt sunk in despair, because now I knew.

"Nagata had a flat tire on Lunalilo Street." I wanted to say something, it didn't matter what.

The car turned the corner into Wilder Avenue. It wasn't far at all to Punahou, thank goodness. Duke and Holly would be there, chattering I hoped. At least they'd be there.

I had known already, really. Of course I had known. But . .
Until now I had been able to pretend to myself that it might not be so.

Beside me, Meg made a sudden swift movement. She was searching through her book bag.

"Look." She took out the envelope in which the mysterious valentine had been on her desk that morning, and drew out the red heart.

Holding it out toward me, she read:

> "Roses may be red,
> Violets may be blue—
> The only thing that matters is
> That I love you."

I could scarcely see it. Shameful tears were starting.

"I knew right away that it was from Edgar," Meg said quickly. "I know his printing, and—he's the only one who would write anything so sentimental. Even though he'd never in the world say it," she added, laughing rather shakily. "It was kind of embarrassing, having him right there when I got it."

That was what had made her blush, then.

She was busy putting the envelope back into her bag, and looked out of the other side of the car as I brushed hurriedly at the corners of my eyes with a finger.

Oh, Meg! I thought. You *are* nice. She had given me the one scrap of comfort that she could.

17
Dread Disease

We children were never allowed to catch the measles, mumps, or chicken pox. So when our friend Randy was discovered one day while playing with us to have spots, he was hustled home up Nuuanu Valley so fast that he might have thought himself on the fringe of a hurricane.

It was measles, and someone at Lanai School came down with them, and several at Punahou. We were whisked out of school and every day Melbie examined each of us carefully with her glasses on. But such was the discipline at our house that never a spot dared show up on the backs or opu's of Holly, Duke, or me. Keiki was two years old and for a while she was kept strictly separate from us. I missed her a lot. And Ka-chan too, and the baby boy at their house.

Misao had to keep Ka-chan near home. Sometimes we'd see her running after him in the yard, holding up the skirt of her kimono, and taking him home. We would call, "Hello, Ka-chan!" and wave to them. Misao waved the little boy's hand back at us, because he was too shy to do it himself. One day, two bright paper fish fluttered in the breeze on a pole in front of their house. "That's because it's Boy Day," Otoru said.

We kept up with our lessons, with Melbie. At times it seemed as though she didn't agree with the way things were put in our books, but she taught us as it would have been done at school.

She took us on long walks while we were being kept out of school. My favorite walk was up a block on Nuuanu Avenue and then to the end of Judd Street, where it curved round into an uninhabited area, in which we could clamber over the hills.

Holly said one day, "Last night I dreamed that I went to Oz."

"What happened?" I asked eagerly.

We lingered behind Melbie, who disapproved of Oz. Once she had told Holly that she was getting too old for such nonsense. I couldn't understand it, knowing that she came from the country that had produced Hans Christian Andersen. I'd never be too old for Oz!

Duke marched on ahead, whistling. He whistled most of the time when he was out of doors, because of the rule: "No whistling in the house."

"The Cowardly Lion took me for a ride on his back. And I met Ozma, and Glinda too. They were so beautiful! Different, of course. Glinda was a little scary—austere, you know."

"I'm going to dream about it, too," I said.

"You can go to the Land of Ev," Holly decided. "I nibs Oz."

That would be just as good. Sky Island, too! Every day after that, we told each other long stories on our walks, of what we had dreamed—or might have dreamed. My mind was filled with the fascinations of imaginary places.

Some days we went into Nuuanu Cemetery and played among the marble headstones, and wondered what the people whose names were on them had been like. It was peaceful here, and there was a kind of friendliness in thinking of the people who had lived in Honolulu before us. The shower trees were coming into bloom, pink and golden, and the plumerias with their fragrant, pale-colored blossoms.

Another good walk was up the grassy sidewalk of Nuuanu Avenue as far as the Country Club Road, or on to where Nuuanu became the Pali Road, and back down the other side. We knew who lived in most of the houses, many of them our friends, or our parents', or Grandma's and Grandpa's. A special friend of Kirey's lived quite far up the Valley; I had been there to tea with her two or three times.

Many of the kids were in school, braving measles, but now and again we'd see someone who, like us, was being kept at home. Melbie would hurry us past these gateways. "Their incubation period may not be over," she would say.

Lots of the yards were big, with large trees—kukui, monkey-pods, poinciana regia with their brightness of flowers, coconut and date palms. One driveway, like ours, was lined with royal palms; this one had two entrances on the Avenue, and the drive swept round past the big white house. The boy who lived there was at Punahou with Duke. He had caught the measles, and Duke and I watched for him at an upstairs window but never saw him.

"They keep you in the dark when you have measles," Holly said. "Pitch dark, so you can't read or do anything."

"Not pitch dark," Melbie corrected. "But very dim. And certainly, no use of the eyes is permitted."

I remembered a birthday party that boy had had, when a screamingly funny man had got his foot caught, way up high over a branch of their banyan tree. He had kept whistling and beckoning to the foot, and finally, when we thought he was stuck there forever, hopping on one leg, he had got it back over.

We were allowed to go to Kirey's, of course—but never to Misao and Nagata's, because of Ka-chan and the baby. Kirey asked us over for Cambric tea, often. When she poured from the china teapot, sometimes she'd say, "The cup that cheers, but not inebriates."

Then there were drives with Grandma and Grandpa. He would come into the hall and whistle his special call—Grandpa was exempt from the rule about no whistling in the house! Often we went out to Waikiki and the turning-around place near the Diamond Head lighthouse. Taka sat squarely at the wheel, his shoulders broad for a Japanese, his pace with the car slow and steady, twenty miles an hour. The three of us children took turns sitting in front with him.

Or sometimes we drove up to the Pali, from where we could look out over the other side of the island and its shoreline, far below, like some distant unknown land. Our eyes followed the course of the narrow, winding road as it twisted its steep way down the face of the Pali. When you got out of the car, the wind nearly blew you over!

Grandpa told us how the Oahu warriors had leaped over the cliff to their deaths, rather than be conquered by Kamehameha's invading army from the island of Hawaii. And how Lili'uokalani, when a princess, had composed *Aloha'Oe* while riding up what was then a horse trail. One of the men in her party, a dashing young colonel on her brother Kalakaua's staff, had fallen in love with a beautiful girl when they had stopped to rest at Maunawili, before the ascent. The song was their farewell.

Grandpa took us to the Bishop Museum and Kamehameha School—we weren't allowed to go near the students, of course. At the Museum we saw the mammoth whale, and the exhibits of old Hawaiian life. We went to Lunalilo Home for old Hawaiians, and to Kalihi Hospital when Grandpa went there to see a friend of his. This was where the people with leprosy lived, if there was a chance of their being cured and not having to go to the Leper Settlement on Molokai. We had to stay in the car with Taka, while there.

Sometimes Grandpa read to us, often poems by Wordsworth. One day, as Grandma sat crocheting at her end of the koa lanai table, it was the one that begins, "She was a phantom of delight." Near the end he stopped to say, "I think this part was written for your grandmother. Listen:

> *" 'A perfect woman, nobly planned,*
> *To warm, to comfort, and command;*
> *And yet a spirit still, and bright*
> *With something of angelic light.' "*

Some days he would write verses to us, as one beginning:

> *"There are many boys and girls,*
> *And they are not all alike.*
> *Some have tow heads, some have curls,*
> *Some are gentle, some will fight."*

During this time, he taught us to play dominoes. He would take each of us in turn and explain exactly, in what Holly called "his legal way." We started playing with each other at home, but it was always more fun with Grandpa, and a better game.

"I'll teach you cribbage next," Grandpa said. "Or perhaps Miss Kire would be a better teacher." He and Kirey had a running cribbage match going—first one would be ahead, then the other. They tallied their games, which were already in the thousands.

"Four can play, can't they?" asked Holly.

"Yes! We'll have foursomes of cribbage, with Kirey."

Thus began our introduction to the two games beloved of Grandpa. Both were fun, and we became quite spirited over our contests. I especially loved dominoes—the black tiles with white dots fascinated me and I liked to pick one up and place it firmly on the table, no uneven edges.

One day cribbage had just ended with Kirey's, "Fifteen-two, fifteen-four, fifteen-six, and a run of three—and one for His Nibs!"

Duke said then, "Tell us about when the Queen was asking for your head, Grandpa."

"That was during the Revolution of 1893. Some of us felt

that for the sake of Hawaii's future, it must be under the protection of the United States. Others didn't agree. If the Islands went our course, it would mean no more monarchy— no queen."

"And she hated you!"

"Yes."

"And asked them to bring her your head."

"On a silver platter!" said Holly.

"The Hawaiians did not behead people," Grandpa said. "When someone had to be killed in ancient times, he was most likely hit over the head with a war club. Later, of course, there were rifles and other guns."

"So your head would have been cut off *afterward*?" Duke asked interestedly.

I shivered. But it was like a story, not like anything that really could have happened. Not to Grandpa.

Kirey said, "You children know, don't you, that Lili'uokalani and your grandfather became friends later."

"We saw her greatness after all of the trouble was over," Grandpa said. "When she was no longer on the throne, nor kept under guard. Her true greatness, I've always felt, was in her ability to forgive. She felt that she had been wronged, but she overcame her bitterness and came to understand our reasons, even though she may never have quite believed in them. And she was a fine enough person not to let past differences—very great differences—stand in the way of friendship for some of us who had opposed her."

"Did you and the Queen talk to each other in Hawaiian?" Holly asked. "When you used to go and call on her."

"Not always. She preferred English, sometimes, when we were together. She spoke in Hawaiian, of course, to her own people."

"Could she speak English well?"

"My goodness, yes! And write it, too. She was a fine linguist and spoke both Italian and French as well."

Kirey went home before we did that day, and we stood at

the lanai door watching her go along the walk toward Bates Street. Her back was straight, her figure trim and neat in its long crisp cotton dress.

Grandpa said, "It's been my privilege to know a number of fine women. And not the least of them is Miss Kire."

"Kirey and the Queen," Holly said thoughtfully.

"How unlike, outwardly, could two women be? Born and bred halfway around the globe from each other."

"You'd never call Kirey great."

"I could, and do," Grandpa said positively. "She is a strong woman. When Miss Kire has a problem, or trouble of any sort, she goes right up to it and looks it in the face. She's alone, you know. No husband, no family within ten thousand miles. Yet she doesn't falter."

"She has us," I said.

Grandpa put his hand on my shoulder. "Kirey has you, and all of us. And we have her, and are the richer for it."

"Kirey says people ought not to worry." Holly frowned. "I don't see how you can help it, though."

Grandpa smiled down into her anxious face. "Kirey's right, you know. There's a world of difference between worry and concerning oneself with a problem. Come, I'd like to copy down for you what someone wrote about worry."

We went with him to his big roll-top desk at the back of the lanai, and he sat down at it and opened one of the drawers to rummage around in it. "This is where I keep things of the kind that I want to remember. It was my friend Mr. Bishop who wrote it, an older man than I but always kind to me. Ah, here it is."

He took out a piece of paper and copied from it, dipping the long slender pen with its nib into the inkwell on his desk: "Worry is never in any way profitable. Many people go through life, much of the time carrying loads of 'borrowed trouble.' "

He gave what he had written to Holly. "You're the eldest. You can remind the others."

"I'll tack it up where we can't help seeing it," she said seriously.

Grandma came in with a plateful of oatmeal cookies, and Grandpa said, "Just what we're wanting! Come and sit down and I'll read to you from a letter I've written to that cousin of yours, Diane."

"How's Diane? Have you heard from her?"

"Have I! You'll never guess what that girl has done now. Bobbed her hair!"

"Oh, I'll bet it looks peachy!"

Uncle Henry was Delegate to Congress now, since Prince Kuhio had died, and he, Aunt Ella, and Diane were living in Washington.

"I'll read you my pearls of wisdom on *that* state of affairs." Grandpa sat in his big chair at the end of the long table, and took the letter from its envelope. "Here is my advice to the young flibberty-gibbet:

'I understand that you have bobbed your hair, which seems to be the first step towards becoming a dangerous flapper; and I give you warning that if you continue in your mad career, you may expect the wrath of your grandpa to descend upon you in large quantities.

'To think of you, my dear, loving, sweet granddaughter frisking around with bobbed hair and skirts built so as to show your attenuated limbs! Do turn from your evil ways while there is yet hope.

'I believe that there are persons who think that girls with bobbed hair ought to be exterminated.

'Your loving but anxious Grandpa'"

18
Bourn, Broc, Bruoh

While we were being kept home from school, not catching measles, I spent much time at the brook that ran across the bottom of our yard. One day, as I went down the slope toward it, there began going through my mind in a jingly sort of way:

> *"I come from haunts of coot and hern,*
> *I make a sudden sally,*
> *And sparkle out among the fern*
> *To bicker down a valley."*

The lines weren't right for our brook. We had read the poem in school, but I had never thought of it in connection with this brook.

Surely there were other things that sounded more like it? Back at the house, I went to the little den, in a corner off the dining and living rooms. Scanning the shelves that went up to the ceiling, I found two or three likely looking volumes.

Many of our books were on Maui now, where my mother had had shelves made for them in almost every room of the Ranch House. At Brookside, outside of our children's books and Melbie's Danish ones, most of them were here in the den and in our parents' bedroom at the head of the stairs. In their room, a platform across half the length of it, an alcove, had been made into a very cozy place. Deep chairs, lamps—and books.

My mother found me there, looking over the poetry shelf. "Want something special, darling?" she asked.

I hesitated, not wanting to tell anyone what I was looking for. "Is there any way—" I began, unsure quite how to ask. "When you want to look something up—not a dictionary . . ."

"Some books have indexes," Mother said. "If it's poetry, there are often lists of 'first lines,' too."

"But if you don't know the first line—and it might not be poetry, even."

I wasn't sounding very coherent but my mother came over to the shelves and, running her hand along a row of books, took out a thick one. I always noticed how she liked to touch books, hold them in her hands. Perhaps that was why all our bookshelves were open, nothing behind glass.

"This is a book of quotations," she said. "Sit here with it and look up the word you want, or the idea. See, this is how it works—an index in the back third or so, telling you where to look in the front part. Then if you want more on any subject, you can find the book that the quotation is from."

She switched on a lamp for me and left right away. I was grateful to her for realizing that I wanted to do my own searching and for not asking what it was that I was looking for.

When Melbie came to the door and said, "Bath time," I couldn't believe the whole afternoon had gone by. I had found several books to take to bed with me that night, and the next day some of them went along to the brook with me.

It seemed the right place to read about brooks, there on the bank with the sound of moving water in the air, and the wild smell of water plants and damp ferns all about me.

I found many names for "brook," some that I knew and others unfamiliar: burn, bourn, ghyll, rill, the Old English broc, the Dutch broek, the Old High German bruoh, the Spanish arroyo, the African wadi. The ones that began with "b" sounded more right.

One bit felt appropriate:

> "With spots of sunny openings, and with nooks
> To lie and read in, sloping into brooks."

I read: "The moon looks/On many brooks . . ." and thought, But none like ours! Some night I would come down here. The only times I'd seen the brook after dark had been in going across to the cottage now and then with my mother, depending on who was living there. And, of course, in looking down on it from a car going over Nuuanu Bridge.

I learned the lovely lines:

> "And this our life, exempt from public haunt,
> Finds tongues in trees, books in the running brooks,
> Sermons in stones and good in every thing
> I would not change it."

The Forest of Arden—or the wilderness? It could be either.

I saw the brook on days when its waters moved slowly between the banks, went hesitantly, yet with a constant murmurous song, curling round stones high now above the surface. There were times when sunlight pierced the leaves of the great monkey-pod trees to dapple the water, to lighten it so that here and there it mirrored branches from above, and occasionally a big stone appeared to have a double, under water. On some days the brook lay in shadow and glided by dark and mysterious, silent.

When rain fell in a first spattering of huge drops, each would start its own small current outward, until the water was speckled with tiny, widening pools. As the rain came faster, more heavily, the little pools vanished in the splash, splash of a hundred drops, a thousand drops, stirring, churning, casting upward a spray of brook-drops that mingled with the rain to become a mist just over the surface of the water. Water of the air, and of the earth, in communion.

There was a day when the brook was a tumbling flood from the mountains. I went up under the Avenue bridge, where its torrents thundered, filled my ears! The coldness of its passing was on my cheeks, and the wetness of a cascade as the brook, a mighty force now, struck the great stones and plunged on through the tunnel.

I knew where the brook came from; I had been to its marshy source, far up Nuuanu Valley. On a day like this, what was that like—when spring water merged with rainstorm? The storm clouds were there; I could see them, away up over the Pali.

"The lofty surge . . ." Where it came from, yes. But where did it go? To the sea? Some day I would follow it all the way . . .

One evening, I did go down to the brook. The moon was high, and bright enough that I could see the monkey-pod leaves folded for the night.

I sat on the plank bridge, legs hanging toward the water, and watched it coming toward me from the high tunnel. Flowing endlessly. It seemed to me that the brook had a life of its own, like no other life I knew. And at the same time, as if it belonged to the course of life itself.

For a moment—the space of a breath?—the brook let me into the stream of its being, its place in the universe and in time. I could see it as all these: one of "the brooks of Eden," the brook of which for an instant I was a part, and one that would be forever as it was this night.

19
Kaneohe
Weekend

I could hear the bell—three rings, pause, three rings—and then Kit's voice answering: "Kaneohe funf neun funf."

"H'lo. What're you and Sut doing?"

"Oh, I dunno. Waiting for you guys."

"I'm all packed. So's Duke."

"We never have to pack much—we leave a lot of stuff here at the beach house."

"Do you want to hear that record I was telling you about? You know, the one that goes, 'High, high, high up on a hill.' I'll play it for you now. Just a sec."

As I turned away from the telephone corner, my mother came out of her bedroom at the head of the stairs. "My goodness!" she said. "And you're going to see Kit in an hour or two?"

I was busy putting the small Victrola on the telephone table and cranking it up. "She wants to hear this song," I explained. "It's really super. You ought to listen."

"I can hear it!" said Mother, going down the stairs. "And I have a feeling I'll soon know it by heart."

When the last strains had creaked away, Kit said, "Did you

see them throw Bubblehead in the Lily Pond after school?"

"No, darn it! I had to go to Pa Robby's office for half an
hour."

"What'd you have to go for?"

"Oh, I'd been swallowing air in recess so it would come
up in Study Hall right after. Dopey old Madame Ketchup
reported me."

"Just your luck to have her that period! She never misses a
thing. You should have seen them giving Bubblehead the
Punahou Swing. One, two, three—and splash! He went right
under."

"What'd he get thrown in for?"

"He'd been trying to cut Lawrence out with that new girl,
Carmelita, the nut. Lawrence likes her, you know. As if B'head
would have a chance!"

Rice Hall, which housed Junior Academy, had a splendid
view of the Lily Pond; I regretted having swallowed air.

"Let's sing 'Wherever you go,'" suggested Kit.

We sang in our concept of harmony, then she said,
"Speaking of Carmelita, everybody thinks she's the biggest
vamp."

"Everybody!"

"Well, not only Lawrence."

"Carmelita thinks so, too."

"She thinks she's Dolores Costello. Well, anyway, she
sang this song, a Spanish one. It really sounded pretty good."

"Like what?"

"Like this." Kit rendered her version.

"I like 'Balencia' better."

"You mean 'Valencia.'"

"No, B. Isn't it? Say! Where's Yani? I can hear Yame right
downstairs."

"Wait—I'll go find him."

Otoru was married now and not at Brookside, and Yame
had taken her place in the house. She had very fair skin for a

Japanese, which made her hair in its huge bun a shining, jet black. Yame moved gracefully, and her dainty kimono was always just so, pulled out a little at the back of her neck to show the nape. She was very pretty, not any prettier than 'Toru, but different. We didn't feel quite so close to her, and couldn't behave quite so familiarly—the one exception being when we could trick her into talking on the telephone to Kit's family's chauffeur, Yani. It had started because their names sounded so much alike.

I ran downstairs calling, "Telephone, Yame!"

"For me?" She paused and turned slowly, one shapely forearm extended toward the painting on the wall that she had been straightening. She answered on the back porch extension, and when she returned to the hall, her face its usual cameo-like mask, I ran up three at a time to continue my chat with Kit.

When at last we were urged by our families to hang up, she said, "Auf Wiedersehen."

Duke and I were to spend the weekend with her, Jake, and Sut at their beach house. Nagata drove us over the Pali to meet them and Yani at the Kaneohe Ranch headquarters. We tried to get Yame to come along for the ride but she laughed and said no. She didn't giggle the way Otoru would have and we didn't dare tease her into it, as we would have with 'Toru.

At the Pali, I wanted to get out and let the wind blow me backwards, and look out over the sweep of windward Oahu, flat-looking below the steepness of the cliff in spite of hills and ridges and valleys. The sea curved round the shore, white band of beach edging a bay here, jutting out to the headland Mokapu above the beach house, making its slow in-and-out way along the coastline and out of sight.

When Nagata put the brake on, Duke said, "Let's keep going. You don't have to do kid stuff like getting blown backwards," and Nagata turned the Studebaker into the narrow roadway that plunged in sharp bends against the cliff wall.

The road went through a large stand of coconut trees at Kailua, their slim trunks and high fronds letting sunshine slant in so that the grove held a kind of living light that you felt you could touch. We met the others just beyond, at the Ranch office, stables, and branding pens. Yani was driving the station wagon, and we got in with him, Kit, Sut, Jake, and the Great Danes, Pulya and Patsy. Then across the flat land of Kaneohe Ranch, where black Aberdeen Angus grazed, and past horses in the pasture near the house.

Kit cried, "There's Kua, see?" and from Sut, "And Hana!"

Kit's horse was a sorrel with a Roman nose, Kuahiwi, meaning "Mountain." Sut's bay was called Hanalei; he had a curiously innocent expression. Each of them seemed to suit his owner in looks, perhaps because the sight of Kit with Kua and Sut with Hana was a taken-for-granted one.

Pulya and Patsy bounded out as Yani stopped the car near the house. We went in through the front door and were at once enveloped in the inviting, relaxed air of that place.

In a corner of the living room was an enormous hikie'e, covered in monk's cloth and with dozens of small colored cushions. Stretched out on it reading a magazine, back against the cushions, was Dee, a friend of Kit's mother. She looked up expectantly, and though she smiled cheerily and crinkled her eyes and said, "Hello, kids!", I had the feeling that she was watching for someone else.

" 'Lo, Dee," we said, and met Kit's mother coming from the bedroom end of the house. She made Duke and me feel welcomed by her faintly lopsided smile and by the amused, friendly light of her violet-blue eyes. She said, "How are you two? Run along in with your things," allowing us to feel at home there as always.

It occurred to me sometimes that she was beautiful, and this took me by surprise because we knew her so well as Kit's mother that we simply accepted her as she was. We accepted too that in childhood, as the single girl with many brothers, she had been such a tomboy that only one neighborhood girl had been allowed to play with her—yet now she was the most feminine of women. The girl who had been allowed to play with her became our mother.

Kit, Sut, and I went past the boys' bedroom to ours at the end and I dumped my suitcase down.

"Let's ride first," Kit said. "I've got to have a ride on Kua."

We rode bareback, with the wind from the sea blowing through our hair and bringing its saltiness to complete my illusion of being far-from-Honolulu. Then we swam. Sut, running ahead past the sand dunes on which grew naupaka-kai, called back, "Waves O.K. today," to reassure me. They knew I was scared of towering surf and hoped always it would be no more than rough water. It was always at least that at Mokapu. Jake and Duke had been playing pitch-pitch, throwing a baseball back and forth, and they joined us in the ocean. So did Pulya and Patsy. At least, they got their paws wet, venturing into the froth of waves on sand, then springing back to race along the beach, barking with excitement.

Dressed in pajamas and kimonos, we went to sit with the grown-ups before dinner.

"Wet hair?" asked Kit's mother, touching our heads with her hand. "A bit damp—I thought you looked rather slicked down! But it's so warm tonight, I suppose you'll do."

Conway was there, smiling at something Dee had said. He had just got up to wind the Gramophone and put on a record, and she asked, "What are you going to play?"

"'Let me call you Sweetheart,'" he answered, and Dee said, "Sure," with her crinkle-eyed look.

He went back to the hikie'e looking complacent, but after they'd been bantering for a while, she said teasingly, "I'm tired of talking with you. Leave me in peace," and turned to her magazine.

He loved this; it gave him an excuse to sit close to her, feigning interest in the fashions she was looking at.

" ' You just know she wears them,' " he said. "You do, of course?"

"Wouldn't you like to know!"

" 'Holeproof Hosiery.' H'mm." Conway examined Dee's elegant legs, stretched out before her.

Dee flipped a page, ignoring him.

Conway tried again. " 'A skin you love to touch,' " and after a few silent moments, "I hate those cloche hats, or whatever you call them."

"I adore them." Dee smiled to herself. "I've just got a new one."

Kit's father laughed softly, looking across at them, musingly. The dogs lay at his feet. He was dark, and good looking: a "man's man." He got us to play games that we loved, games like foot polo, and contests of strength or skill in which the "booby" was paddled with a flat board—one hard swat from each of the others. He wrote scenarios for us and had us act them out. He, as director, would shout instructions such as, when we were Indians crawling on the ground on our opu's: "Get your okole down, Bobora! What do you think you are, a shimmy dancer?" He filmed one of these plays, everywhere at once with his movie camera, and called it *Mike's Bar*.

He turned now to us and said, "I'll beat the dickens out of all of you at Hearts, after dinner."

"We'll see about that, Ancient One!" Kit said, with a light pat on his black head. She put *The Prisoner's Song* on the Gramophone. "I love this. It's on the Hit Parade . . . 'I'm tired of living alone. ' "

Before we had to turn out the lights, we got out the inevitable movie magazines. The three of us sat on one bed to look at them, and swooned equally over Ronald Colman and Vilma Banky. "Isn't she *gorgeous*," we said of Pola Negri. "A real vamp—not like Carmelita."

"I like Douglas Fairbanks," Kit said. "Wasn't he super in

'The Thief of Bagdad'!"

"But you like Ronald Colman better."

"Yes." We all did. "Especially in 'Beau Geste.'"

What could it be like to be one of these fabled beings? A movie star! Movie stars were beyond anything one could aspire to, and at the same time they were intimately known through movies and, especially, through their pictures in these magazines and the fascinating details of their lives, loves, longings—the things that made of them an enchanting but quite believable mixture of familiarity and awesomeness.

I had just got an autographed picture of Rudolph Valentino and had left it between the pages of Screen Play for Kit and Sut to find.

"'I'm the Sheik of Araby,' without a shirt," Kit sang. Sut and I joined in, through "'Into your tent I'll creep,' without a shirt," to the final "'. . . A-ra-by.' Without a shirt."

I told them I had decided to find a Ranch Boss and marry him.

Sut said, "That's what I want to do, marry a Ranch Boss."

"*I* don't want to get married!" Kit said scornfully.

Neither did we, we explained, not really. But if we ever had to, this would ensure living the kind of life we wanted.

We drifted then into a favorite pastime: telling each other romances featuring ourselves and the boys we knew who could ride and rope and do the things we admired. Not strictly romantic in content, say a tale of chasing after the wild cattle that roamed the far slopes of Haleakala, with the boys letting us go for a change. But romantic as being spun by three girls who avowed wanting nothing of men but the opportunity to live the ranch life.

When we had put out the lights, Kit said, "Do you know the story about the student nurses playing a joke on one of the others?"

Her voice sounded like a ghost story, so we stayed on her bed.

"The interns had been dissecting, and gave them a hand to

scare somebody with, so they put it under the covers of this new little student's bed. They all waited for her to scream, or something. But nothing happened for ages so they opened her door. She was sitting up in bed—her hair had turned white and she was eating the hand."

At that moment, a hand rose from the darkness under the bed and closed over my arm. My scalp prickled. This is what it's like to have your hair stand on end, I thought. I couldn't possibly have shrieked but made a sort of gurgling sound.

"What's the matter?" asked Kit.

Muffled sounds of mirth from the floor under us; Jake and Duke couldn't hold out any longer. I never did know whose unearthly hand it had been.

When Sut and I got into our own beds, she said, "Good night, good morning," and we responded in kind. This was Sut's time-honored entreaty that a new day might dawn. "Schlafen sie wohl," added Kit.

We woke to the everlasting current of the ocean, waves traveling toward shore, breaking to roll up onto the beach and be swept back under the next.

"Let's ride up Shady Hill today," Kit suggested.

After breakfast we caught and saddled the horses and, going toward the kitchen for a bag of sandwiches and hard-boiled eggs and a canteen of water, passed the two boys looking as if they didn't quite know what to do.

"Where're you going?"

"What's it to you?"

Jake shrugged. "Keep your shirt on, we're just asking."

"Well, we don't want any boys tagging along, if that's what you were thinking of."

"Don't flatter yourselves!"

We rode first across the flat sandy pasture toward Kaneohe Bay, in order to swim our horses from one side of an inlet to the other. Then to the wooded hill. A wide cart track wound up it, protected from the already hot sun. We could hear bird calls from the trees and see an occasional flight from branch to branch. Some of the black cattle had climbed the slope to graze in this cool place.

We sang as we rode along, with room for the three of us abreast.

" 'Oh, Rose Marie, I love you, I'm always dreaming of you.' "

There was no sound but the clop of our horses' hoofs, birdsong, gently fluttering leaves, and our own voices. Kit ambitiously swung into the *Indian Love Call*, but we decided that one was better on the Gramophone. " 'Tea for two, and two for tea . . .' "

"Where are you going to start looking for your Ranch Boss?"

"Why not right here?" I asked recklessly.

All of us knew how far-fetched this was. Kit and Sut's father was the Ranch Boss here! But in that quiet, enchanted place, a thousand miles from Punahou, anything might happen.

Kit looked over her shoulder and said, "I thought I heard horses on the trail behind us."

We reined in and listened.

"I must have been hearing things."

As we rode on, she and I sang our own harmonic arrangement of *Imi Au I'a 'Oe* for Sut's benefit.

Sut said, "I've heard better," but this comment failed to lower our spirits.

"Supposing that *was* a Ranch Boss I heard!" Kit said. "He's riding along behind us on a beautiful white stallion, like the ones in Vienna. When we get to the top of the hill and are about to have our sandwiches, he'll come charging out of the trees and pick you up with one arm, fling you across his saddle, and make off with you."

"Why can't I have lunch first? I'm getting hungry."

"You are romantic."

"Or we could give him a sandwich too, and then he could make off with me."

"No!" they both shouted, and Sut added, "He ought to come tearing out of the wood, the way Kit said. And you'll disappear into the trees and bushes on the other side of the path."

Like Tom Mix. No—he'd be even more dashing and exciting. Handsomer!

"And then what?"

"He'll make his way to the edge of Kaneohe Bay, a secret cove, where there will be a canoe waiting."

"And you'll sail away, round the point at the other side of the Bay."

"Never to be seen or heard of again!"

By this time we had reached the hilltop, so we dismounted and tied up, and unstrapped the bag of lunch and the canteen from Kit's saddle.

Kit dropped the bag and said, "Confisticate it!"

"It'll crack the eggshells, that's all."

"I was startled. I thought I heard something again."

We all kept still. There *was* the crackle of twigs snapping, and hoofbeats dulled by the grass that grew more plentifully here than on the flat below. Someone was keeping out of our sight. It couldn't be—it couldn't *possibly* be the Ranch Boss. My heart began to thud.

"Who's there?" called Kit.

"Maybe just cattle."

Oh, no! What a letdown. I was hardly even hungry by now.

"Come out of the trees!" cried Kit, and Sut shouted, "We can hear you."

With war whoops, three horsemen were upon us.

"Only them!"

But Jake, Duke, and our friend Allen from Kailua Beach were well enough satisfied by our looks of dismay as they galloped into view.

"You don't think you're going to get some of our lunch, I hope," Kit remarked.

"Course not," said Jake airily, getting off and tying up his mare. "We've got our own, and so has Allen."

Well, it could have been worse. Allen was, in fact, one of the better looking boys in Kit's, Duke's, and my class—blond with blue eyes, and skin deeply tanned because of the fishing that was his favorite pastime.

"I suppose you were telling some of your stories," said Jake shrewdly. "Well, we thought we'd give you the thrill of thinking it was going to be a true story."

All the boys laughed raucously at his wit, and we settled down to a lunch of cracked eggs and squashed sandwiches. The boys had brought lemon and cream soda water and root beer, two apiece, and with remarks suitable to their generosity, gave a bottle to each of us.

We rode home across the pastures with Allen, and galloped our horses on the hard sand at the edge of the sea. They splashed in and out of water as waves pounded the shore.

A half dozen or so families had beach houses at Kailua. We knew them all and stopped to chat here and there, then rode on to Mokapu for a swim before dinner.

Driving home in the station wagon late Sunday, Yani having come back to the beach to pick us up, we were quiet as the car followed the track over the ranchlands. Kit and Sut had called last farewells to Kua and Hana, and our minds must all have been looking back to the beach house and its adjacent pastures.

I had scarcely given a thought to the world of school and Honolulu, until Kit said as the car rounded curve after sharp curve of the road up the Pali, "At least we didn't have to go to the Cops and Robbers party!"

Actually, beforehand I'd had a passing regret at missing it, but now it seemed far removed from us. Cops and Robbers was the usual Saturday afternoon game, when we didn't go to the movies at the Hawaii or Princess, or to a football game or track meet. Boys and girls took turns at being cops or robbers, and when a robber was found by a cop, lurking under a bush or in a tree or greenhouse of the host's yard, he (or more often she) was kissed and thus caught.

Johnnie would have been there, I thought fleetingly, driving in on his new motor scooter. But I'd see Johnnie at school.

"*Kissing* games!" said Kit derisively. "I can't stand them."

"Me either," Sut and I said. But was I being just a shade untruthful? Cops and Robbers *was* a good fun game. Especially if Johnnie was playing it.

"I'll bet Carmelita was there!" someone said.

"With bells on."

"Well, anyway, she can't wear her Spanish shawl to a Cops and Robbers party."

"*I* think she's sappy."

"Cuckoo!"

But this was empty defiance. The weekend was over, the next day was Monday, and school pitilessly approached.

"Damn, damn, double damn, triple damn, Hell!"

I hoped Yame would be around somewhere when Yani deposited Duke and me at Brookside. But she wasn't. Was Yani looking for her? I couldn't be sure.

The two of us stood watching as the station wagon went on round the side of the house to go out through the Bates Street gate, and waited for it to reappear and pass the entrance on Nuuanu Avenue. Then we silently picked up our suitcases and went up the steps to the lanai.

20
Ranch Boss

"Melbie, I don't want to go to school any more. Why *should* I? All I want to do is marry a Ranch Boss and live all my life on a ranch." This had been not long after the weekend at Kaneohe, the school year before this last.

Melbie had considered me gravely for a few moments and then said, "I think you should finish elementary school, at least. Through eighth grade."

I groaned. "Two more years! I *hate* school."

"I'm afraid you'd be sorry later. There are so many things to be learned—and it's good to make friends at your time of life."

"I've got friends. Kit, Sut, all my cousins, and Miya and Jannie and Meg, and—oh, lots of people."

"Yes, that's true," Melbie agreed. "Those are all good friends."

"Well, then—"

"I think too that your Ranch Boss would appreciate your having had some more education."

I thought for a while. "But after eighth grade, then?"

187

"If you still want to do this. You'll be rather young to marry."

There was that. Still, school seemed then to stretch endlessly ahead of me. "I won't want to go any more, after that."

"All right. Eighth grade—and then your Ranch Boss."

I found him that very year, during seventh grade. Kit, Sut, and Jake each invited a friend to go on a riding trip to Pa Lehua, in the mountains of Oahu. There was a house there, which could be reached only on horseback, and Duke and I went along on the trip.

Count was the manager of the ranch from which we rode. He lent all of us horses, and he and his brother and sister-in-law were our hosts.

It was glorious. And Count was my Ranch Boss come true. He rode beautifully, he looked just right in his sombrero and cowboy clothes, he was so wonderful that my heart tripped and skipped. He wasn't handsome, but he had the kind of looks you couldn't help liking. And he was terribly funny. We nearly died laughing.

I didn't see him again until the summer after Duke and I had finished eighth grade. It was on Maui, at the Fourth of July, and there was a round robin series of polo games among the teams of Maui, Oahu, and Army.

It was the day of the Maui-Army game. Kit and I were "holding sticks" at the white rail, and beyond us Sut was on the bell platform; she had been entrusted to clang the big bell at the ends of the chukkers, and a large clock stood importantly on the platform rail in front of her. I had my father's mallets to mind, and Kit had my uncle's, as her father wasn't playing that day; his was the Oahu team. We had to be ready when one of them came galloping by, shouting, "Fifty-one!" or whatever length he wanted. He would drop the damaged stick on the grass at our feet and take the one held out to him, scarcely slowing for the exchange as he slipped his hand into the looped thong at the end. The three of us, Kit, Sut, and I, were wearing yellow as a matter of course. If Oahu had been playing, they two would have worn blue, and I also if the game had been against any team but Maui.

Cars lined both sides of the field, which was surrounded by acres of sugar cane. Holly with her brand-new license had parked as close as she could to the center "players' section," where we were. She and Vilmy were sitting on the fenders; and Count was on the grass, leaning against the front of their car. He was with two or three girls. This time my heart stopped completely. There he *was*.

I had to give credit to Melbie. She had not gone back on her bargain of "Finish eighth grade before you marry your Ranch Boss." The time had just, somehow, come and gone.

Count saw us down the line and waved frantically. The girls he was with must be from Honolulu, older than we—we didn't know them. Their laughter told us that he was keeping them entertained, and quite often he looked up to say something to Holly and Vilmy, too.

We could hear Holly saying to Vilmy, "I don't think Nat is so good looking."

"He's not good *looking*," Vilmy said condescendingly. "It's that he's so rugged, and masculine. He's got sex appeal. He must eat a lot of lettuce! The way he looks at you—doesn't it give you goose bumps?"

Holly didn't reply, and I wondered if Nat did look at her the way he looked at Vilmy. Holly had been seeming different to me lately, more grown-up—sophisticated, to use one of her own words. But next to Vilmy, she seemed younger again, not quite sure of herself. Holly was as pretty as any girl I knew, especially now with her hair up, but there was something slinky (again, Holly's word) about Vilmy that made her friends seem almost awkward. Vilmy with her smooth brown hair, creamy skin, and rather narrow face, reminded me of some sort of dog. A Russian wolfhound? She looked elegant. Her name was really Ruth but she wanted everyone to call her Vilma, because of Vilma Banky. We called her Vilmy instead.

We watched the Army player, Nat, riding onto the polo
field, saluting his wife Pat with his mallet before settling it
back against his shoulder. He looked well on his pony, which
counted more with Kit and me than good looks. You could see
how strong he was in the way he sat the black mare; he was
muscular, in his short-sleeved red Army shirt—his muscles
showed right through. All of the players looked spic-and-span
at the start of a game, in their starched white breeches, polished
boots, and white helmets. The Maui players were always more
splendid than any, I thought, in gold shirts numbered in black.
The ponies' coats shone, their tack gleamed with care whether
old or new, they stepped high in their "boots" protecting
forelegs, and arched their necks in eagerness for the game.

Pat stood at the rail at a little distance from us, in her
leghorn cartwheel; she was holding Nat's polo sticks for him,
naturally. "Nat and Pat" was almost one name, or so we had
thought, though Vilmy's remarks had disturbed this concept
somewhat. Pat was slim in her cotton dress, and very pretty in a
fragile sort of way. She and Nat were staying with us, in the
guest cottage.

A number of the players were now galloping slowly,
taking practice swings to warm up or "knocking balls" down
the length of the field. My father was among them, mounted on
Red Wine. It made me proud to see him out there. He rode
with the straight ease of the natural horseman, schooled to ride
in youth. To my mind, he was the finest rider I had ever seen,
and the best polo player, not only the top Number One of his
time in the Islands.

The referee blew his whistle, balls were hit off the field,
and the eight players gathered at the center: three of each team
facing each other, the Number Fours to the rear. The referee
held the ball behind him, threw it, and the game was on.

To me polo has always been the greatest game in the
world, especially the outdoor game as it was played then, four
men to a team, a field three hundred yards long, and a white
willow ball whose "crack!" to the thundering of hoofs is the

very sound of polo. Once in a while you were lucky enough to get your hands on a discarded ball—and how it was treasured!

When the play rushed past you along the foot-high sideboards that bounded the field, it was almost more than you could bear in excitement. And when a player had a clear field and took the ball the length of it, it was the kind of performance that made you conscious of breath held: controlled swift motion in both man and mount, swing, crack, spinning ball ahead, ponies racing in position behind, sweating, mouths lathering, thrusting forward, spurred but more crucial to the game, on balance, than their riders. "Performance" is not the right word in the sense that any participant was aware of an audience. Swearing, hurled with such volume that it reached our ears from any corner, was proof of that! Yet performance it was, the most stylish, the most thrilling, the most heart-breaking or heart-filling imaginable. When a goal was scored, horns blared in applause and in recognition not only of the scorer but of the teamwork that had made his goal possible.

In a lull that followed the horns, while ponies went to their positions at the field's center, Kit and I could hear Vilmy's low, drawling, half-laughing voice, though not what she said. My hands had been gripping the rails so hard, at either side of my carefully arranged polo sticks, that there were dents in the palms and fingers, and whitewash had come off on them. Dusting them against each other, I said in a quiet tone, "Vilmy does a sexy-sounding voice on purpose."

"Hmph!" said Kit. "I wonder who else thinks it's sexy— maybe only Vilmy."

"Nat?" I suggested tentatively.

"Not when he's playing polo, anyway!" We agreed on that.

Soon after, when the bell sounded just as Nat was getting a new mallet from Pat, he turned and rode slowly past us toward the stable. Kit called out, "I like your mare. But why do you call her Nightie?"

Nat cocked his head toward us, grinned, and said, "Because she pulls up so easy," and rode on.

"The *nerve*!" Kit whispered. But a small giggle escaped her, and in a moment we were both shaken by horrified mirth. People didn't *say* things like that. But when they did!

We were helplessly laughing when Sut called over, "What's the big joke, for Heaven's sake?" We could only sputter in reply.

During the intermission most of the spectators walked around, stopping to chat with those sitting in their cars, or just stretching their legs. In practice games, twice a week— Wednesday and Saturday afternoons—this was the time when Duke, Jake, and a few of my cousins rode onto the field and "knocked balls," getting the feel of it for when they too would play. But not on a tournament day. We could see the boys roaming along the rail, or stopping to sit on a car's hood or on the grass, not able to stay still for long.

Count came up to speak to us, with his wide smile, and it was wonderful to see that humorous, craggy face again. I could hardly think of a word to say, but it was so good to be near him after these two years, the first months of which had been filled with daydreams of him.

When he had wandered on, Kit, Sut, and I went through the stable archway, past the big saddle room, to the open space behind the long rows of stalls. Here there was an atmosphere of suspended action. Two or three players were examining their mounts for the next chukker, or giving orders to the grooms; others splashed water on their faces and arms, drying with towels which they hung around their necks; one player was lying flat on the saddle room floor.

We looked over brown Kona Coffee's stall door, and as we moved on to the next, the player called Major Patton paused beside us. Together we peered in at a handsome bay, Kama'ole. The major's rather stern face relaxed and he said, "A beauty, isn't he?" We chorused an agreement of yesses, and he smiled at us, his face lighting in a way we hadn't seen it do before. Major

Patton had the reputation of being the toughest, most hard-boiled of any Army player. All we had seen of him was hard, rough riding, and strong hitting, and all we had heard was rougher and stronger language from the field. Later, he was to be known in war as one who "fought to the last ditch." Now, his smile made him a man like other men, taking the time to admire a superb animal with us.

We went the length of both sets of stalls, divided at the center by the archway and saddle room. Of course we stopped longest by our fathers' ponies, and even as we did, a young hapa haole groom came for my father's mare Colleen, named by the Irishman in charge of the polo stables. Daddy and everyone else called her Co-leen. His favorite was Leihulu, or Feather Lei of Royalty, and I felt sure he was saving this one for the final chukker.

"Time!" said Sut, and we went back to our posts.

The game was hard-fought, with the edge appearing first to be in favor of one side, then the other. Major Patton rode harder, slammed into the pony he was "riding off," hit harder, and swore with such violence that we trembled. The tide could easily turn against Maui. Once he galloped over the sideboard just in front of Count and the Honolulu girls.

The girls squealed, and Count said, "What you do is make a noise like a saddle slicker. Most horses are afraid of saddle slickers." It made me think of how we used to go into stitches over the things he said.

A pony went down, and in a flash, while the rider was still recovering himself, Major Patton was off his own mount and at the animal's head. The pony lay, winded and hurt, near enough for us to see with what tenderness the major quieted the frightened mare, how gently he spoke to her, though we couldn't hear the words. Someone took his reins, and with infinite care he soothed the fallen mare and helped her to stand. She was badly lamed, but no more.

"And that's your tough Patton!" a man behind us said. "The rough and tough Patton is a legend."

But when play resumed he was riding, fighting, swearing as hard as ever. In the end, the game was resolved by a "sudden death" period, with Maui winning by a goal.

The Maui team gathered on the field and, raising their helmets with each cheer to their opponents, shouted: "Hip-hip-hooray! Hip-hip-hooray! Hip-hip-hooray!" and the Army responded by cheering Maui. This was always a thrilling end to tournament play.

After the game, there was an informal gathering at the Ranch House. Nat went to the cottage to shower, and Pat went with him, of course. My father and two or three other players showered and changed at the house, the rest wore towels around their necks and jackets over their red or gold shirts. Their breeches were no longer white.

Kit, Sut, and I went into Holly's room, downstairs at the front of the house, where Vilmy was staying with her. Vilmy sat now before the dressing table mirror, brushing her hair with slow, graceful strokes and putting it up again.

"Hello, little ones," she drawled to us, regarding us in the mirror with amusement. She made us feel like shuffling our feet and stuttering. She and Holly stopped talking, as if they had been saying something private, and Vilmy began to put on rouge with her little finger. "You put it on in a triangle. Slanting up your cheekbone first . . ."

We washed our hands and faces in the bathroom, ran combs through our hair, and went out to the lanai. A bar was set up there and we sidled over to it and asked Fuji for lemonade. There was spiked punch for the grown-ups.

Count was standing not far from us. He seemed to be watching the door that led from the living room to the lanai, and didn't notice us. There was a kind of tightness in him that was not typical, a sort of worried expectation.

Kit said to Sut and me, "Gee, what a game that was!"

"Wasn't it super! How did you like the sound-effects from Major Patton's direction? I knew all the time that Maui would win, because Army scored the first goal. Bad luck!"

"You weren't acting all that confident."

We saw the major standing across the lanai, looking tough and handsome, laughing and talking with Brownsey and an aunt of mine. Even while chatting thus in a friendly way, there was something rather forbidding about him, something that said, "Don't take any liberties with me." As if anyone would dare! Then I remembered the gentleness in his face, as he knelt on the field beside the injured pony.

Count was still facing the door, and a change in his manner made me turn in time to see Holly and Vilmy come through it. Good Lord, was he falling for Holly? My Ranch Boss—how ironic that would be. My own sister!

Count drifted up to talk to them, but before long Holly was there beside us.

"I thought you were with Count," I said, looking at her questioningly.

She gestured toward him and Vilmy and said, "Thought I'd give him a chance." Count was leaning toward Vilmy, and speaking more seriously than he usually did. "Vilmy has It. Count's got a pash for her, didn't you know?"

Vilmy! They simply weren't the types. Now, if it had been Holly . . . Vilmy was batting her long-lashed eyes at him. *Vilmy.*

Nat and Pat came in from the cottage, a striking couple, partly because they were so different. Fragility and masculinity. They stood together at the edge of the lanai.

Brownsey said in passing us, glancing back toward Nat, "God's Gift to Women." There was that little chuckle in her voice that took the sting out of whatever she said. "Talk about bedroom eyes!"

Holly called to Duke, who stood nearby re-playing the game with the other boys, "Get Nat and Pat some punch, why don't you, Duke?"

"You must mean lemonade," Duke said. "Nat and Pat are in training, remember? One more game for Army." He went off toward Fuji's bar and got glasses of lemonade for Nat and Pat.

Someone else was going toward them, not obviously, stopping to chat here and there along the way. Vilmy, of course. When she reached them, Nat gave her one of those goose bump looks.

Poor Count! He was standing alone, watching her. I went over toward him, beckoning Kit and Sut to follow. It didn't matter what we said. Just something to distract him, to give him something to think about, the smallest comfort. My Ranch Boss . . . there would perhaps be no other. Ranch Boss, goodby. Two years ago, it would have been unbearable. Now— it was a surprise, and a sentimental but not really hurting farewell.

"Remember Pa Lehua?" I asked.

"That was a good trip, wasn't it, kid? We had a lot of fun. You and Kit had just learned about double chins, and you kept saying, 'Hold it up,' to each other."

"You taught me something that first day, as we started out along the road. You were riding a big gray who was a fast walker, and you said he had been trained to it by being ridden on a hard road while he was being broken."

The boys came along, the four of them: Duke, Monty, Cho, and Jake. We surrounded Count. No one but me, I felt sure, knew that *he* needed *us*. We seemed to be a bunch of kids who needed him: his wit, his warmth, his trick of making us laugh.

"Nat wants to ride on the Ranch tomorrow," Duke said. "One of the others, too. Guess I'll be elected to take them."

"They sure look funny when you put them on a Mexican saddle," Monty said. "So darn sissy with their stirrups about a mile too short, and holding their reins in as if they were going to be run away with. And they either post, or bounce all over the place. Some of them even start off at a gallop. Maybe I'll go along, just for laughs."

"Those fellers are damn good riders," Count said. "You

guys don't always look so hot on a polo saddle. But you're learning!"

Yame passed a tray of kalua pig, on which was a wooden cellar of Hawaiian salt, pa'akai, and a pepper mill. We all took some, and as Count was grinding the mill, he said, "Which is this—red pepper, black pepper, white pepper, toilet pepper?" We giggled, and the boys guffawed.

"Wanna go with us tomorrow, Count?" Duke asked. "Maybe we can get *you* on an English saddle!"

Count moved so that his back was to where Vilmy and Nat stood, grinned, and said, "Sure." He turned then to Sut and asked, "Where did you ever get that name?"

She started to explain that it had come somehow out of "Sister," and he smiled his broad, contagious smile and said, "She was running along on a slippery road and she sut down. Was that how it happened?"

All right for you, Vilmy! I thought. You go ahead and flirt with Nat all you like. *We're* cheering up Count.

21
Wild Cattle Couldn't Drag Me

"Opala!" Duke shouted, branding iron in hand. "Whatcha doing?"

Monty, on his horse in the Olinda corral, looked across the fence and called, "Why aren'tcha in the pen? Go get your horse, Opala. We need you in here." He tilted his sombrero back and grinned at the young man who was loosening Oregon's saddle girth for Holly, while she tied the tall bay's neck rope to a fence post.

Opala waved toward the boys. "Be right with you!" Turning back to Holly, he said, "I like your papale."

She was wearing her very wide brimmed lau hala hat and I wasn't surprised that he liked it—or her wearing it. All of us wet our lau hala hats to shape them. Holly looked awfully nice, I thought. Her blue bandana was fastened by one of the kukui nut slides that Duke made for us, from the tree in the Ranch House yard.

"Thanks for your help, Opala," said Holly, who could quite well have attended to Oregon herself. "Now get in there and show those dumbclucks how to rope."

In the pen, he caught a calf by the neck, and Cho's lasso neatly looped its hind legs. The calf bawled in a half-strangled way as the two cow ponies braced to hold the ropes taut.

Kit and I, perched on neighboring fence posts, could feel the sun's warmth through our blue and white checked palaka shirts with their rolled-up sleeves. We liked these best when they were soft from many washings and faded by the sun.

That clear stillness of air that is peculiar to mountain slopes; the tall, quiet eucalyptus trees beyond the pens; the lowing of cows in the pasture and the clamor of calves being branded; dust stirred up to drift about the horses and riders; scents of burning wood for the irons and of scorched hides—all of these were so familiar that they took on a dreamlike quality. There was a sort of pattern to the way in which horses crossed the pen, ropers twirled their lassoes and threw, and spurred their mounts to tighten the lines for the branding process. When a group of calves was released into the pasture, cows trotted up to sniff them, each reclaiming her own. I was glad these calves weren't being weaned yet. Sometimes you could hear the mournful cries of their mothers night and day, after a drive.

All of the ropers' and foot workers' faces and clothes were showing signs of the dust. Jake was roping, several of the cowboys, and Sut and our friends the Hatch-Patches, Hattie and Patch. Duke and Lorry were on foot with others of the cowboys—throwing roped calves, and holding them down; taking irons heated on the fire and marking flanks with "a c," the Ranch brand; snipping a bit of ear as a further protection of ownership; castrating; dehorning; giving injections for blackleg.

I said to Kit, "I think Opala likes Holly."

"You do?"

"You saw when he loosened Oregon's girth."

"Just because of that, you think he likes her?"

"It was the way he looked at her."

Kit shrugged. "You mean you hope. *I* didn't notice

anything." After a minute she added, "Holly's only two years older than you."

"I know. But she's more grown-up, kind of."

"You just think that because she was at boarding school for a year. She's not old enough for him."

"I bet she thinks she is. Opala looks like the Arrow Collar man, don't you think? We can make up a story about them, some night when we're telling stories."

"That's a terrible name to call him," Kit said. *"Rubbish."*

I thought about this nickname bestowed by our brothers and my cousins. "It's really because the boys like him so much."

We watched the branding in silence for a while, then Kit said, "Louis has eyes like a smouldering volcano."

Louis, a good looking Portuguese, was herding a reluctant calf toward the gate into the pasture. He looked up at us, spat, swore at the calf, and flashed us an only half-apologetic grin.

"I still like Mahi'ai best."

We had learned from Sadie, years ago, how to get an 'akulikuli hat lei from a cowboy, and it had become a game with us on each cattle drive or branding day. The Hawaiians always had the freshest and gayest ones, so they were our main targets. At lunch time, I thought.

Kit yawned and said, "I'm getting sleepy, sitting in the sun. Guess I'll go and rope now." She climbed down from her post and went for Kua.

My father rode across the pen and reined in his big chestnut Maneli, still his favorite, beside me. "Lots of manuwahi cowboys today."

There weren't any who were really malihinis to branding that day, or at least there were none trying to rope. My father said "for-free cowboys" jokingly, but he was always careful about whom he asked to try a hand at it, and he kept watch over the younger ropers and the unaccustomed. "It's so much easier than they know, to get into trouble," he would say.

My mother and Kit's, and a few other women, were sitting on boards of the roughly built "spectators' gallery." Mother was having another baby, and didn't look as if she felt very well. A broad brimmed hat shaded her head from the sun.

A visitor at Kit's family's log cabin had been riding side-saddle. This fascinated us. We had seen sidesaddle riding only in pictures. One of the pictures, of course, was of Kirey in her days of riding before her back began to trouble her.

Cowboy lunch was salt beef, pa'i'ai, cold boiled potatoes, and soda water. We sat in the tall grass of the pasture slope above the pens. Inevitably, when slices of watermelon finished the meal, one of the boys put a piece of it down Opala's neck. He retaliated, but soon had Cho, Jake, Monty, and Duke soaking him with watery handfuls scooped from their slices.

The girls came to his rescue, and Hattie and Patch, Kit, Sut, and I were quickly engaged in the struggle. Holly, looking amused at such foolery but not joining in, sat a little apart. When we all emerged dripping from the scuffle, Opala went to sit beside her, mopping face, neck, and arms with a red cotton bandana.

Opala was very special to all of us, especially to those of us who went to school in Honolulu. He had a cattle ranch on Oahu and many were the weekends that we spent at his house near the ocean: riding, swimming, playing baseball or cards, and herding cattle through kiawe trees when we were lucky enough to be there for a drive weekend. Without our realizing it, he was a strong influence on our impressionable youth. He was friend, judge, hero; and near enough in age to be involved in such high-jinks as a watermelon fight.

Just supposing he and Holly would *really* . . . Ever since I had thought momentarily that Count was interested in her, I had been wondering when romance—real romance—would come to her. And if it should be Opala!

Kit said, "Wouldn't it be fun to try the sidesaddle?"

"Yes! You ask if she'll let us."

Each of the five of us—Kit, Sut, the Hatch-Patches, and I—
took a turn at it, and found it much harder than we had
expected. The trick of balance was different from that of riding
astride. How *could* Kirey have done it?

Walking through the pasture gate near the pens, on our
way back to join the others, we picked peaches from the tree
that grew there. How good they tasted, right from the tree! As
guavas did, when we came across a bush while riding.

We disregarded Cho, who said, "You'll all have opu aches.
Those peaches are green."

Hattie had lingered behind us, and spoke to a cowboy who
was mounted to return to the branding pen. We saw why soon,
when her new Stetson was bedecked in the bright mixed colors
of a lei. "I got the first one!" she said.

By the end of the afternoon's work, all hands were hot and
dusty. The sisters Hatch-Patch and I, and quite a number of
others, were to spend tonight at Kit's family's mountain house,
as we had last. Our parents too had guests, and we parted. Most
of them and the cowboys rode down through the pastures to
the Ranch headquarters, but my father drove Mother down the
road, giving Maneli to someone to be led.

This baby, like the rest of us, would be born at Brookside.
How well I remembered the night when Keiki had arrived!
Lights in the upstairs hallway, hushed urgent voices,
hastening footsteps. And, terribly, moans from Mother's room.
My father told me later that for a week or so after the birth of
each child, he couldn't stretch out his arms to full length,
because Mother held onto his hands during labor.

Now as I untied Ke'ala from her fence post, I talked to her
as I had to so many who had come before. Ke'ala—My Sweet.
"You *are* my sweet." She was a palomino mare, slenderly built
and with a beautiful head and gentle but alert eyes. There had
been many since Jack. After Kula Boy had come 'Ilima,
inherited from Duke; Lady Gray and then Rosy Dawn from
Holly; lively Kilauea, neck always arched; the Thoroughbred

Quick Step; my father's small Moa Ula, the Little Red Hen. My whole heart had been Jack's, and now it was Ke'ala's. Differently, as Daddy had told me it would be. A less passionate, all-consuming love, but love nonetheless.

It was quite a cavalcade that climbed through pastureland and eucalyptus wood to the rough roadway.

Kit said, "Think of the times we've had to walk home in the rain and mud after a party." During rainstorms, chains had to be put on wheels of cars ascending the Olinda road, and at times nearing this highest house, a car would skid to a halt despite them. Carrying stockings and evening shoes, we had sometimes walked the rest of the way in the dark.

Patch said: "Let's play Sardines tonight. Or Murder!"

The five of us rode in a group. Ahead were Kit's parents with the sidesaddle lady, a friend of theirs whom we had nicknamed Alekoki, and their husbands. Holly and Opala were just in front of us, and noisily bringing up the rear were Jake and the other boys, Monty, Cho, and Duke.

The driveway was shaded by tall stands of eucalyptus, and it led upward to a clearing. Here were the two houses, the log cabin and an old building that had been a barn. There were masses of deep blue hydrangea, roses climbing a trellis, and a grape arbor. This was Mahuilani, the Gathering Place of the Clouds. Today it was clear, but many were the times when mist circled wraithlike through the trees to veil the hillside in silver gauze.

The grown-up women left their horses at the stable for the men and the younger ones to unsaddle, and walked across to the cabin for the first baths.

"Look there." I nudged Kit and we watched Opala at Holly's side again, helping with Oregon's tack.

She was saying, "Remember that time when you were so late bringing Duke home to Brookside, after one of your cattle drives at Koko Head?"

"Do I! Melbie was waiting for us at the front door."

"It was after dark," Holly said, "and she was wild. She

didn't say anything but we could tell."

"I'm terrified of Melbie. When she looks at you that way, it would be better if she did bawl you out."

Holly giggled. "I never dreamed that *you* were afraid of her!"

Opala looked at her, smiling, the bridle in his hand.

I said in a low voice to Kit, "Sardines would be better. You can hide *with* somebody in that game."

Patch overheard and said, "Mercy! Do you mean you think that those two—?"

After dinner we sat round before burning logs in the lava rock fireplace and on the big hikie'e in the corner. Kit's father and the sidesaddle lady's husband were playing dominoes at the card table. Sut, Hattie, and Patch were near the front door, putting one old favorite after another on the Gramophone.

As *Cielito Lindo* came to a wavering end, Monty was saying, "Let's go after wild cattle tomorrow, Opala. We'll ride up the mountain over on the Kula side. O.K.?"

"Tomorrow!" exclaimed Opala. "We've just had two hard days' work and so have the horses."

"You're lazy, that's all. We'll use the horses we rode yesterday."

"Good idea," agreed Cho. "You can count on us to get you out of bed. We'll set the alarm for three."

Kit's father looked up from his game and seemed about to say something, but chuckled and remarked, "I'll leave this to Opala, I think."

After a few moments, he looked across at the woman who sat in one of the log armchairs at the fireside. "Let's have *Alekoki* now, shall we?"

The lovely dark-haired woman known to us by the name of this song stood up and sang the lilting melody that told of the desolate love of a royal prince, beside a pool and waterfall of Nuuanu Stream.

We were quiet for a little, the spell of that haunting

adoration still upon us. Until someone said, "Lights out! It's time for Murder."

"Sardines," I said quickly, but was shouted down.

Hattie said teasingly, "What you want is to hide under the table with one of the boys."

"Don't be such a dope," I retorted indignantly. Already slips of paper were being handed out, kerosene lamps turned down and blown out, and I was caught up in the excitement of wondering who would draw the lot of Murderer.

In the dark, you tried your best not to touch anyone, in case it should be that fearsome being. I stood in a corner, as small as I could make myself, and listened to the wandering footsteps, the brushes of one against another, the startled *Oh's* and quick retreats. Maybe Opala was the Murderer, and he would track down Holly, and instead of striking her dead he would kiss her.

At last, the cry of "Murder!" Lights went up and found Monty, to his chagrin, murdered by Patch. "Mercy!" she said, seeing who it was she had foully done to death.

Holly and Opala were at opposite ends of the room from each other.

We went off to bed with calls of, "See you at three, Opala!" and "Go right to bed now, so we'll be able to get you up," ringing in our ears.

All of us younger ones were housed in the remodeled barn, five of us sleeping in the room that had been a hayloft. Holly had a room to herself, and the boys were in the other upstairs rooms. There were three old high-backed double beds in our room, and we slept two to a bed with me as odd-man-out.

My bed was nearest the large window that went right to the floor, through which hay formerly had been tossed. The moon had risen beyond eucalyptus trees of the paddock, and I lay looking out at darkness streaked by moonbeams, and listening to the night sounds: the creak of tree trunks, the shifting of a hoof, a dulled snort from one of the horses.

After a time, I became aware of another quiet noise. A shadowy figure was coming toward the barn from the direction of the log cabin. Who could it be? Opala, come to gaze romantically at Holly's window? Maybe it *was*. But the figure went out of my sight, toward the lanai.

I got out from under the heavy blankets, shivering, and crept along the hallway to the top of the narrow, ladderlike stairs.

Footsteps below—and there he was at the bottom. It *was* Opala. Perhaps he wanted her to come out for a walk. A walk under that rising moon!

"Do you want me to call her?" I whispered down.

Not hearing, he started up, going sideways as you had to on that steep flight.

"I'll get her for you," I said when he was closer. "I know what room she's in."

"What? Oh, Bobora—what in the world are you doing up?"

"I heard you, saw you coming."

"You're cold. Back to bed—but first, show me what room they've got it in."

It! What did he mean, it? I couldn't have heard him right. "This way. Sh."

"Sh, you bet! Don't wake them, for the Lord's sake."

"In here . . ."

He shone his flashlight round the room. A startled exclamation, and then, "That's Holly!"

"You mean you—who are you looking for?"

"The boys will be in the other rooms. Quiet, now."

Boys! All he wanted was the boys.

He went softly into the room across the way, stealthily searched with his flashlight until its beam found the alarm clock.

He switched it off, sighed in relief, and said, "Back to bed now. And *don't wake up the boys*."

22
Medal and Mask

Jannie, Kit, and I climbed our way up the bleachers beside the ROTC grounds until we found good seats, near the top.

We were ahead of time, and Jannie said, "What are you going to wear to Fanny's party tonight?"

"Mine's Indian," Kit said. "Pocahantas, I guess."

"Oh, swell. I'm wearing my father's kilt. Everybody will think I'm a boy."

This seemed highly improbable, even with masks. Jannie's face was round and cherubic, and wisps of yellow hair were sure to escape the Scottish cap that accompanied the kilt. Besides, though she was slender, her figure wasn't exactly a boy's.

I felt halfway between being embarrassed and pleased by the costume that had been made for me. I might as well tell them, so they wouldn't be too surprised. "Mine's a ballet dress. Red, with a skirt that sticks straight out, and long red stockings." They were the daring part. Red stockings! The embarrassing bit, that it wasn't at all the kind of costume for a girl who scoffed at most things that hadn't to do with horses

207

Kit, Sut, and I had our horses at the polo stables now—
Kuahiwi, Hanalei, and Keʻala—and we rode in Kapiʻolani
Park and on the race track and polo field, and up the path on
the slopes of Diamond Head.

"Music!" cried Jannie. "They're coming!"

This was the day when the Battalion Commander, Hendy,
was to receive the Best Soldier Award. And it was to be
presented by Holly! She was back at Punahou to graduate,
after her year of boarding school, because she had been so
desperately homesick.

Holly was Battalion Sponsor of Rotcy, and Hendy was not
only the recipient of the coveted award, he was Senior class
president, captain of the football team, and the best looking
boy at Punahou. He was half Hawaiian, tall and one who held
himself straight, with bronzed skin and black hair, and such a
knockout in his uniform that I didn't know how Holly could
bear it.

My heart seemed to beat in rhythm with the school band as
it strode smartly onto the field to the strains of *Ka Moʻi
Kalakaua*. Hendy marched at the head of the Battalion. I
spotted Duke in the ranks of younger boys, their faces serious
under peaked caps, concentrating on keeping the pace. We all
stood as the Colors went by, the U.S. flag and the Hawaiian.

How snappy the Sponsors looked in their Buff and Blue
uniforms of crepe de Chine! Holly and the three Company
Sponsors were on the reviewing stand with the General, the
Major, and the school President. I could feel with her as she
was called upon to step forward. How could she stand the
excitement of pinning the ribbon to Hendy's uniform!

When the *Star-Spangled Banner* and *Hawaii Ponoʻi* had
been sung, and the Battalion had marched off the field, we
milled around under the spreading monkey-pod trees. We were
too shy to congratulate Hendy; he wouldn't even know who we
were! He was the center of attraction, anyway, and we'd never
have been able to reach him.

What would it be like, I wondered, to be such a hero? This

was his day. Oh, if only, *only* he and Holly . . . It was her day too, after all.

Lately, my stories of romance to Kit and Sut had been of Holly and Hendy. True, I still had hopes for her and Opala. But here was someone right on the scene! Very much on it.

Wouldn't it be natural, when she was Battalion Sponsor, and Hendy was Commander? *Wouldn't* it? Once I mentioned this to Holly and she laughed, but in rather a pleased way. "Aren't you being a bit previous?" she commented.

Girls from our class came now to join the three of us. It was the thing to have boys' names, so there were Billy, Bobby, Ray, even Harry. "Wasn't it super? Hendy looked absotively marvelous." "Lucky Holly! Let me touch you, her sister." "What are you going to wear tonight?"

Tonight, tonight. It was there at the backs of all of our minds.

We had been drifting closer to some of the Seniors, who still clustered about Hendy. "OpI thopink hope's topoo dopivopine!" someone said rapidly.

"Lopuckopy yopou!" to Holly, who answered, "OpI'opll nopevoper foporgopet thopis dopay, opif opI lopive topo bope opa hopundroped."

The P.D.Q., talking Op as usual. Holly would never tell me what the intitals of the club stood for. We guessed that the Q. was "Quintet," but that was as far as we got. At football games, rallies, often on school days, the five dressed alike: white flannel skirts, double-breasted jackets (very stylish), one of these in yellow, two in light blue, two navy. They would walk with linked arms—yellow at the center, light blue at either side, navy at the ends.

Members of the P.D.Q., naturally, were going to the Rotcy Ball that night at Pauahi Hall. We younger ones went up the wide flight of stone steps to the Auditorium, transformed for the occasion. Near the ceiling, red, white, and blue streamers led to each corner from a magnificent array about the center light. Above these, balloons in the same colors floated, their strings hanging to where tall boys could reach them.

Oh, surely, surely this would prove to be the setting for my Holly-Hendy plans to flower! She was going with Bill, faithful Bill. "He's no ball of fire," Holly admitted. "But he's awfully nice, really."

It was a Program Dance, and I had examined Holly's Program with anticipation. Hendy was down only for the first Extra. But with the stag line, and cutting in! I could picture her entering the ballroom with Bill, and Hendy giving a start as he gazed at her across the big room, as if he had never seen her before.

Driving to Fanny's party on Alewa Heights, Kirey was the chaperone in our car, sitting in the front seat beside Nagata. It was easy for six of us to fit in the back, with the "little seats" that many of the cars had, which folded over when not in use. Duke and his best girl, Harry, were on them tonight. He had his license now and drove us to school but he wasn't driving at night yet. On the way to or from school, he loved to have a policeman stop the car and ask to see his license, so he could produce it from the back pocket of his cords.

Kirey was our favorite chaperone. She never turned around or attempted to talk with us. When we were dropped, we called goodby to her and Nagata, knowing that this discreet pair would be back for us at the designated hour.

Fanny's house was lit by Japanese lanterns suspended from the ceiling. Through the painted paper came but a glimmer of light, casting over us a borrowed magic, a spell of enchantment such as we had never known. Fanny and her parents, with their easy welcoming ways, allowed no sense of strangeness nor shyness to arise. Strangeness only in that the evening was bewitched.

Far below were the lights of the city, so far as to set us apart in space and time. Holly and Hendy were down there somewhere, at the Ball.

Here at Fanny's, boys who beforehand had made wisecracks about our attire now became one with the scene: the pirate with his skull and crossbones; the moustachioed villain; the cowboy with high-heeled boots, silk bandana, and Stetson; a fisherman with throw-net in folds over his shoulder—"My net's to catch a girl." We could tell that it was Allen. And the sailor boy—I recognized him at once, mask or no. I had hoped against hope that he would be here; in these unfamiliar surroundings, he might even notice me.

Fanny herself, of the curly brown top, was in something that sparkled and glittered mysteriously in the half-light. Ida, with the trace of Hawaiian blood that gave her voice a lilt, wore a holoku of old rose satin, its long train held by a loop over her wrist; Meg, the pale golden beauty who had been kind when soccer-playing Chuck had loved her instead of me, was a Grecian girl in silver chiffon; Kit might have walked out of an Indian forest; Jannie's kilt fooled no one. Gentle, shy Miya wore a fabulous kimono and obi; we had never seen her in kimono before. "It was part of my mother's trousseau," she said. Her hair was up, with a comb in it like the one Toru used to wear.

Music from an unseen Victrola was of the romantic variety—then suddenly a gay, sad, unknown gypsy tune. There was a real gypsy too, in her little booth, her crystal ball telling us all manner of wondrous happenings in store for us. We could believe anything that night!

The sailor boy did dance with me and said I was someone he'd never seen, in my red mask. I could believe that, too! None of us were ourselves.

"I've seen someone at school who's rather like you," he said. "But I'd never have dared dance with that girl."

Never have dared! But then the thought came, It's a line. Holly had told me about lines.

He was part Hawaiian, enough that his slow, kind smile took a special kind of warmth from his eyes. Tonight his mask nearly hid those eyes but I knew the warmth was there. His curly, light brown hair was topped by a sailor cap set rakishly.

He was going on seriously (perhaps it wasn't a line?), "That girl is always going around with a bunch of other girls, at school."

A bunch of girls . . . Could he be shy? Were boys shy, the way I was myself?

Emboldened by something—the lantern-light?—I said, "Sometimes we see you practicing for track on Alexander Field."

He looked down at me questioningly.

More diffidently, "Would you mind if we sat on the bank and watched you?"

He hesitated, considering. "Not all of you. I'd be too scared to run. But if you like, you can go up with me sometime. Any afternoon you like."

The red ballet dress had brought me luck. No, it wasn't just that, or the masks, or the fortunes. It was the whole of this party, this becharmed night so unlike anything we'd known. Tomorrow we'd be the same people, so well known to each other. Or little known, depending. But maybe, maybe—Pete really might take me up to the field with him, some day.

"You could time me for the four-forty, with my stop watch," he said smiling.

Ready for bed, I sat in the dark at the window, watching for Holly to come home with Bill.

The air was quiet, the trees hushed, and from above, a myriad of stars shed a pale glow over their tops. I could see the royal palms clearly, lining the drive. Thick, straight, tall whitish trunks, with gold-touched fronds fanning outward at their crests. No wonder they were called royal. Beyond, wide-reaching trees sloped toward the brook. If only I could go down to the brook tonight. But I dared not miss Holly.

At last, headlights turning in between the stone pillars! Bill's flivver made such a racket, it would be surprising if the whole household weren't awakened. There was the slam of a car door and footfalls on the lanai steps.

Holly reached the top of the stairway and put her head in at Mother and Daddy's room so they'd know she was home. As she opened the screen door to the dimly lit upstairs hall, I slipped out of my door at the other end.

"Holly!" I stage-whispered. She was wearing her new white dress, short but with a long, sort of pulled-up panel at one side. "Gathered," Holly called it. Bill had brought her a red carnation lei, and she had stuck the blossom intended as a boutonniere into her shingled hair. She looked beautiful.

"Still up, infant?" she asked softly. "How was your party?"

I followed her into her room. "Oh, wonderful!" How to describe it? "But I want to hear about *yours*."

She sat on the bed and took off her silver shoes, wriggled her toes, stretched her arms above her head, and yawned.

"It was divine, simply divine."

I couldn't wait another minute. "And Hendy. You danced with him?"

She smiled at my eagerness, and said, "Yes."

"Oh, go *on*."

"Besides his number, he cut in on me—once. We danced the Charleston."

"Is that *all*?"

She laughed and said, "There's a girl he's giving a big rush. And she's a sireen!"

"But you and he . . ." I wasn't quite taking it in, after my fantasies about them, my hopes.

"We're good friends. Oh, he's a peach! Marvelous. And pinning the medal on him this afternoon was probably the biggest thrill of my life. But—I hate to disappoint you—no romance between him and me."

I sat at the window again, for quite a while. Something sweet-smelling wafted up from the garden. Naturally, I had known it was all in my own mind, this affaire de coeur of Holly's.

I wondered if Fanny were looking down over the Valley, over the tops of our trees to the city below. My evening—this evening made by Fanny—would stay with me. Not real either? In a sense. But what *was* real? The still trees in the garden seemed to hold the answer, and just for a second, they gave it to me. What you believe, what you feel, what you dream . . . Yes, what you dream—that's real.

I turned quickly away, before the trees could change for me, and got into bed.

23
Dear Editor

During the summer before I first went away to boarding school, Jannie came from Honolulu to spend a couple of weeks with me at the Ranch. We agreed that life on Maui was duller than it had been. Cattle drives were fun always, or riding in the pastures, and we loved to swim at the beach and cultivate our tans. But most of the boys we knew were my cousins, whom both of us had known all our lives. It was true, there had been romantic interludes—but it seemed to us now that we knew them all entirely too well.

We sat on the lawn under the camphor tree late one afternoon, feeling listless. A shaft of the setting sun streaked the bole of the tree and sparkled on the wall of the Ranch House. It lit Jannie's blond head to gold. Aikane, the Llewellyn setter, lay almost asleep on the grass near us, letting life pass him by. Well, why not? He was old.

I sat looking at Jannie, chewing on a blade of grass and frowning. "There's the dance on Saturday. Might be fun."

She sighed. "Nobody will be there."

"Maybe somebody will come up from Honolulu, or

215

something."

"But nobody we don't know already. Why don't we ever meet anybody new?"

"Let's think of something to do, not the same old thing all the time."

Afterwards, it seemed that the idea had occurred to us simultaneously, as if it had been hovering about us in the still air.

"A letter—"

"To the paper . . . ?"

"Ranch girls."

"Looking for husbands!"

When we composed the draft to be dispatched to one of the Honolulu newspapers, we changed "ranch girls" to "good looking ranch girls." We signed ourselves "Violet and Rosa" and gave my address, in care of the Ranch.

"Somebody might answer that we could write to," Jannie said. "When you're on the mainland, you'll be glad to get letters." We didn't admit to wanting any more than that, even Jannie who was to stay at Punahou. How I envied her!

In the morning, we sought out the boy who rode to the post office each boat day for the Ranch mail.

"Wheelie." It was a little embarrassing to have to explain. "We might be getting some letters addressed to 'Violet and Rosa' and if we do—could you give them to us privately?"

Wheelie looked at us and smiled, and we wished we hadn't had to mention it. He was the son of Masa and his Portuguese wife. In Wheelie, this combination had produced a strikingly handsome boy. His dark eyes flashed a conspiratorial glance.

"Sure, no trobble. I won't let anybody see."

An uneasy feeling stirred in me. I looked at Jannie and could see that she too was beginning to wonder just what we had done. We walked slowly back to the house.

My cousin Monty was there with Duke. The boys had just been released from their jobs on the respective family ranches and were planning a camping trip into Haleakala Crater before having to go away to school.

Monty said, "Why, it's the gruesome twosome! How are you, Jannie-benannie?"

Jannie blushed, as she always did when he called her that.

He grinned at us with an eyebrow raised, which made him look like a small boy pretending to be grown up. Monty had freckles and sandy hair, and reminded me of a rangy pup that hasn't filled out to the size of its paws. His grin could never go unanswered, and we both smiled back.

"When are you going in?" asked Jannie eagerly. "Who else is going?"

"Tomorrow, if it's any of your business. And no *girls* are going—in case you're getting ideas."

"Are you riding Whisky?" I asked Duke. Whisky was a little mule he often took when the going was to be rough.

"Natch. Who else?"

"Will you be going up Lau-ulu?"

We knew, of course, that they would be, but a crater trip was fun to talk about and contemplate. It would be an all-day ride to the camping grounds at Pali-ku—first up the side of the mountain Haleakala, then the steep, rocky trail into the dormant volcano, and from there across the floor of the crater. Lau-ulu was a high ridge above the camp site.

"Sure, we'll go up Lau-ulu. More goats there than any place."

"Don't take a bag for the goats!" Jannie warned. "Bad luck."

"We know *that* much."

As the boys left us to see about pack mules, a tent, and blankets at the stable, Monty said, "Hey, Duke. D'ya hafta go to that dance on Saturday?"

"Yeah," said Duke resignedly.

"Maybe we should take these two wahines, since we've gotta go anyway. You can have Jannie-benannie."

"Well, thanks! I'd sure like to take my own sister."

When they had gone, I said, "If we could only meet

somebody cute! Have a date with someone besides kids we've known all our lives. And who would ask us as though it sounded like a date!"

"We prob'ly wouldn't be allowed to," said Jannie practically. "But if we just *knew* somebody else . . ."

Two boats a week traveled between Honolulu and the seaport of Kahului. A few mornings later, we wandered out to the stableyard at about the time Wheelie would be riding up with the mail. There wouldn't be anything, I told myself. Yet—perhaps just one?

As we went through the gate in the stone wall from our yard, Wheelie had tied up his horse and was carrying the leather bag, made double to fit across the saddle, into the Ranch office. Well, we'd known there wouldn't be anything. We could go across to the stable to see Masa, maybe have a ride.

Wheelie called to us as we walked toward the tack room. "Hey!" We turned, and he winked at us, slapping one half of the bag. It looked fatter than the other.

Had there been a letter then, after all? He came back down the steps and we watched as he opened the bag and took out a handful of envelopes. All sorts of handwriting, all shades of ink, some typed . . . Never had we seen so many letters.

"Here, you better carry it in this." He thrust the saddle bag at us, after taking out the mail for the office.

As we reached the lanai door, my mother was coming up the brick steps of the terrrace. Now that we weren't having school at the schoolhouse on the hill, she had taken it over as a studio. She painted there, and wrote poetry, and carried on a voluminous correspondence with someone in Haifa.

"He's the Guardian of the Cause," she had told us.

Mother had become a Baha'i, and there was no longer any automatic writing, or concern with numerology or other of her old interests. Her faith as a Baha'i was to sustain her all her life.

Over the studio fireplace hung a portrait of Abdul Baha,

and on a wall, a sign in Persian that read plainly: "EVIL." We used to tease her about that sign but she never minded, or paid any attention.

"Has Willie come with the mail yet, I wonder?" she said now. "I'm expecting a letter."

"I—uh—yes, he has."

"Oh, you have the bag there."

"Yes, but he left—uh—your mail at the office."

"Would you run over for me, darling?"

"All right." I backed away from the door, knocking my lopsided burden against it.

"What have you got the mail bag for?"

"There's some stuff in it." We fled, taking Wheelie's telltale bag with us.

Mother's letter with its foreign looking writing and stamp was at the office and, thankfully, we realized on our return to the house that she had forgotten what else I carried. We left her carefully slitting the envelope with a letter opener. Her missive would begin: "Dear and valued co-worker," and would be signed "Shoghi."

We sorted our letters in my room and, with a sense of stunned disbelief, began to read them. There were thirty-odd for each of us. Many were from soldiers at Schofield Barracks. Soldiers! My spine tingled. Soldiers were older than the boys we knew. One of them was in the cavalry and he had sent me two snapshots. The one of him on horseback, waving his hat, was inscribed: "To my long-distance little friend from Raphael." The one in which he wore a bathing suit read: "Remember me. I am Raphael."

About half of the letters proposed marriage. One young Chinese man who worked at a bank in Honolulu had written us separate but identical letters, offering his hand.

We giggled, then Jannie sobered. "They're all so—well, they don't really sound all that grown-up, but they must be. People who work, and are soldiers."

"We did say we were looking for husbands."

We stared at each other. Husbands! Why hadn't we said—correspondents? Boys our own age.

One of the last we read was from a tourist. It was the only one addressed to both of us.

"He doesn't sound like an ordinary malihini," Jannie said thoughtfully. "More a—well, almost like a beachcomber." She gave a shriek, and held the letter out to me in a hand that shook a little.

I read: "I been thinking about going on over to Maui and seeing your Island. Guess I might take the Boat tonight along of this letter. Be seeing you."

We didn't speak for a long minute. Then Jannie said, in a strangled sort of voice, "He won't be able to find us."

"But we gave the Ranch address! He'll come up here."

"What shall we do?"

"He'll go to the Ranch office first. Maybe we could get Wheelie to—"

"What if he does go to the office! No one there will know who Violet and Rosa are. And we can warn Wheelie."

Relief descended upon us like a blessing, and we began to laugh.

The next day, we took our lunch and went for a long ride. We sat on a hilltop washed in sunlight for our picnic. The sun, scents of warm grass and earth, the barely heard rustle of eucalyptus leaves, even the distant overhead caroling of a skylark, combined to make us feel sleepy. Our horses, tied to trees of the nearby grove, had partly-closed eyes. We tipped our sombreros over our faces, and lay for a long time in the tall grass.

Back at the stable, as we were unsaddling, a car came along the road and stopped. A man leaned out to call, "This the Ranch here?"

We said yes, and he got out. "Thanks for the lift, buddy." He waved the driver on.

"Say," he said, coming toward us. "I'm looking for somebody. Might be you could tell me where to go."

He wouldn't have been bad looking except that he needed a haircut and a shave, and he wore Japanese slippers with dirty bare feet instead of shoes. We didn't like his appearance. A grown man, to be so poorly groomed . . .

"Who do you want?" I asked, hosing down Ke'ala.

"Couple of young ladies named Violet and Rosa."

I stared at him across the mare's back, while water from the hose made a pool in the dry dust. Jannie paused in the act of unbridling, and gaped too. We were alone there—everyone had left the stable and the office hours ago.

My voice quavered a little as I said, "There's nobody here named that."

"There sure is." He dug into a pocket and brought forth a folded newspaper clipping. "Says so right in this letter. And I've had a hell of a time bumming a ride up here to see them."

Curiosity overcame other emotions. I turned off the faucet, and both of us went to look at the scrap of paper in his hand. It was the first time we had seen our letter in print. The paper must have come in the mail of the day before, but we had been too much occupied in reading the resultant communications to think of looking up the letter.

There it was, ranch girls, husbands, and all. And at the bottom, "Violet and Rosa" and the address.

The man seemed very close to me and I moved a little away.

Jannie said, "It must be—a joke, or something."

"Joke! Listen, I came from Honolulu to see these dames, and if they're going to give me the run-around—"

"But you said you were coming anyway!"

Jannie, the man, and I must have realized at the same moment what I had given away. The three of us stood there, not moving, while a leaf floated down from one of the silky oak trees that lined the roadway, slowly on an unfelt current of air, as in a dream. It lay for an instant at the man's feet, each feathery prong distinct on a mound of red earth, before his slipper ground it into the dust.

"Trying to kid me, are you?" He smiled, as if we were sharing a secret—as, indeed, we were. I didn't like his smile; it was a sort of leer, that made him look—not nice. "Well, I can take a little kidding. I like girls with some spunk to 'em." Spunk was the last thing that I felt I had, right then.

"Which is which, now? Are you Rosa?"

I shook my head dumbly and pointed at Jannie.

"Rosa," he said slowly. "And Violet. Good old-fashioned names." He looked from one to the other of us, and his eyes made me turn from their gaze. "But you're not old-fashioned girls, writing a letter like that. Are you?"

The sound of hoofbeats had been somewhere in the background, but did not register in my mind until five boys on horseback and two pack mules rounded the bend of the road and jog-trotted into the stableyard.

"Jannie-benannie!" called Monty. "What are you doing? Did you miss me?"

Duke clattered up on his little mule. "Whisky, you've earned your rest tonight!"

The world, all at once, seemed to be full of boys. Boys dismounting, starting to unsaddle, unloading the pack mules, clumping about in their high-heeled boots, boys everywhere, boys' voices.

"Jannie-benannie, come help me with this blasted pack saddle."

"Where's the key to the tack room? Is it open?"

"Lemme have that hose."

"My horse is lame. That damn stone he picked up on the trail."

"You wahines shoulda had some of the goat stew we made."

The man moved closer to Jannie and me. "Friends of yours?" He gestured with a sort of amused contempt toward the boys. "You girls don't seem to be sure what league you belong in." He laughed unpleasantly.

I could feel my cheeks growing warm, and Jannie was

scarlet. She made a motion toward grabbing the clipping but he returned it to his pocket.

Monty, the pack saddle from the mule's back in his hands, walked over. In his cowboy boots, he was taller than the man, but next to him the other suddenly looked older.

Monty's expression was puzzled. He glanced at Jannie and me, then said politely, "Their batting average is fairly high, though."

I could see that the man was going to reply sarcastically. He would tell Monty, all the boys, what we had done! They would never let us hear the end of it.

His hand was reaching toward the pocket that held the clipping. The finger nails repelled me; they were dirty, unkempt. How very unattractive he was.

It seemed that Monty felt aversion for him, too. He looked at the man for a moment longer, but with distaste. Then he simply turned away and took the saddle to the tack room.

Other boys crowded up and, with a non-committal "Hi," to the stranger, began to tell us about the goat hunt on Lau-ulu Ridge.

Jannie and I kept an eye on the man, trying not to appear to notice him. After two or three minutes we saw him shrug elaborately, cast a look of scorn at us and the boys, and begin to saunter off down the road.

When the horses had been let into the corral for the night, Monty gangled against the gate and said, "Say, you two," including both Jannie and me in his eyebrow-raised grin. "If you think Duke and I are going to take you to that dance tonight, you'd better go and get cleaned up."

Jannie laughed up at him. *"We'd* better get cleaned up!"

He was streaked and grimy with dirt, disheveled, his crumpled jeans smelled of horse sweat and mountain goat, there was a sparse growth on chin and upper lip that ill became his funny, freckled face.

I knew why Jannie was looking at him the way she was. To me, too, he looked wonderful.

24
The Sawmill

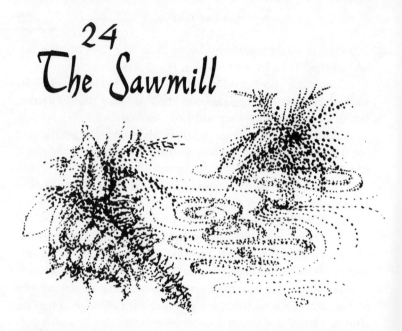

Mother looked up from her scratch tablet, her eyes abstracted. "Well, darling," she said, realizing that I was there. "You'll be able to wear your new dress for the wedding. Christen it!" She smiled sweetly but vaguely and turned again to her list.

"Wedding!" I added scornfully under my breath, "New dress." I didn't want to make a fuss about that, though, because I might really want to wear it.

On the sofa, in the corner nearest my mother's chair, I noticed that the faded blue of my jeans and checked palaka shirt looked washed-out against the chintz. The yellow in it and a bowl of poppies on the round brass coffee table were bright notes in the Ranch House living room, always dark by day. It was a restful darkness, though.

Mother's lamp cast a circle of light on the ceiling and illumined an arc of book bindings on the shelves of the bookcase. The glowing textures made me want suddenly to take the books down, read them all. But later.

After a time she looked up again, as if aware with mild surprise that I was still there. "Aren't you riding today?"

"Ke'ala's lame."

"What about one of the others? Quick Step."

I wasn't in the mood for riding. I wanted to talk with my mother. But her face had resumed its detached gaze. She settled her writing board, shaped like an elephant, on her lap and poised the pencil. After writing two or three words in her upright hand, she put down the pencil and took a sharpened one from a china mug on the table.

Shifting my legs from one side to the other and curling them up under me, I said contemptuously, "I can't see why Nora would marry him!"

Mother raised her eyes slowly and looked at me uncomprehending, then said, "George is very nice." She took off her glasses and her rather studious aspect was gone. Her eyes were strangely youthful in the middle-aged face. There was an air of impending movement about her now, when she was no longer concentrating on her tablet.

"He's a friend of Anthony's, you know. And Anthony is such a dear."

Anthony was the poet who was living in the Ranch cottage far up the mountainside.

"George can't even ride," I said quickly, before she could get up and go.

"Isn't this Thursday? You'll have to study for tomorrow."

"I will, sometime." I was being tutored in algebra two mornings a week. It wasn't that school had been so hard of late; it had been hard to pay attention.

"Better do it this morning, because of the wedding."

She put away her tablet and writing board neatly, and stood up. "Riding isn't everything," she said. "George has never had the opportunity, you know."

That was the trouble with Mother these days, it seemed to me. When you got her to stop thinking about something else, so that she might talk to you, she was off and away.

Standing in front of the house, I felt the sun's warmth on my back. A page of my algebra book came between me and the sunny summer day, and I thrust it aside. The trees on the lawn, the camphor under which I stood, the kukui, the ancient towering eucalyptus, all were motionless as though better to absorb the sunlight. Fat white pigeons whirred in sudden descent from the roof, cutting through the stillness.

I saw Duke and shouted to him.

"What'sa matter?" He stood waiting impatiently.

"Let's do something. Climb trees in the gulch?"

He guffawed, and ambled off toward the garage. "Climb trees! When are you gonna grow up?"

I'm never going to grow up, that's when, I thought. In my teens . . . Well, no matter how old I got, I'd remember what it was like being this age.

I didn't need Duke to climb with me. I thought of the mango trees at the bottom of the gulch, and the jacaranda with its canopy of lavender bloom. But I didn't turn in that direction.

Aimlessly I wandered back across the lawn and through the gate in the stone wall to the stableyard with its red saddle room, warehouse, and blacksmith shop. Back of them was an old building, and I went toward it.

The smell of curly flakes of wood and sawdust mingled with mustiness here in an intoxicating fusion, not of scent alone. The great saw at the center of the room took shape in the dimness, boards creaked as my bare feet walked across them, the air on my cheeks was cool after sunshine. Peace enveloped me, a safe, secret peace.

I strolled about the room for a while, examined the saw whose every angle was known to me, rubbed my fingers along the smoothness of a newly cut board. The day before, I had heard the whine of the saw. I seldom came here when the mill was in operation, but loved the screeching wail from a distance.

Up the steep, rickety stairs at the back—they swayed under me—and across a vacant space to the little room. Its floor descended steeply from each wall to a square at the center, and at the far side was a small window. This was the most mysterious and secret part of the sawmill, this little forgotten, unexplained room. Bending under the ceiling and gripping with my toes, I crossed the slant.

The window looked down over the tops of the Dairy buildings, across the plain at the foot of the mountain to the West Maui range beyond. Blue and green, light and shade, creviced valleys that were dark caverns, their ridges knife-sharp. The high peak above Wailuku was a light-washed carving upon the shadowed canyon behind it.

Somewhere at the back of my mind persisted the image of my algebra book, and of Nora's forthcoming marriage. But I let them float away.

The church was decorated with white flowers, as at Easter. Between Duke and my mother, I wriggled in the new dress and wished there were colored flowers. On Sundays there were, usually from Aunt Ella's garden at Olinda. Pink, blue, lavender, yellow. The oak paneling glowed with a warmer luster when the massed flowers were in color. Or perhaps it was that the light was different in the morning, streaming palely through stained glass at the opposite side. I loved this church, a memorial to my Maui grandfather. Here, I could feel that I had known him.

Why wouldn't Duke stop fidgeting? He had made such a thing out of having to wear a suit. I suspected that he really enjoyed being dressed up. I turned my head to tell him to sit still, and he whispered, "Why do you keep *wiggling*?" The annoyance on his face, lengthening now from its former roundness, struck me as funny and I almost giggled. He turned away with dignity.

The new dress didn't feel quite comfortable. It was too something. Grown up? Anyway, it didn't seem like mine, not yet. It was linen, really a very pretty color, sort of apricoty, and at the square neck and short sleeves there was a cutout design of flowers. Duke had said, "What a waste time dress," and the lack of conviction in his voice had made me feel that it was going to be a success. Then the usher who had brought me to the pew had held his arm for me as if I were a lady. It was Anthony, who lived in the mountain cottage. He said, "I hardly recognized you," and when I didn't answer but just looked silly, had added quickly, "It's not many girls who can wear both cowboy and party clothes."

He came up the aisle now, walking as though in unconscious time to the organ. He was very handsome in his blue coat and white flannels, hair dark and glossy, face and hands deeply tanned. In the subdued light of the church, his eyes were startlingly blue. Seeing him in profile, I thought, He looks like a poet. He turned and his eyes met mine, and I looked away quickly. For goodness sake, why hadn't I just smiled? My cheeks burned.

Nora was very pretty in her dress with its long train, and cream-white pikake leis over her arm instead of a bouquet. Their fragrance lingered in the aisle after she had passed. The bridesmaids were in white, too—a "white wedding." Diane was matron of honor. Mr. Holliday, holding his prayer book, looked solemn, George looked scared. When he turned to stand beside Nora, I could see that his knees were shaking.

Nora had asked me one day what color George's aura was. It seemed to me now that surely I must only have imagined seeing people's auras, when I was younger. "Brown," I had answered crossly, upset that she was marrying someone from away.

The wedding was like a ceremony in a dream. The music was making me sleepy; it almost was a dream. The first chord of the Recessional made me jump.

The reception was at Nora's house, farther along the mountain than the Ranch House. Nora's house no more! She was going to live on the mainland. What got into girls, anyway? Catch anybody getting me away from the Islands!

At the punch table in the dining room were Duke and Monty, stiffly elegant and superior—they did like wearing their suits!—and my cousin Cathy. There were two bowls of punch, spiked and unspiked, at opposite ends of the table.

Cathy had on the kind of dress I had worn until now. Today I felt the two years' difference in our ages, and something made me straighten my shoulders and lift my head.

"Come and get some punch." Cathy's eyes were gleaming; she loved weddings.

I walked slowly up to the table and accepted a glass from Monty. He had been about to drink it but, to my surprise and probably to his, offered it to me instead. What made him look so young today? Being dressed up?

After several glasses of punch and a dozen or so cookies, he said to me, "Wanna dance?"

The music was gay, and there was something infectious in the murmur of talk on the broad lanai, something that made me want to be a part of it, yet kept my eyes roving over Monty's shoulder as he guided me rather jerkily. I didn't know what I was looking for until I saw Anthony, standing absorbed, watching the steel guitar played by a large Hawaiian. Monty swung me around, and he was gone.

When the dance was over, Monty said, "Shall we go in and get some more punch?"

"No thanks, I don't want any more." Lightheaded in bravery, I said, "Let's go over by the music."

But Anthony wasn't there. Sick with disappointment, I watched him dancing with one of the bridesmaids when the music boys began to play and sing, "I love a pretty Maui girl."

Later, Cathy and I stood at the lanai railing. Each of us held a box of wedding cake, to sleep on. Seven slips of paper, six of them labeled, to go under the pillow, one to be drawn out every morning: the one you loved, someone you hated, the names of four other boys—and the most exciting of all, the blank slip.

"Will you dance?" At the quiet voice, so near me

unawares, a delicious agony overtook me. My hand trembled and spilled punch onto my dress.

"Oh, what a shame," Anthony said. "Here, let me." He took my glass and put it on the railing, and with a deeply creased, monogrammed handkerchief dabbed at my skirt.

"Oh, it's all right, never mind, it doesn't matter." But I couldn't move or take my eyes from that brown, shapely hand. The nails were well cared for, the fingers slender. I thought of a violin bow.

"There, it will soon dry off. Come along."

Circling on Anthony's arm, I felt as graceful as the bridesmaid had looked. Anthony danced slowly and with infinite grace, his hand at my back was firm. Faces swept by, Cathy's goggling, the music boys laughing as they played, other dancers. I missed a step, and transferred my gaze to Anthony's dark blue shoulder.

The music over, he said, "Let's watch the sunset."

He pulled round a wicker settee, away from the players, got us each a glass from the punch table, and we sat with our backs to the party. Below us, the mountainside fell away in a long rhythmic sweep to the plain and the West Maui Mountains thrusting into the sea. Bright arrows at the horizon became pale slanting shafts above 'Iao Valley.

"We were nearly too late," he said. "This is the hour I reserve for sitting on my porch."

"How do you like it up the mountain?" I looked sideways to watch his face as he answered.

"It's the most perfect place I've ever lived."

"You don't get lonely?"

"Heavens, no! You don't mean that, do you?"

"Well, no, I guess not. No."

"You love the mountain, too. I've seen you riding. You wouldn't be lonely there, either."

Once I had been riding Ke'ala through the Mountain Pasture and had seen smoke rising from his chimney, a phantom pillar against the eucalyptus grove above. He had been wearing jeans and a flannel shirt, looking neater in them than anyone I knew would have, and was building something with stones. He called to me to inspect the ones he had found. "Aren't they beauties? Look at these, with moss growing on them. They're my favorites—except this, almost a perfect oval, just enough off. And this one like a small idol. Perhaps it's been that." He set it on end on a level bit of ground. "They're nice," I had said. "What are you making?" "A barbecue, can't you see?" His smile, gently teasing, had made me say, "I'd better go along," even while it awoke an unaccustomed glow in my chest.

"How's your barbecue?" I asked him now.

"It works splendidly. You must come up sometime and let me broil you a steak."

"Oh!"

"I'll ask Duke to bring you up one evening. Do you remember the idol? I've put him on my mantelpiece."

"My father found an idol on the mountain. He left it where it was. He's found adzes too, and quite a good poi pounder. And a round kind of stone the Hawaiians used to play a game with."

"It's easy, in some places, to picture the people who lived here long ago. In the native forest, for instance. I walk into it quite often. Do you like the forest?"

"I love it. We have wonderful hunts there—pheasant, you know. Do you shoot?"

"I don't, no. I should imagine that gunfire was rather out of place there."

This was a new idea, but perhaps he was right.

"Glorious shapes those trees take, with their moss-grown branches like ghostly arms. There's an atmosphere there quite different from anywhere else, an old feeling, as before the monarchy. I lie under the trees for hours."

"What do you think about?" I added hesitantly, "Do you make poetry?"

"I just let impressions come and go. Now and then, when

I've been very still, I've seen native birds. Tiny green ones, and once a red one. Like a lehua blossom."

"That must have been an i'iwi. You ought to have a horse. Why don't you ask Daddy to lend you one?"

"I like walking."

"But don't you like riding?"

"I've never tried it."

That was natural, perhaps. He had grown up in a city. "I ride to the forest sometimes, and take my lunch along."

"You've been rather a tomboy, haven't you?" What did he mean, been one? "That's the best thing for a girl. She grows up to be the most feminine woman." I thought of Kit's mother, such a tomboy that only my mother had been allowed to play with her. And look at her now!

Cathy's voice was behind us, and I thought, Don't come, not yet. I sat very still until she must have moved away. Anthony too was silent, but I was aware of his presence as never before of anyone else. I wanted to look at him, to see the shape of his head and the way his hair grew, with its suggestion of a wave.

The atoms of darkness had gathered while we talked. Lights at the shore and at the foot of the West Mauis were shimmering patterns in yellow and white. A cane fire billowed heavy smoke, shot with flame. Reservoirs on the plain were like diamonds fallen from a giant's necklace.

The music from across the lanai slowed in rhythm, somehow mingled with my thoughts so that it almost answered my underlying question. "I don't want to be feminine." It should embarrass me to say this to Anthony. But it was important.

The deep blue eyes smiled into mine. He didn't reply at all.

On the way home, Duke said, "They're going to tear down the sawmill tomorrow."

I froze, and said when I could speak, "How do you know?"

"Daddy said. They're moving the saw over to the cowboy stable. The building's too rickety, liable to fall down."

Before daybreak the next morning, I was climbing the teetering stairs. The faint square ahead, the little window, was just visible.

Crouching beside it, I saw dawn come to the West Mauis, watched as the last pale star dissolved like vanishing hope. The first sunlight touched the mountain's jagged crest, free of clouds at this hour, and traveled with slow precision down its sheer ridges, into the deep valleys. The mountainside below me, and the plain, were shadowed still.

I wanted to feel intensely, to know that this was my farewell to the sawmill. I looked round the slanting little room, its odd contours retrieved from darkness, and tried to feel the way I should have felt. But it was like finding an old photograph, like a dream remembered. In some way I couldn't understand, the room and the sawmill were already gone.

25
Why Are You Blue?

Danny put me into his car and went round to the driver's side. We were under the porte-cochere of his mother's house in Nuuanu Valley. As he got in, he put an arm along the back of the seat and sang softly, " 'Brown Eyes, why are you blue?' "

My eyes filled with tears and I couldn't look at him.

"It'll be bad, awfully bad the first year," he said. "I don't suppose there's anything much worse than being homesick. But there are good things, too."

What was there that could be good about going away to boarding school? Looking toward the lanai of his house, I was afraid that tears would roll down my cheeks.

Danny's house . . . the good times, happy times at Danny's house. His mother had parties for him and his friends, or asked only two or three at a time. Perhaps this had a good deal to do with my relationship to Danny. I knew him as part of a family, not just as a boy who "took me out." Tonight, the second to the last before Holly, Duke, and I—and Danny too—were to leave on the boat, it had been a party. An evening of easy companionship, like so many others.

The evening had included, as often before, a game of billiards. I was hopeless at billiards, which afforded Danny much pleasure. He did try to teach me, though. Everything about this night had been familiar, friendly: the buffet supper of curried chicken with baked bananas, and a huge coconut cake; at the table, everyone making his water glass sing by wetting the bottom and running a finger around the rim; the parlor games afterward, chief among them tonight the one in which we sat on the floor in a circle and each in turn traced with his finger an imaginary design on his neighbor's face—imaginary with one exception. The object of the game was revealed when a mirror was passed from hand to hand, and Meg had streaked Danny's cousin Dick's face with charcoal. "Hey! Look what Meg's been doing! She can't do that to me—I'm a misogynist."

It was only when Buck got out his ukulele that I thought, This party is a "last time." He had taken it from its case and, handling the koa wood instrument lovingly, begun to play.

Buck's Hawaiian heritage was apparent in his gentle yet assured manner, and in the music that was so much a part of him that we scarcely understood the birthright that it was. He had blue eyes and thick brown hair, and enough of Hawaiian blood blending with Caucasian to give him a charm peculiar to the Islands.

We sat around on the floor and on chairs, sometimes just listening. But we all sang the *Hawaiian War Chant* with him, and swung into "Kiss me, my darling . . ." When he began, "'Across the sea, an island's calling me,/Calling to the wanderer to return,'" I said to Danny, "I've got to go."

The scent of my lei, there in Danny's car, was almost more than I could bear. That day, he had taken me to a beach picnic at La'ie, on the other side of the island. Driving up the forest-bound road to the Pali, he had stopped the car where a Hawaiian woman made ginger leis at her little house surrounded by trees, and strung them on a line before it. He got me a yellow one, my favorite. Wild yellow, elegant white—

nearly always, I wanted the yellow.

The top of Danny's convertible had been down, the woods at either hand rose high above us. The sun of a summer sky was warm on our heads and arms, there were pools of light here and there among the trees; beyond them, the walls of Nuuanu Valley stood brilliant and clear-edged. The trade wind was in our faces and blew my hair back, and the fragrance of ginger was all about us. Summer in Honolulu: a ginger lei. Up the winding, narrow road, past the Upside-down Falls where the Pali winds blew a waterfall against the cliff in a spray of sun-shot sparkle.

Then, I had not let myself think, It's the last time.

I said now to Danny, "What is there that's good about school? Nine months away from home!"

He hesitated a minute. "There's no way I can kid you about its being bad. But there are good fun things."

"Like what?"

"Well—there's the Hawaiian Reunion in New York."

"I'll bet they won't let Kit and me go."

"My gosh, you'll have weekends away from school, won't you? Sometimes!"

"Only Seniors are supposed to. She and I might have just one, at the beginning when our families are still there. Because we'll be from so far away—New Girls don't get weekends. Why don't they have the Reunion at vacation time?"

"Most of the kids can get away, I guess. Well, you'll have vacations, even if not weekends."

Yes, at Cleveland with Sadie! Not only that, she was actually going to be at school, had been there for a year already. Thank the Lord for that, and for Kit. I could never have stood it, otherwise.

When Danny had brought me home and I was getting ready for bed, I hung the lei on a hanger with my dress. It would be wilted by morning, but I wanted to smell it during the night.

The next day I spent at home, roaming about the house and yard, seeing all the people there that I'd be leaving, hugging Keiki. She was seven now. I thought back to when I had been seven, the summer the Clevelanders had been on Maui, and she seemed much more of a little girl than I had felt. I knew my arms would ache for her, as once they had for Teddybear.

The new baby, a boy, had duly been born—at Brookside of course. But instead of in Mother's bed this time, on a Chinese table known thereafter as the Light of Day Table. He was beginning to run around now and called himself "Mister McKee" after a Scotsman in his favorite picture book. It was hard to catch him long enough for a hug. He would whirl off, prattling, "Me, me, I'm Mister McKee!"

The one place I didn't want to be was in my own room, because of the nearly-packed trunks. The steamer trunk stood on end, with clothes for the boat and for New York before school. The big chest-type trunk, which would travel in the "Hold" of the ship, contained blankets, bed linen, towels, and clothes for school: khaki uniforms for day, white voile for evening, colored velvet capes to go with these, a camel's hair coat, black bloomers and white middy blouses for hockey (which I knew I'd hate), thick lisle stockings in beige and black, Spalding saddle-shoes (these I liked), knee length woolen socks. And a dozen white collars that had to be pinned to the khaki dresses, fresh every day, and black ties. Everything, of course, sewn with name tags.

Holly, Duke, and I—each in a different school. Holly's was to be in New York and was called a "finishing school." Mother and Daddy were going with us, and would spend a few weeks in the East.

In the afternoon, when Grandpa was home from his office, I went across Bates Street to see them all there. He and Grandma were on the lanai, and Mutie came downstairs with an amber necklace in one hand, a tourmaline choker in the other, and a box of candy for Duke.

"I've strung these for you and Holly, to have while you're away."

Amber! Was Holly old enough to wear amber, as Mother and the aunts did? And I to wear tourmaline? It was hard to say anything. "Thank you, Mutie."

She stayed for a bit, talking about the East, especially New York where she had known the Baha'i leader, Abdul Baha. After a while, she kissed me and went back upstairs. To string more beads, perhaps.

Grandpa said, "Don't forget, you're going to the place your forbears came from, Connecticut. In a sense, you'll be going home."

Home! *This* was home. Brookside, and the Ranch. I sat on the footstool beside his chair. Grandma was at her end of the koa table, knitting a blue baby blanket. "For Diane," she said. Think of it, Diane was having a baby!

"Write to us about all you see and do," Grandpa said. "Especially when you're missing home, as you're bound to do. And we'll write to you of Bates Street and Brookside, your very own home."

"What about your real, own home, Grandpa? Before Honolulu. It was on Kauai . . ." I kept forgetting that, and thought of him and Grandma as always right here. She had lived on Maui as a girl.

"Yes, Kauai." His eyes seemed to be looking back, with a light of times remembered. "I was born on Kauai, you know that, in Koloa. My father was both a doctor and a minister there. The only doctor on the island, for many years. I used to ride horseback with him to all parts of it."

"Do you miss your home there?"

"Sometimes I miss it very much. Often I dream of it. But you see—" he frowned, trying to tell me exactly what he meant. "My home on Kauai is a part of my life for always, even when I don't go down there for years at a time. Someday, you'll know this too. One goes on through life—the old, the new, the in-between—all of it together forms a pattern, makes a lifetime."

Brookside will be my home always, I thought. And the Ranch. But always I'll come back to Brookside and the brook. These are mine, they're the place where I belong.

"Success all through life depends on persevering effort, notwithstanding discouragements. Profit by these. Take a far look. Look forward and upward." He sat thinking for a minute, and went on, "New places, new friends, learning both in class and at other times, a countryside that your great-grandparents knew. All of this, besides being lived at the time, will be preparing you for what comes when the three years are over. You'll be growing up."

Anthony had implied that I'd be growing up. But, "Three years away!"

"With summers at home, of course. And all of us you've left behind will be your link with home."

Ara came in with oatmeal cookies and guava juice, squeezed from the fruit that grew on Grandma's bushes. I wondered if anyone on the mainland knew what guavas were like, sweet and tart at once. Not in the East. It would be cold there, it would snow. Even handling the camel's hair coat and woolen stockings, I hadn't been able quite to believe it.

Kirey came to meet me at her door. "Come in, child. I'm just going to make tea."

I had "real tea" with her now. No one could make it so well as Kirey. She gave it to me today in the cup wreathed in pink roses and green leaves.

"I have something for you," she said.

After tea, she brought it to me: a small framed painting of a Honolulu garden, with a pink shower tree in bloom, done by her friend Mrs. Dranga. On the back, Kirey had written: "A little bit of home while at school."

"I'll put it on my bureau." I couldn't imagine any bureau of mine so far away.

"I'm glad you're going to an Episcopal school. Think of home when you're in chapel. The hymns will remind you."

Could I bear it? Supposing we should have to sing *Now the Day is Over*. We did, kneeling, during a Sunday evening chapel service, and Kirey came very close to me.

On leaving Kirey's, I went down the slope and flung myself to the ground under the monkey-pods, where I could look down on the brook. I dwelled on my misery, and the unfairness that was taking me from the people and places I loved.

Floating in my mind that day had been the unacknowledged thought that all of it would be here for me when I returned. What Grandpa had said and Kirey's giving me "a little bit of home" had strengthened this tenuous thread of awareness.

Gradually, the sounds around me embraced me, until they flooded through every sense of my being. My ears were filled with the brook, my eyes with dark water flowing forever, my head with the smell of water plants, as I lay on the soft yielding grass.

At dinner, Holly told us about skyscrapers, hotels and restaurants, streets jammed with traffic.

"But I've seen all of those things in the movies," Duke said. "I know what it's like already."

"Wait till you see some musical comedies!"

Duke scowled. "I'd rather go to the Princess and the Hawaii, right here."

"And all the big stores. They make shopping exciting."

"The Paia Store is good enough for me."

This kind of talk went on about me, leaving little impression. Disbelief and non-acceptance had taken hold again. I *couldn't* be going away . . . but I was.

After dinner I followed Mother into the den, where she stood looking for a book. She held out an arm to me and said, "When you're at school, find the library. It will be a nice quiet place, and there's such comfort in books." Looking at the rows and rows of shelves, I knew it was what I'd have to do.

Rain had begun to splash on the window panes, and instead of joining the others in the living room I went to the lanai to look out into it, listen to its steady streaming onto grass, its bouncing from driveway and granite steps.

Daddy followed me there, and stood with his arm around me. He gave me his handkerchief and said, "Even the Heavens weep when you're leaving, my dear."

On Steamer Day, I couldn't believe that these things were really happening. A truck came to take all of our luggage to the *Matsonia*—Holly's, Duke's, and my steamer and "Hold" trunks, Mother and Daddy's steamer ones. Then came quick goodbys across Bates Street, except for Grandpa, who was coming to the boat. At Kirey's, she put round my neck several strands of fragrant pikake, ivory-white jasmine. Misao and Otoru were in the house, and Holly and I kissed them goodby at the door. Yame and Yani were married now, and she lived at Kit's family's.

'Toru hadn't lived at Brookside since her marriage, but she had come to see us. They gave each of the three of us a plumeria lei of a different color, and a box of Japanese candy, tomoe ame.

Driving over Nuuanu Bridge I saw the brook below, already removed from me. Along tree-lined streets, I tried to impress everything on my mind, to remember. I looked hard at the policeman under his umbrella at a cross-street as he turned his sign to "Go."

At the wharf, we shook hands with Nagata. Grandpa bought an armload of varied leis from two or three of the lei women at the entrance. At the foot of the gangplank, the band was playing *Mai Poina 'Oe Ia'u*, Forget Me Not. On board, stewards were passing trays of confetti streamers.

All of our friends who were staying home, or taking the boat next week, were there to see off the travelers. Soon we had

leis up to our noses. All shades of carnation, lavender
maunaloa, white crown flower, gardenia, tuberose, pakalana.

"Don't forget to throw them overboard at Diamond
Head."

"You won't come back unless you do!"

"*Write*, now."

"We'll think of you when we read in the Advertiser that
it's snowing where you are."

"And then we'll go to the beach and get sunburned."

Nearly everyone, going or staying, was a kama'aina. It was
easy to recognize the few tourists, though one couldn't have
explained how; they just looked different.

Buck came and gave Duke and me leis. "I'll be on the next
boat. Another week at home!"

"Lucky stiff!" said Duke.

Meg was there, and Jannie, and Sut and Jake. Kit would
be on the boat with us, and her parents.

Jannie gave Kit and me each a little book. Kit's was *The
Prophet*, and mine *The Forerunner: His Parables and Poems*.

A steward walked along the deck, striking a gong. "All
ashore that's going ashore!"

Grandpa kissed Holly and me, shook hands with Duke,
and was gone. I watched him walking down the gangplank,
tall and erect in his pongee suit and Panama hat, the "ever-
present walking stick" in his hand.

We tossed confetti to those on the wharf; boat and wharf
were joined by a hundred streamers of blue, pink, yellow, red.
They broke as the *Matsonia* pulled away, with blasts of her
whistle, and a streak of water widened between her and the
dock. The band was playing *Aloha 'Oe*. It wasn't real, it
couldn't be true.

Harbor, then shoreline, receded. A wide expanse of blue
separated us from the coconut palms along the beach. We
could see the brand-new pink Royal Hawaiian, and the white
Moana Hotel with its banyan tree and its pier. Then Diamond
Head, a crouching lion. Honolulu—Fair Haven.

Passengers lining the rail began throwing their leis. All colors of flowers, so far below, rose and fell with the tide, floated away from the ship. I took mine off slowly, let them over the side one by one. Last of all was Kirey's pikake, crushed and its petals turning brown, heartbreakingly sweet. I watched its descent, but it was impossible to find it among so many on the water. Even so, I thought, it will bring me home.

26
The Brook

My father came into the den and said, "The old gentleman's gone."

I stared for an instant, unable to realize that it was true, then rose from his chair. This was partly an automatic gesture, because we always surrendered the chair to him; he would never have claimed it, but the old leather rocker was so much "Daddy's chair" that it would have been unthinkable to remain seated in it while he was in the room.

The little den, off the great high-ceilinged rooms at side and end, was a haven to me. I loved its shabbiness in contrast to the long pillared living room and the elegance of the dining room with its wallpaper depicting castles; loved the big koa desk, the book-lined walls.

I had been sitting there thinking of my grandfather. The day before, which was the day of my return to Honolulu from my first year of boarding school in Connecticut, had been the only time that he had not met the boat when any of us were coming in: from school, from a trip, at six in the morning from the Ranch on Maui. Searching the wharf from the deck and not seeing him, I had known something was wrong. The brilliance of the city beyond, trees so green that they dazzled the eyes, sunstruck ridges of wooded valleys, had accented the shadow of foreboding.

My father said now, "Your mother's still there. Would you like to go over and see her and Grandma?"

"No!" I began to tremble. "Daddy," I implored him, "did he—" but I couldn't go on.

He put a thin brown hand on my shoulder. His touch and his voice were calming. "He suffered some, but the end came very peacefully." His eyes, so blue in the tanned face, were kind.

His face blurred, and I went out of the room. From my first realization, I had known that I must go out of doors.

The Cold Lady in the windowed alcove of the living room stood serenely on her pedestal, one arm raised to balance the urn on her head, her robe rippling in peaceful folds.

Peace . . . The end had come peacefully.

Funeral. There would be a funeral, and I would be expected to go. I had never been to a funeral. I couldn't! I wouldn't!

In the hall under the long wide staircase curving upward, the echo of his own "Are you there?" whistle hovered. Down the front steps, I didn't turn to look toward where the old gentleman lay in his room across Bates Street. The poinciana regia tree flamed before his house, a scarlet umbrella. This I knew without looking, and knew too that it was said always to be so at a time of death. A splendor of farewell to one who had always seemed old to me.

I can't go to his funeral! I won't. I'll get a cold—anything, to keep from having to go.

I had known, really, when I saw Kirey the day before. She had waited for me at her cottage, as if she understood that was where I'd like to see her first. I threw myself into her arms, clung to her as I had done when a child, had that safe, happy feeling of being with her again, enveloped in the scent of Lavender.

But when I drew back and looked at her, her face told me how sick Grandpa was. Knowing, I couldn't accept it.

Now, going toward the brook, the grass was good under my bare feet after a year of shoes. Down the flight of stone steps, along the edge of the brook, from stone to stone. The water eddied and swirled, but quietly, slowly. Reeds and clover on the lower banks stirred gently. How many times had I searched for a four-leaf clover, never finding it!

I stepped into the water. Some of the coldness of mountains was in it. In the middle, it was up to my knees, and as it swept round them and bubbled past stones, I looked down to the streambed that lent its darkness. The crest of a miniature range of hills, a boulder the size of my little toe. A clawed dragon slithered by; a freshwater 'opae.

In the high, wide tunnel over which passed cars and streetcars of the avenue, I felt removed from the dull rushing of city sounds. Somehow, the day before had gone by without my having visited the brook. There was a sense of homecoming here that had been absent in my return—except for those first brief moments with Kirey—because of the atmosphere caused by illness, by foreboding and strangeness. Here there was a remembered dampness of earth and foliage in the air, the brook chuckled about its rocks as I had heard it, five thousand miles away. The monkey-pods let sunlight lie in shifting patches on the water. The street was far away.

It was possible here to imagine the street as it had been long years ago, when a low bridge had crossed the brook in place of the tunnel I had always known. And for the first time, sitting on the slanting concrete like a continuation of the bank, and thinking of those days, I could picture my grandfather as a younger man. Black moustache and hair instead of white, the same erect carriage, now without a cane. For the first time, it did not seem like a story to me that Queen Lili'uokalani had demanded his head on a silver platter.

The Queen's order had struck to the heart of a small girl, my mother, a fear that never left her. Guards were placed about the house, grown-ups whispered and cast uneasy glances. A phrase overheard here, a word there. Terror lurked beyond each corner, stalked her bed so that she pulled the covers over her head. During this time, Grandpa himself was mostly away from home, at his office conferring with colleagues. He came in for a bath and a change of clothes, a quick meal.

Later, of course, Lili'uokalani became his friend.

My mind went back to another occasion that had seemed not quite real to me. Now, it was no effort to picture a young man of twenty-three planting a sapling on Maui, sent by missionary friends in India, a plant that would grow into the largest banyan in the Islands. It seemed to me that he must have known then that it would be a special tree, that would thrust outward in all directions, sending down roots from its branches which became tree trunks in their own right, until it was a giant, spreading tree supported by a dozen trunks. A tree that would shade countless people, down the years, from the hot Lahaina sun.

Here, with the strength of slow-moving dark water at my feet and the remoteness of the city overhead, I felt older than the man who lay on his bed across the street. (Did he lie on it still? Was there a coffin yet?)

I *was* older, by eleven years. "Will Owen is as bright a boy as any mother ever called her own. He gallops about on his broomstick and whips up. 'See, Mama, see horse kick!' And see his rogueish black eyes, his ruddy, full cheeks and prominent forehead. I think you would love to call him Grandson." Will Owen became, for me, a four-year-old boy: my grandfather. The coffin was for his little sister. And it had taken six months for the letter, telling of the coffin, and of Will Owen, to reach his grandparents in Connecticut. The writer of the letter had had to go to the funeral of her child.

If the coffin had been Will Owen's, I wouldn't be here beside the brook . . . It *was* Will Owen's, three-quarters of a century later.

"Grandpa," I said, choking.

Will Owen, four years old, was mine now, and so too were the young sheriff planting the banyan, and the man who had been hated and feared by a queen, and loved by an ex-queen. The man with the cane had always been mine—who walked me home along the path through our yard after dinner at his house, taking off his hat as he kissed me good night, his moustache tickling my cheek; who went to the bank for shiny new quarters, and brought us those long boxes of wonderful molasses cookies; who took us to band concerts at Kapi'olani Park, and to Kawaiaha'o Church, where part of the service was in Hawaiian; who in the grown-up world was attorney general and senator, but to me, opponent in dominoes and cribbage, reader of Wordsworth. Who had always been there on the wharf . . .

Going back, stone to stone, I saw a four-leaf clover on the bank. It had been waiting there for me. I plucked it, touched it to my lips and held it above the brook for an instant before letting it drift to the surface of the water. Caught up by the current, it sailed downstream, a moment green before it went out of sight.

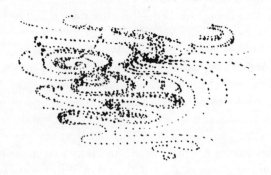